François Jullien's Unexceptional Thought

Global Aesthetic Research

Series Editor: Joseph J. Tanke, Professor,
Department of Philosophy, University of Hawai'i

The Global Aesthetic Research series publishes cutting-edge research in the field of aesthetics. It contains books that explore the principles at work in our encounters with art and nature, that interrogate the foundations of artistic, literary, and cultural criticism, and that articulate the theory of the discipline's central concepts.

Titles in the Series
Early Modern Aesthetics, J. Colin McQuillan
Foucault on the Arts and Letters: Perspectives for the 21st Century, Catherine M. Soussloff
Architectural and Urban Reflections after Deleuze and Guattari, edited by Constantin V. Boundas and Vana Tentokali
Living Off Landscape, or, the Unthought-of in Reason, Francois Jullien, translated by Pedro Rodríguez
Between Nature and Culture: The Aesthetics of Modified Environments, Emily Brady, Isis Brook, and Jonathan Prior
Reviewing the Past: The Presence of Ruins, Zoltán Somhegyi
François Jullien's Unexceptional Thought: A Critical Introduction, Arne De Boever

François Jullien's Unexceptional Thought

A Critical Introduction

Arne De Boever

London • New York

Published by Rowman & Littlefield International Ltd.
6 Tinworth Street, London, SE11 5AL
www.rowmaninternational.com

Rowman & Littlefield International Ltd. is an affiliate of Rowman & Littlefield
4501 Forbes Boulevard, Suite 200, Lanham, Maryland 20706, USA
With additional offices in Boulder, New York, Toronto (Canada), and Plymouth (UK).
www.rowman.com

Copyright © Arne De Boever 2020

All rights reserved. No part of this book may be reproduced in any form or by any electronic or mechanical means, including information-storage and -retrieval systems, without written permission from the publisher, except by a reviewer, who may quote passages in a review.

British Library Cataloguing-in-Publication Data

A catalogue record for this book is available from the British Library.

ISBN: HB 978-1-78661-575-6
  PB 978-1-78661-576-3

Library of Congress Cataloging-in-Publication Data

ISBN: 978-1-78661-575-6 (cloth : alk. paper)
ISBN: 978-1-78661-576-3 (pbk. : alk. paper)
ISBN: 978-1-78661-577-0 (electronic)

∞™ The paper used in this publication meets the minimum requirements of American National Standard for Information Sciences—Permanence of Paper for Printed Library Materials, ANSI/NISO Z39.48-1992.

Printed in the United States of America

Contents

Acknowledgments — vii

A Note on Translations — ix

Introduction: "Not the Exceptional, but the Unheard Of" — xi

1. Chinese Utopias in Contemporary French Thought — 1
2. In Between Landscape and the Nude — 35
3. In Management as in War — 69
4. François Jullien in Dialogue — 103

Conclusion: For Future François Julliens — 125

Index — 139

About the Author — 151

Acknowledgments

This book grew out of a long-standing research interest of mine—namely, the presence of the Far East in contemporary French thought. The book wouldn't have happened without Joseph Tanke's recommendation, offered one fine evening in Honolulu, that I read François Jullien's book *In Praise of Blandness*, which Joseph described as "one of the most beautiful books ever written in the French language." He understood, before I did, the connections between that book and my critique of Western exceptionalism. I followed his recommendation and read *In Praise of Blandness*—and many more books by Jullien. I think it's only fitting that this book ended up in the Global Aesthetic Research series that Joseph edits.

Olivia C. Harrison kindly picked up some Jullien books for me in Paris and discussed the introduction and chapter 1 of this book with me. I am also grateful for Olivia's extensive written comments on chapter 1. Martin Woessner heard me out about chapter 3 and provided comments on an early version of chapter 2. He also commented on early versions of chapters 1 and 3.

During the 2018–2019 academic year, I was able to work closely with my graduate student research assistants Carl Schmitz and Clara Wenrong Lee on each of the book's chapters, which helped push the book forward at a steady pace. Some of the work I did with my graduate student Rose Sheela on critical surf studies also resonates in this book's third and fourth chapters. I am grateful to the provost's office at the California Institute of the Arts and its Research and Practice Fellowship Program that helped support that work.

A version of chapter 2 was originally published as "François Jullien's Unexceptional Thought" in *boundary 2* 47 (1) (2020): 1–42 (republished by permission) and benefited from the peer review that I received as part of that process. Some of my early thoughts on Jullien ended up in *Against Aesthetic*

Exceptionalism (2019), and writing that short book contributed significantly to the work that ultimately ended up in this volume.

In an interview, François Jullien resists the notion that because one writes a lot the work must by necessity be of poor quality. I hope my work, too, can contribute to that resistance.

A Note on Translations

Unless otherwise indicated, all translations in this book are mine.

Introduction: "Not the Exceptional, but the Unheard Of"

Étudier dé-familiarise (Studying defamiliarizes).

—François Jullien, in interview with
Nicolas Martin and Antoine Spire[1]

POINTS OF REFERENCE; OR, FRANÇOIS JULLIEN'S SECOND LIFE

Born in 1957, François Jullien obtained his degree in philosophy in the mid-1970s and left to China to study at the universities of Beijing and Shanghai. In the late 1970s, he moved to Hong Kong to take up a position at the French Centre for Research on Contemporary China. Later still, in the mid-1980s, he was a researcher at the Maison Franco-Japonaise in Tokyo.[2] After holding several prestigious academic positions in France, both as a sinologist (president of the Association française d'études chinoises, for example) and a philosopher (president of the Collège internationale de philosophie), he became the Chair of Alterity—a peculiar title, given the criticism he develops of alterity in his work—at the Fondation Maison des Sciences de l'Homme. Over the course of his career, Jullien has published more than thirty books in French, about half of which have been translated into English. His work has been the subject of both lavish praise and harsh criticism. While Jullien has received several major awards for this work, he does not have the same renown in the English-language world as other contemporary French philosophers. This may be because much of his work is classified as sinology and thus seems to cater to a more-specific audience than the French philosophy that is often simply marketed as (universally appealing?) "theory." However, for contemporary Western theorists to leave Jullien aside because he is a sinologist and does not address what preoccupies Western thought would be a grave mistake. Jullien is precisely always working in between the Chinese and Western traditions of thinking, and when working on the one he is often speaking to the other directly in an attempt to draw out what he calls the "unthought" (*l'impensé*) of each. Sinologists, too, would be mistaken if they read Jullien solely within the limits of their discipline. The point, rather, is to always operate in between so as to see what such a balancing act might yield.

Having returned to European thought after what he often refers to as his "detour" through China, Jullien has now arrived in the late phase[3] of his work, in which the full arch of his adventurous thinking is becoming clear. Marking that trajectory is a recently published and monumental *Cahier de l'Herne* dedicated to Jullien, which includes three sections authored by Jullien himself (they wrap up parts II, V, and IX of the volume). Titled "De l'écart à l'inouï—repères I, II, III" (From divergence to the unheard-of—points of reference I, II, III), those sections take the form of a dialogue between Jullien and an unnamed *lecteur attentif* (Jullien 2018, 78; hereafter "Points of reference")—presumably Jullien himself—who questions Jullien about his entire oeuvre. As such, these sections provide great insights into Jullien's work as a whole. I propose to spend some time with them here as a way to introduce the reader to my own study of Jullien's thought.

I should probably note from the outset that as such a study *François Jullien's Unexceptional Thought: A Critical Introduction* does not pretend to be comprehensive, and it does not discuss equally all of the books that Jullien has published. Rather, I focus on certain books and topics that stood out to me within Jullien's work and in relation to the present moment as worthy of inquiry. That said, my selection of texts and topics nevertheless touches upon many of the key concerns in Jullien's work, and in that sense the book can provide something like an overview of Jullien's thought and provide a variety of pathways into it and some of the important debates it has triggered.

The form of Jullien's "Points of reference" evokes, perhaps, postmodern literary experiments like Jorge Luis Borges' "Borges and I" (and Borges plays a role in Jullien's oeuvre due to Michel Foucault's reference to his work in a famous passage where Foucault writes about China; Foucault 1973). Or the "Points of reference" may evoke the Platonic dialogues, at the origin of the Western thinking that is central to the current phase of Jullien's work: Jullien's book *L'Invention de l'idéal et le destin de l'Europe* (The invention of the ideal and the destiny of Europe) offers a reading of Plato *de Chine*, "from China" (Jullien 2009b).[4] Certainly the dialogue (in the form of the interview) takes up an important role in Jullien's collected work. For this study, for example, I have drawn from innumerable interviews that Jullien has given throughout his life and that, in one case, constitute half a book (the other half is writings about Jullien by Nicolas Martin and Antoine Spire, who also do the interviews; Martin and Spire, 2011).

More importantly, however, a strong philosophical notion of dialogue appears frequently in Jullien's work about the universal, the uniform, and the common, where he argues that the West "s'est mis à 'dialoguer' avec les autres cultures" because "il a perdu sa puissance" (the West has begun to enter into dialogue with other cultures because it has lost its power; Jullien 2016a, 83–84). But Jullien harshly criticizes this "falsely peaceful" and "falsely egalitarian" dialogue, which is most often held in "globalized English or *globish*" (Jullien 2018, 84), and rejects it in favor of what he refers to as a "strong" (ibid., 85) understanding of the word "dialogue" as evoking both the "in-between" (*l'entre*) and a "path." The *dia* in the Greek word "dialogue" marks both the in-between that distinguishes the dialogue from a "monologue of two" and the bridging path that makes the dialogue possible (ibid.). This is why to translate one of Jullien's key terms, *écart/divergence*, as "gap" is not quite right, as Jullien points out; *écart* translates as "gap," but it *also* names the bridge across (ibid., 120). That particular kind of dialogue can only develop over time, Jullien insists, since each point of view needs to slowly "reflect itself in relation to the other" so as to lead to an "effective encounter" (86). Jullien understands this as a process of developing a "common" that "does not do away with the in-between" or bring some kind of "forced assimilation"; instead such a common is *produced* and *promoted* by the in-between (ibid.).

Central to Jullien's method is translation. As he writes in *This Strange Idea of the Beautiful*, following a characteristic passage where he develops his criticism of a French translation of Zong Bing's fourth-century treatise of landscape painting[5]:

> The non-sinologist is no doubt weary of these remarks concerning translation, but it should be understood that all of these small additions, serving as compromises and rendering the translation "smoother," mean, in the end, that we are always dealing only with variations of the same and that, while believing we are reading Chinese texts, we are still sitting at home. (Jullien 2016b, 178)

The remark comes in parentheses, but it may just as well have been bolded. One may want to turn it around: even a nonsinologist cannot fail to be engaged by Jullien's remarks concerning translation, which seek "to restore Chinese texts to their strangeness," to paraphrase the title of the final chapter of *This Strange Idea*.[6] Jullien's remark about translation arrives some ten pages after a passage in which he writes dismissively about how "the steamroller of theoretical globalization" has Westernized Chinese thought (Jullien 2016b, 165). Jullien's translations, crucial to his work overall, seek to bring some relief, even if he also grants in *Book of Beginnings* that "the principal notions of Chinese thought are not directly translatable" (Jullien 2015, vii).[7]

If translation (and commentary on translation) has an important role in Jullien's work, it is because for him it is the language of the in-between, as he explains at the end of *Il n'y a pas d'identité culturelle* (There is no cultural identity): translation opens up the in-between, and "la traduction est la langue *logique* de ce dialogue" (translation is the *logical* language of this dialogue; Jullien 2016a, 88, emphasis original). The in-between is, for Jullien, associated with a "fecundity" that is generated by divergence's "de-coincidence" (Jullien 2018, 233). It's in this "de-coincidence" that we see "the negative" (rather than "evil") at work as what Jullien terms the "neg-active" (ibid.). He has developed this part of his thought at length in *L'ombre au tableau: Du mal ou du négatif* (Casting a shadow: on evil or on the negative; Jullien 2004a). The task of philosophy is partly to separate out a "sterile negative" or "negative negative" from another, motivating negative or neg-active that is productive (ibid., 126) or intensive. Jullien in part praises G. W. F. Hegel and his dialectics (ibid.),[8] even if he has also deems Hegel's work on the negative insufficient for his own project (the neg-active "ne se range pas pour autant sous les lois de la dialectique," "does not fit under the laws of dialectics"; Jullien 2010, 62–63):

> Un des grands problèmes de notre époque est de penser le négatif fécond, ce que j'appellerais le "nég-actif," sans le faire basculer dans une dialectique de reconciliation hégélienne. (Interview in Citot 2009, 31)[9]
>
> One of the great problems of our time is to think the fecund negative, what I would call the "neg-active," without making it tip over into a Hegelian dialectic of reconciliation.

It's on this understanding of the neg-active that Jullien's notion of existence is based, as what names the de-coincision of the self as the *process* or better: *passage* (to evoke the *dao*—道 or "path") of living: *ex*-istence. Hence Jullien's interest in the notion of "a second life" (Jullien 2018, 235), one that is lived in perpetual de-coincidence with the first and in fact enables one to live a better life.

One could, then, read these "Points of reference" in which Jullien enters into a dialogue with himself as a formalization of the idea of a second life—of the de-coincision of Jullien with himself that establishes an in-between at the same time as it produces a bridging path from the one to the other. Such an autocritical, philosophical process can only develop slowly, and it is not surprising that Jullien would engage in it only late in his career and life, at a time when he is able to assess his lifework's full trajectory—and specifically his study of Greece after the extensive detour through China that he has accomplished.

CHAPTER SUMMARIES

It is with the mention of the detour through China that the first "Points of reference" section begins, with the solicitation of Jullien's entire work to leave behind the major philosophemes of the West—"Being, God, Truth, Liberty" (Jullien 2018, 78)—but without becoming "sinized" (ibid.). Insisting that his work is not "comparativist,"[10] in the sense that it does not "proceed through resemblances and differences" (ibid., 79), Jullien points out that by working in between European thought and Chinese thought he allows both to reflect themselves in each other so as to uncover each thought's "unthought" (ibid.). Both European thought and Chinese thought, therefore, "deconstruct" through the encounter with each other, and in Jullien's view one can only really think from that "unthought" (ibid.). Otherwise, "on ne pense pas" (one does not think; ibid.). To philosophize means, precisely, to "sortir du chemin déjà frayé," "to stray from the path already forged" (ibid., 120). Jullien's friend Alain Badiou has characterized him on those grounds as an "apostate" (Badiou 2018, 97). A library, in Jullien's view, is nothing but a "juxtaposition of divergences" that trigger thought (Jullien 2018, 120).

All of this also means there is no essentialism in Jullien's thinking. By "Chinese thought" Jullien simply means "thought that was written in Chinese"; and to say so does not mean that Jullien adheres to a linguistic determinism, as he insists (Jullien 2018, 79). In *Chemin faisant. Connaître la Chine, relancer la philosophie* (Step-by-step[11]: getting to know China, relaunching philosophy), a book in which he explains his methodology, he suggests that language merely "predisposes" thinking in certain ways (Jullien 2007, 52). Still, from a historical point of view, it should be pointed out that by "Chinese thought" Jullien mostly means pre-Buddhist classical Chinese thought; he frequently distinguishes between Daoism, Buddhism, and contemporary Chinese thought, all of which appear in his work. His overall focus, however, is on Daoism. He will often work across traditions that are generally opposed—Daoism and Confucianism, for example—to discuss those elements on which they agree (see Jullien 2004c, 94–95). Certainly—and this has irritated some of his critics—there is ample hopping around within and between his books. Part of the problem is also that Jullien often works metonymically, allowing the work of an individual author or painter to stand in for a much larger tradition of thought or aesthetics (see Harrist 2011, 252). All of this leaves Jullien open to the charge of generalization and essentialization (though the latter would be hard to push, given the extensive criticisms of essentialism scattered throughout his work).

Many of those issues are reflected in the list of critical points that Jullien's interlocutor—Jullien himself—raises and that I intend to address at various points in this study: the instrumental approach to China that the very phrase "China as detour" evokes, if not the essentialization then the generalization of both "Chinese thought" and "Western thought" in his work, and the fact that Jullien's work abstracts from case studies into concepts and thereby tends to ignore specific contexts[12]; and some have also pointed out Jullien's "tendency to overstate" (Wang 2008, 242). Jullien also recalls in "Points of reference" the nondebate with Swiss sinologist Jean François Billeter, who published a short polemic titled *Contre François Jullien* (Against François Jullien; 2006), to which Jullien responded in his book *Chemin faisant* (Step-by-step)—or, rather, to which he offered a reply.[13] In a review of Jullien's book *The Great Image Has No Form, or On the Nonobject in Painting*, Robert Harrist bluntly states that, "at the great height from which Jullien surveys [historical phenomena], far removed from the experience of making or looking at paintings, art and its critical discourse in China become as blurry as in the landscapes [Jullien] so admires" (Harrist 2011, 253). Clearly Jullien has triggered no small amount of criticism over the course of his career. In "Points of reference," however, he notes that all of those criticisms, to which he has replied on numerous occasions, "no longer concern him": "Je ne m'en soucie plus," as he puts it; "C'est passé"—"they're in the past" (Jullien 2018, 81).

I will address most of the critical issues I mentioned in chapter 1, which focuses on a problematic that has received very little sustained discussion in this context—namely, Jullien's orientalism.[14] I pursue such a consideration in part to lay out the key terms of Jullien's late work on the universal, which seeks to capture the overall methodology of his thought. Although many points of criticism may be in the past for Jullien, they are difficult to avoid for any new reader of this work, and a responsible study of Jullien's thought cannot but begin, in my view, with a consideration of his method and, if you will, its ethics and politics.

Having dispensed with the more-obvious criticisms, Jullien's autocritique quickly dives into the philosophical stakes of his work—specifically, the "deconstruction from the outside" (*deconstruction du dehors*; Jullien 2018, 81) that all of his work pursues and that uses China to break out of Western ontological and metaphysical thinking. As I explain in chapter 1, the phrase "deconstruction from the outside" is meant in part to distinguish Jullien's approach to China and the West from that of Jacques Derrida, who always finds deconstruction "within" (Martin and Spire 2011, 135) (and in whose work China was implicated, as I discuss in chapters 1 and 4). In Jullien's view, Derrida ultimately remains too much within the Western,

Judeo-Christian tradition, even if Islam plays a role in his work. Islam, however, does not truly provide an outside-to-Western thought, Jullien points out ("l'Islam fait partie du monde occidental"; "Islam is part of the West"; Jullien 2004b, 96); it does not provide the "exteriority" that interests Jullien. Derrida ultimately remains too "biblical" (Jullien 2008a, 155). Exteriority for Jullien is associated with distance and divergence; alterity, which Jullien rejects as a philosophical construct (rather than an objective fact) is the logic of difference and distinction (Jullien 2018, 119; 2007, 34). Alterity operates within the logic of identity and opposition, which Jullien rejects (Citot 2009, 28). Jullien turned to China not as an alterity but because of the objective fact of its elsewhere, of its language being outside of the Western languages, and of its thought having developed for a long time outside of the European tradition (Jullien 2007, 33).

In her contribution to *Cahier de l'Herne*, Jullien's Chinese translator, Esther Lin, recalls that, during a conference in Pisa on the work of François Jullien, Italian philosopher Remo Bodei proposed the notion of the "exoptic" to characterize Jullien's approach (Lin 2018, 45). Lin also explicitly mobilizes the notion in contrast to the exoticism with which Jullien is sometimes charged, and Jullien himself has taken up the notion in his work (Jullien 2007, 18). Here is Jullien in conversation with Nicolas Martin and Antoine Spire, distinguishing his work from orientalism and exoticism:

> J'appelle *ex-optique*, en revanche, le travail qui consiste à produire les conditions d'un recul permettant de découvrir du dehors ce qu'on ne perçoit plus du dedans—ce qui est une autre façon de nommer la déconstruction que j'opère. Mais attention: lire *du dehors* n'est pas lire *de loin*, comme on pourrait le croire; c'est au contraire lire de plus près, en s'appuyant sur un effet de contraste rendant plus saillant l'implicite. (Martin and Spire 2011, 171; emphasis original)

> I call *exoptic*, by contrast, the work that consists in producing the conditions of a withdrawal allowing the discovery of an outside that one no longer sees from within—it's another way of describing the deconstruction that I pursue. But note: reading *from the outside* is not *distant* reading, as one might believe; it's on the contrary reading more closely, by relying on an effect of contrast that makes the implicit stand out more.

As far as the philosophical stakes of Jullien's deconstruction go, in "Points of reference I" Jullien discusses ontology first and how *l'écart* (divergence) and especially *l'entre* (the in-between) replace the Western ontological notion of "being" in his thought. Jullien arrives at this replacement, of course, by way of China, through the detour via China, which offers in itself a thinking of the detour. Central to this kind of thought are the notions of the "allusive" and the "evasive" (Jullien 2018, 82), which are opposed to the Western ontological thinking of presence.[15] In "Points of reference II" Jullien speaks of the in-between as a "deontologizing concept" (ibid., 119), a notion that recalls one of the subtitles of his book on "literati" painting, *The Great Image Has No Form*—"An essay in de-ontology." "*L'entre* n'est pas de l'*être*," "the *in-between* is not *being*," as he puts it (ibid.; emphasis original), suggesting that in the Western world perhaps only modern art (Cézanne, Braque, Picasso) has been able to think this in-between.

This relates to Chinese thought's criticism of metaphysics: the idea that something is beautiful because there is an ideal of beauty that stands behind it, or is above it, and that delivers the structuring rupture between the sensible and the intelligible that is so typical of Western thought. Jullien's interlocutor—Jullien himself—points out how this "modelization of the beautiful" is "incarnated in the nude" (Jullien 2018, 83), which Jullien considers typical of Western art. In China, by contrast, the nude (or at least the nude as it is construed in the West) is missing, as Jullien discusses in his book *The Impossible Nude: Chinese Art and Western Aesthetics*. In chapter 2, I show how a sustained inquiry into aesthetics in Jullien's work can help to lay bare these philosophical arguments—specifically Jullien's "Chinese" criticism of Western ontology and metaphysics. While such a project needs to pass via the nude, it also has to consider the reflection on the Chinese landscapes of the Southern "literati" school (as well as landscape in general) that extends throughout Jullien's work, from his dissertation to some of his most-recent books. Indeed, if the nude is associated first and foremost with Western thought, landscape helps Jullien lay bare Chinese thought, and it is in the divergence between the two, in the in-between that it produces, that a philosophical dialogue between the West and China becomes possible. Still, it is in landscape that the Chinese thought of process and what Jullien calls "correlation"—the relations between things—becomes most visible (Jullien 2018, 84).

One of the more-peculiar aspects of Jullien's work is its contributions to both military studies and management studies. This can be traced back to Jullien's study of the Chinese notion of efficacy, which extends over three books: the dense academic study *The Propensity of Things: Toward a History of Efficacy in China* (1995); the much-shorter study of the Chinese art of war, titled *A Treatise on Efficacy: Between Western and Chinese Thinking* (2004c); and, finally, Jullien's still-untranslated *Conférence sur l'efficacité* (Lecture on efficacy; 2005), which summarizes Jullien's *Treatise* as a "lecture for managers," as I discuss in chapter 3. Carefully considering the transfer between military theory and management theory in Jullien's work as well as its reception, I derive from Jullien's approach a Chinese managerial conception of sovereignty that, I argue, provides a useful lens through which to view not only the current global economicopolitical situation but also Jullien's insistence, in this context, on European approaches to both war and management (Jullien 2018, 85) that can be played out critically in relation to Chinese thought.

Central in Jullien's analysis of efficacy is the Chinese notion of "silent transformations"—or slow, gradual process. One of the issues Jullien has with Hegel is that, even though Hegel thought the motivating force of the negative, he did not think its silent transformations—Hegel was too event focused, too focused on a history made by great men, to consider this. This also means that Jullien is no fan of writing history through its revolutions (Jullien 2004a, 144ff.). The notion of silent transformations operates in a divergence with the Western notion of the event, which has thrived in European philosophy. Whereas the latter is associated with the European thinking of sovereignty, the former—especially in its association with management—is much closer to what Michel Foucault analyzes as governmentality/biopolitics and its central, liberal/neoliberal imperative of "laissez-faire." Historically, this notion translates (as I discuss in chapter 3; but the translation ought to be criticized as well) the Chinese notion of *wu wei* (無爲), which names the efficacy that rules without exertion and enters into Western economic thought via the physiocrats' eighteenth-century work on Chinese politics. Jullien opposes such a Chinese model of political manipulation and regulation to the Western/ Greek model of politics through persuasion (rhetoric). It's the tragic, head-on clash familiar from Greek theater versus the Chinese oblique approach—and Jullien clearly seems to prefer the latter, as Roger-Pol Droit, for example, has noted (Droit 2018, 38).

As critics will note, Jullien is not the only one to have developed such a criticism of Western thought via China. In her article "French Feminism in an International Frame," literary theorist Gayatri Chakravorty Spivak points out that "French theorists such as Derrida, Lyotard, Deleuze, and the like have at one time or another been interested in reaching out to all that is not the West because they have, in one way or another, questioned the millennially cherished excellences of Western metaphysics: the sovereignty of the subject's intention, the power of predication, and so on" (Spivak 1981, 157). But should Jullien's work be inscribed in this lineage of "French theorists . . . reaching out"? Spivak's specific charge in this context becomes that Julia Kristeva, whose book *About Chinese Women* is the example she analyzes, does not have any deep knowledge of the Far East and ends up speaking only about herself in her attempt to "[touch] the *other* of the West" (Spivak 1981, 158; emphasis original).[16] What is launched in Kristeva's book as speculation becomes fact over the course of less than one hundred pages; the reader is treated to "the most stupendous generalizations about Chinese writing" based on no evidence whatsoever, "no primary research" (ibid., 160). Chinese thought is distorted so as to assimilate it into the West, exactly as eighteenth-century sinophiles did (ibid.). Kristeva criticizes those—but she is guilty of the same (ibid.). Is this Jullien's situation as well, as the already-mentioned Jean François Billeter, for example, as well as some of Jullien's reviewers have argued? Or is Jullien a different kind of philosopher, and do his references to Chinese thought ultimately lead elsewhere? Furthermore, is this situation mine? Dear reader, might it be yours?

Let me be very clear about my own project: I seek to offer a study about Jullien's oeuvre in order to explore the divergences it lays out between Western and Chinese thought (thought written in various European languages and thought written in Chinese). I myself am largely assessing Jullien's oeuvre from the Western side, in view of the divergence it opens up in relation to Western thought. In other words, my ultimate reference point is "the West," and I think this ought to be possible without falling prey to the kinds of distortions that Spivak (and Kristeva, oddly) draws out. In Jullien's thought, the criticism of Western thought is developed through a study of Chinese thought. But I myself come to Chinese thought as a nonsinologist, with limited knowledge of the Chinese materials that Jullien studies.[17] I note, however, that, contrary to the work of the theorists that Spivak mentions, Jullien is known as a sinologist and his work is based on primary research into Chinese materials (as well as secondary research in Chinese, I should add; I say this even if Jullien's work overall—like the work of many of his French colleagues—appears to be a little thin on the secondary sources, which were either not consulted or may have remained unacknowledged so as to not overburden the work with reference notes[18]). Additionally, Jullien's already-mentioned use of translation as a method appears to reveal more than basic linguistic competency in Chinese. (I should add that I know no Chinese.) Certainly it appears that part of what Jullien attacks in his work is precisely superficial references to Chinese thought in Western philosophy—and, more generally, Western culture at large—that claim to find the other where, in truth, they only promote the self. I explore this at length in chapter 1, where I investigate the role of orientalism in Jullien's work. Against the (orientalist) effort to, once and for all, *find* the other, Jullien emphatically works *between thoughts-in-progress*.

For all of those reasons, Jullien strikes me as a more reliable reference than those that Spivak attacks. He himself in fact mentions dismissively the numerous "utopies Chinoises" (Chinese utopias) in which French thought has been caught up (Jullien 2012, 61). Still, some have argued that Jullien mistakenly construes China as the West's absolute other and participates in a long (French) tradition of China's exoticization.[19] In this book I have tried to provide a more nuanced point of view, but I should grant that I ultimately do not have the full competency to judge this.

Although most of those particular issues are addressed in chapter 1, I return to them in chapter 4, where I explore the relations of Jullien's thought on

China—and the divergence with Western thinking that it opens up—to the work of certain thinkers within the Western tradition. Jullien has occasionally been criticized for writing "in an intellectual vacuum" (Lachman 2011, 233), without referencing other scholars who have done important work in his field. While this is partly due to his essayistic style, this is also because Jullien has tended to privilege concept over context and has focused on logical connections that translate between disciplines rather than on issues that, for example, apply within sinology alone. Chapter 4 draws out some of Jullien's less-recognized interlocutors within the Western tradition, creating a genealogy for his work in Western thought that has largely remained silent in his own writing. It also raises related critical questions about how some of what is characterized as "new" in the Western tradition—I focus on speculative materialism/realism, object-oriented ontology, and new materialism—can in view of the Chinese tradition only be characterized as new based on a Eurocentric lineage of thought. Finally, the chapter argues that Jullien's most-important interlocutors are not necessarily "philosophers" (in other words, thinkers in the Greek, and by extension Western, tradition) but precisely those thinkers who have worked at the limits of Greek philosophy, specifically in postcolonial studies and black studies. There are important resonances, for example, between Jullien's thought and the work of Moroccan poet and theorist Abdelkébir Khatibi (who was very interested in Daoism, as indicated by his long poem from 1976, *Class Warrior—Taoist Style*)[20] and Martiniquan writer and theorist Édouard Glissant (Sam Coombs has in his book on Glissant explored the Jullien/Glissant connection; Coombs 2018), as well as the work of Fred Moten. This will also allow me to close the main chapters of this book with a return to the discussion of orientalism (theorized by postcolonial critic Edward Said; 1978) with which I began.

THE UNHEARD-OF

Toward the end of "Points of reference III," Jullien establishes both a terminological contrast and ultimately a terminological shift in his work through the introduction of the notion of *l'inouï*—"the unheard-of." The ambiguities of the notion are not quite the same in French as in English. The French word *inouï* comes from the Latin *inauditus*—"unheard." According to the French/English dictionary of *Le Robert & Collins*, *inouï* can refer to unprecedented or previously unheard of events or circumstances, extraordinary or incredible news, or incredible or unbelievable speed, audacity, or force. The *Trésor de la langue française* indicates that *inouï* refers to something that one hadn't previously heard of; something that one had never before heard mentioned, that is unknown, unprecedented; something that's extraordinary, surprising, uncommon. It refers to something unbelievable or astounding, something extraordinary and derailing. It's associated with strangeness. The English "unheard-of" covers much of the same territory but includes in both its American (US) and British uses the meaning of unacceptable or outrageous, highly offensive. In English, "unheard-of" tends to have a more negative meaning than in French: in most of the sentences that the dictionary offers to illustrate the term's usage, "unheard-of" has a negative connotation. It's the French *Trésor* that sticks most closely to the literal and in both English and French nearly forgotten meaning of *inouï*/unheard-of: the fact that it references something that is, quite simply, not heard—hasn't been heard before, as the *Trésor* puts it, although obviously when the term is used it's usually in reference to something that's just been heard, that's come out of obscurity as something shocking and new. As such—but this is my interpretation—it also seems to have a hint of futurity built in, since even if it were previously unheard-of, what's just been heard sets a new precedent and seems to anticipate such future occasions of the same.

The unheard-of is *both* what is ordinary and not heard of in that sense (too ordinary to be heard or noticed) *and* what is extraordinary and stands out as never before or extremely rarely heard of (possibly with a negative connotation in English). But the status of this "extraordinary" needs to be nuanced. It's Jullien's interlocutor—Jullien himself, from his second life—who suggests the opposition between the exceptional and the unheard-of: when thinking the fecundity opened up in the in-between that divergence produces and promotes, it seems one needs to think of this fecundity or resource precisely "not as exceptional . . . but as unheard-of" ("Non pas l'exceptionnel . . . mais l'inouï"; Jullien 2018, 241). The exceptional only has value as a rarity, Jullien explains, and in that sense it is a relative notion—unless it takes on an abusive, absolutist form (ibid.). The attention it attracts is bound to peter out (ibid.). The unheard-of, by contrast, is an infinite resource that, without loudly announcing itself, arises from the very heart of both thought and life (ibid.). It's what remains unseen, or unheard—as well as, to hearken back to an earlier part of this introduction, unthought. At the same time, Jullien points out that it "surpasses the imagination," "dépasse l'imagination" (ibid.). In that sense, the unheard of is "the other name of what is so boringly called 'real'" ("L'inouï est l'autre nom de ce si lassant 'réel'"; ibid.).

The challenge is to break with characterizations of the surpassing of the imagination that Jullien evokes as "exceptional." If there is a surpassing, which suggests some kind of rupture or break as well as an upward movement, it is a surpassing into the unheard-of that can be characterized as "unexceptional." This is not so much about a Western thinking of the rupture or break, or what's also called the event; instead, it is about what Jullien analyzes as "the silent transformations"—"silent" as in "not heard of." At the same time, if the phrase "silent transformations" is meant to name the unexceptional, it is worth pointing out the need to rethink the unexceptional as precisely "what surpasses the imagination"—"upward," if you will, but not into exceptionalism.[21]

The particular kind of negotiation that develops here is reminiscent of Jullien's work on "the bland" (*dan*, 淡), a notion that he critically adopts from Roland Barthes' writings about China, which were based on a trip Barthes took to China in the mid-1970s with a small group of other writers and thinkers associated with the journal *Tel Quel*. With its seemingly ironic title, which echoes (as the book's translator has pointed out; Jullien 2008b, 12–13) both Erasmus's *In Praise of Folly* (West) and Jun'ichirō Tanizaki's *In Praise of Shadows* (East), Jullien's book *In Praise of Blandness* evokes Barthes through its essayistic style. Contrary to Barthes, Jullien *praises* blandness as the aesthetic that comes closest to Chinese thought.[22] It is worth noting, however, that *A Treatise on Efficacy* (originally published in French in 1996, which is five years after the first French publication of *In Praise of Blandness*) ends with a chapter titled "In Praise of Facility," in whose opening paragraph the "unexceptional" is praised as a key feature of Chinese thought. As such, it is associated in the paragraph with "the evident 'facility' of that which is ceaselessly realized in an unremarkable and unnoticed fashion" (Jullien 2004c, 184). There is a close connection, then, between the facility that is praised in this chapter and the unexceptional—and between the unexceptional and the blandness that Jullien praises as "Chinese" and that has been associated with writers as diverse as Emily Dickinson and Haruki Murakami (see Kang 2018; Row 2012).

By calling Jullien's thought "unexceptional" I want to draw out the unexceptionalizing tendency that Chinese thought brings to Western thought,[23] which Jullien shows to be exceptionalist through and through. Undoing exceptionalism in Western thought—specifically, unexceptionalizing or deexceptionalizing Western thought, as Jullien might put it—can lead us away from some of the more problematic exceptionalisms that have constituted it. The ultimate goal here is not so much to oppose the West and China on this count as two identities—one of which could be discarded in favor of the other (there is unexceptionalism in the West just as there is exceptionalism in China); rather, it is to play out their respective resources in their divergence with each other so as to see what that might yield.[24] As Dirk Baecker in a text about Jullien has pointed out, we are dealing here with different "accents" rather than with completely opposed worlds (Baecker 2008, 32).

For such a project, then, the notion of the unheard-of, which only appears in Jullien's late thought, is a useful one, and it must be considered in relation to terms like "blandness," "facility," and—indeed—the "unexceptional" in Jullien's work. Indeed, as a notion I think it provides a key to Jullien's oeuvre as a whole, connecting to both the terms that established it as well as the thought that has developed from there. One could do worse, in fact, than characterize Jullien's thought as a thought of the unheard-of and the unexceptional as I do in this book. But with that there come, of course, consequences. There is, in my view, no doubt that, while Jullien introduces the unheard-of as a characterization of his work overall—as a name for his interest in uncovering the unthought in both Western and Chinese thought—it's a notion that clearly derives from his study of China first and foremost, and therefore it's something that, I think, he brings to Western thought from China. The unheard-of is, first and foremost, the unthought of *Western* thought. Some philosophers come close, but none quite manage to think, in Jullien's view, the silent transformations that remain unheard-of in the Western tradition.

On the other hand, it is worth noting the rethinking of the unexceptional that the notion of the unheard-of also brings, as what surpasses the imagination and what's so boringly called "real." This rethinking has something to do with the complicated status of the immanent and the transcendent in Jullien's thought—and perhaps (this is at least what Jullien suggests) Chinese thought at large. While Jullien's thought has often been presented as a completely immanent and material thought, Jullien has resisted this, distinguishing his position from Gilles Deleuze's in at least one instance (Jullien 2004c, 183), and developing a notion of internal transcendence as a way to name the combination of the material and the spiritual in the Chinese tradition (in the sense of yin and yang, or the regulatory double movement of respiration—in/out[25]):

> Il y a bien une transcendance en Chine, c'est ce qu'on appelle le Ciel. Mais c'est une transcendance non pas par extériorité, comme celle du Dieu biblique ou comme celle des idées platoniciennes, c'est une transcendance par, je dis souvent, totalisation de l'immanence. (Jullien interviewed in Piorunski 1998, 157)
>
> There is for sure a transcendence in China; it's called Heaven [*tian*, 天]. But this is a transcendence not by exteriority, like that of the biblical god or of the Platonic ideas; rather, it's a transcendence by way of, as I often say, the totalization of immanence.

This may be why the notion of the unexceptional can actually be a productive one in this context: because it retains, in its naming, a trace of the exceptional that makes a bland-bland reading of the bland impossible. This is also why the "unheard-of" is such a good term in this context: because it captures precisely the idea that the bland is not just bland—that the bland always includes a kind of double tendency where a negative limit is combined with a positive one, in the same way that Jullien distinguishes the negative-negative from the neg-active.

All of this is perfectly summed up by the notion of the unheard-of, which captures both these limits. If the notion thus applies to Chinese thought in particular, it's interesting that Jullien also uses it to characterize his thought at large, which supposedly equally draws from Western cultural resources. This is where the exceptionalism of Western thought can in certain cases draw out the unthought of Chinese thought, where Western exceptionalism can bring something to Chinese thought that is valuable. Of course it's not entirely correct to call that contribution "exceptional," since the unheard-of is opposed to that, as Jullien's interlocutor—Jullien himself—notes. But it would still mark the positive tendency of the unheard-of, the way in which the unheard-of names something that stands out. Certainly in Jullien's late work he returns to Western, European thought—Greek thought—to explore its resources: the ideal in Plato, for example, or *logos* in Aristotle. Jullien's work on Christianity, which includes, for example, his book on the intimate, can be read as developing precisely such a negotiation: between the unexceptional and the exceptional.

If in his early work Jullien takes a detour through China to critically assess the Western tradition, in his late work he returns to the Western tradition to develop its resources, often in explicit relation to China (as in his Plato book, for example): "I'm now starting on a new phase, wherein I'd like to try to grasp again what seems to me to constitute the stakes of European thought in regard to Chinese thought" (Jullien 2009c, 184). "Von Griechenland nach China *und zurück*," as Jullien puts it elsewhere (From Greece to China *and back*; Jullien 2008a, 133; emphasis mine). This last move is crucial to his thinking about the universal, which in fact rejects the notion of the universal in favor of the notion of something universalizing, a regulative idea in the Kantian sense that provides a common orientation through "work" and as the result of a "process." Noting—and criticizing—the historical and geographical specificity of the Enlightenment universal ("je me rends compte à quel point les catégories kantiennes sont, elles aussi, marquées culturellement"; I realize to what point the Kantian categories are also culturally marked; Martin and Spire 2011, 139), Jullien nevertheless also draws out the resources of this tradition. Talking about the purpose of Catholic schools in our time, for example, Jullien observes that it no longer makes sense for them to teach students to believe, to teach them the catechism, et cetera. But that does not mean they need to go: rather, the vocation of Catholic schools today can only be to teach the resources of Catholicism in the same way that one can teach the resources of Judaism or Islam in schools associated with those other religions.[26]

Importantly, this is not a relativist position: Jullien criticizes, as I will discuss in chapter 1, what he perceives to be the unequal position of women in

Islam, as marked by the veil whose use he opposes (Jullien 2010, 18). It is the hard-won equality of women in the Western tradition that in his view needs to be valued as a resource against the role of women in Islam. One might not agree with this, of course—or at least argue that it needs nuance (equality of women in the West? Give me a break . . .)—but as a gesture, it is indicative of how Jullien in his late work seeks to play out Western cultural resources in their divergence with other traditions, some of which he might also not have studied as carefully as he has China (I will consider this in chapter 1, when I look at his travelogue about Vietnam). There are, in other words, some clear problems with Jullien's "Greek" turn; but as a gesture that seeks to critically work with the legacy of European/Western thought—and not blindly reject it and throw out the baby with the bathwater—such a project seems valuable and perhaps especially important today, when the revolutionary emancipatory content of the Enlightenment or Western reason often risks being eclipsed by the justified attacks on its "white," "straight," and "male" representatives and (and this is the more substantial target of the criticism) ways of thinking. Jullien may be a white, straight male himself, and may be read in that sense as a representative of the very tradition that is under attack; but his detour through China enabled him to unwork, in my view, the European/Western tradition precisely where it is most white, straight, and male: in its exceptionalism—specifically the metaphysics and ontology associated with sovereignty.

As I have already indicated, there are problems with the use of China as a detour or philosophical tool for a project that ultimately returns to the West; there is, in this context, the risk of orientalism that I consider at length in chapter 1. Indeed, there is the specter of governmentality/biopolitics and neoliberalism that ought to be considered in this context as one economicopolitical form that the detour through unexceptionalism might take—especially in view of Jullien's work with French businesses in China and the reception of his thought in both contemporary military and management studies (chapter 3). None of this is without risk. In the end, however, I find one of his thought's most-important contributions precisely in the relation it entertains with postcolonial thought and the necessity to learn from its critique while not giving up on the resources of European/Western thought.

I am reminded here of Gayatri Spivak, who did not pull any punches in her criticism of Kristeva's (orientalist) use of China, who as a postcolonialist is also a Europeanist and inscribes her work in postcolonial theory explicitly within the Western tradition and its resources. From her extensive introduction to her translation of Derrida's *Of Grammatology*—and her early criticism (as many have since noted) of the role of China in that book (see Meighoo 2008 and Jirn 2015)—to, for example, her dense *Critique of Postcolonial Reason: Toward a History of the Vanishing Present* or the monumental volume of writings in *An Aesthetic Education in the Era of Globalization*, Spivak

Introduction: "Not the Exceptional, but the Unheard Of"   xxvii

has precisely critically mobilized the resources of the European/Western tradition within the very field that took that tradition to task—for its heteronormativity, racism, or sexism and misogyny, for example. For Spivak, however, none of that means European/Western thought should be thrown out wholesale; indeed, where could a thought be found that is entirely free from such or other problems? (Certainly non-European/Western thought isn't.) When a moralizing approach comes to eclipse the real contributions that a tradition of thinking has brought, we will become all the poorer for it. Moralizing without end, ad infinitum, as part of an impossible project, we will progressively become deprived of all of our cultural resources—not only those in Europe/the West—as part of a mad search for a thought without problems. Jullien can show us, rather, that all thought is problematic and unexceptional in that way—even if not equally so; at the same time, no thought is reducible to the ways in which it is problematic, and thought is unexceptional in that way as well. Thought always, unexceptionally, exceeds what it stands out for and is maybe accused of. The point of Jullien's work is to critically cultivate, in this perspective, the cultural resources of a thought, diagnosing its problems and criticizing them, but also facilitating the democratic use of its fecundity for all.

This means that the cultural resources of European/Western thought are there not just for Europeans/Westerners. They are there for all: "Bach . . . is my heritage" (Cole 2016, 11), as Teju Cole puts it in a critical reading of James Baldwin. Jullien would argue that the same is true for any other cultural resources, although one would have to point out from a historical and political point of view that this cannot be true in exactly the same way due to histories of colonialism, for example, or the different power position of a "dominant" culture compared to a "minority" culture. Especially in view of debates about cultural appropriation, it seems some nuance may be needed when it comes to Jullien's plea for the democratic "exploitation" of "cultural resources" across the board. Who can exploit which cultural resource to what purpose? What are the histories and politics of such exploitation? How should those histories and politics be addressed? While drawing out cultural resources requires the slow and careful study of the European/Western and Chinese traditions—if there isn't much in Jullien addressing the issue of appropriation as such, the emphasis on study and the defamiliarization that it brings does address the issue of misappropriation and explicitly seeks to avoid it—it is clear that for Jullien those resources themselves are not identitarian. They do not mark an essential difference through which China and Europe/the West can be opposed. Rather, these are living cultural resources that are in perpetual development, as the resources of cultures that ex-ist and do not coincide with themselves. It is, in that sense, the process of cultures in which Jullien's work situates us, as the living movement of their resource that, in identitarian approaches to culture,

xxviii *Introduction: "Not the Exceptional, but the Unheard Of"*

should be considered "dead," like a "dead language" (as Jullien in his late work often puts it; see, for example, Jullien 2016a, 45–46). Cultures, then, are living languages that, spoken around the in-between of translation, ex-ist in a divergence that lays bare their resources for common use. Diverging from each other, their divergence also produces a bridge between them that promotes and produces true cultural dialogue, at a distance from the relativism or uniformity that have become the order of the day.

NOTES

1. Martin and Spire 2011, 245.
2. See, for example, Piorunski 1998, 151.
3. Roger-Pol Droit characterizes this late phase as "another book" or also as "book 2" in Jullien's oeuvre (Droit 2018, 37; 40). Jullien himself might disagree with this, as he has indicated that he thinks of his work very much as "one book, whose different titles constitute so many chapters intended to back up and prolong each other" (Jullien 2009c, 181).
4. On Jullien's complex relationship to Plato, see Potte-Bonneville 2018.
5. Jullien points out that this is one of the first-known treatises on Chinese landscape painting. The issue he foregrounds in his criticism is that the French translator systematically introduces an "I look" into the discussion of landscape, whereas the Chinese text includes nothing like this.
6. Jullien is, of course, not alone in making this point; his argument here recalls that of Lawrence Venuti in "Translation as Cultural Politics" (Venuti 1993).
7. The strongest objection to such a presentation of Jullien has probably been raised by Billeter, who charges Jullien with denying Chinese authors their specific voices and ultimately offering the reader nothing other than the point of view of Jullien himself. Billeter argues that Jullien's translations are a key tool in this project. See Billeter 2006.
8. Jullien 2004a can be read as a lengthy engagement with Hegel's dialectics.
9. Elsewhere, he also frequently takes Hegel to task for his racist remarks on China (see, for example, Jullien 1995, 17–18).
10. "Je ne fais donc pas de la philosophie comparée" (Citot 2009, 28). See also my chapter 1.
11. Literally, "forging a path," no doubt referencing *dao*.
12. Jullien responds to this by saying that in this call for context he overhears a *fear* of the concept (Martin and Spire 2011, 164). To forge a concept, he indicates in another interview, "is to forge a tool . . . is to forge a weapon" (260).
13. Following Michel Foucault, he explicitly distinguishes between *réponse* and *réplique* in this context, reserving the latter for the kind of rejoinder that Billeter's book solicits (Jullien 2007, 13).
14. One article that engages this issue, though it does so rather defensively, is Kubin 2008. Edward Slingerland's book *Mind and Body in Early China* (2019)

includes a highly critical discussion of Jullien's overall thought and specifically his orientalism, which I will address in my chapter 1.

15. On this count, Jullien has made reference to Schlegel's notion of *Anspielung* and how there may be connections between the German Romantic tradition in general and Chinese thought (Jullien 1997, 208).

16. It is not clear in the review to what extent Spivak considers these points to apply to "Derrida, Lyotard, Deleuze, and the like," as well.

17. My position is in that sense very different from Jullien's, who stands neither within Western thought, as its deconstructor, nor in Chinese thought, as fully sinized (Jullien 2012, 60). Instead, Jullien operates between the two.

18. Consider, for example, a review of Jullien's book on "literati" painting, *The Great Image Has No Form*, which objects that Jullien's "arguments take place in an intellectual vacuum . . . without reference to almost anyone else in the field" (Lachman 2011, 233). While Jullien "quotes extensively from early treatises by Zong Bing, Guo Xi, and Jing Hao," "no previous scholarship on these authors and texts is engaged or acknowledged"; "this near total lack of acknowledgment of Chinese art history as a discipline will cause those from other fields to credit Jullien with far more originality than he deserves" (ibid.).

It's worth noting that this particular reviewer appreciatively mentions Billeter's *Contre François Jullien* (2006) and echoes many of Billeter's charges, ultimately accusing Jullien of beginning "with his conclusions firmly in hand and . . . casting about to justification for them wherever he can" (Lachman 2011, 234). Or, as another reviewer puts it with respect to the same book, "Jullien himself appears to have avoided almost all recent scholarship in the fields of Chinese art and intellectual history. Indeed, rarely does one encounter a publication by a major university press that displays such disengagement from the ongoing scholarly discourses with which it might reasonably be associated. The book is best approached, perhaps, as a work of belles lettres intended for an audience outside academe" (Harrist 2011, 252).

19. See Billeter 2006.

20. See Fieni 2018. The original French was published in 1976, with the English translation first appearing in 2017.

21. When in an interview Jullien and his work are characterized as "exceptional," he responds that this may appear so but then immediately moves away from the term and counters it with his notion of *écart* or "divergence" (Martin and Spire 2011, 214–15).

22. It is perhaps Barthes' work in *The Neutral* that comes closer to Jullien's appreciative work on the bland: see Hansen 2008.

23. I am certainly not the only one to have noted this. In their commentary on the *Dao De Jing*, Ames and Hall, for example, hint several times at the book's challenges to exceptionalism: see, for example, Ames and Hall 2003, 70, 84.

24. Jullien has written most clearly about this methodological point in his most recent works. My sense is that he has focused on clarifying it in response to the charge that he operates within an opposition between Western and Chinese thought and construes China as the absolute other, either to embrace it over the West or to reject it. But Jullien insists this is not so: his is not a thought of identity and difference but

of resources and divergence. Nevertheless, it is not always easy to avoid the suggestion of opposition in his thinking, as Marcel Gauchet in his questioning of Jullien has pointed out (Jullien 2009c, 183), and that difficulty will appear in my reconstruction of his thought here as well.

25. See Jullien 2007, 60; Martin and Spire 2011, 194.
26. Collège des Bernardins 2018.

REFERENCES

Ames, Roger T., and David L. Hall, eds. 2003. *Dao De Jing: "Making This Life Significant"; A Philosophical Translation*. Translated by Roger Ames and David Hall. New York: Ballantine Books.

Badiou, Alain. 2018. "Jullien l'Apostat." In *François Jullien*, edited by Daniel Bougnoux and François L'Yvonnet, 97–98. Paris: L'Herne.

Baecker, Dirk. 2008. "Sinndimensionen einer Situation." In *Kontroverse über China: Sinophilosophie*, edited by Dirk Baecker, François Jullien, Philippe Jousset, Wolfgang Kubin, and Peter Pörtner, 31–47. Berlin: Merve.

Billeter, Jean François. 2006. *Contre François Jullien*. Paris: Allia.

Citot, Vincent. 2009. "Entretien avec François Jullien." *Le philosophoire* 31: 27–36.

Cole, Teju. 2016. *Known and Strange Things*. New York: Random House.

Collège des Bernardins. 2018. "Mardi des Bernardins: Croire ou ne pas croire, une question obsolète?" Filmed October 2, 2018, at Collège des Bernardins, Paris, France. Video, 1:07.08. https://www.youtube.com/watch?v=7nYcZaVAwVw&t=3603s.

Coombs, Sam. 2018. *Édouard Glissant*. London: Bloomsbury.

Droit, Roger-Pol. 2018. "Une vie après la Chine." In *François Jullien*, edited by Daniel Bougnoux and François L'Yvonnet, 37–42. Paris: L'Herne.

Fieni, David. 2018. Review of *Class Warrior—Taoist Style*, by Abdelkébir Khatibi. *boundary 2*, September 12. https://www.boundary2.org/2018/09/david-fieni-review-of-abdelkebir-khatibis-class-warrior-taoist-style/.

Foucault, Michel. 1973. *The Order of Things: An Archaeology of the Human Sciences*. New York: Vintage.

Hansen, Jérôme. 2008. "The Diet-ethics of Blandness." Review of *The Neutral: Lecture Course at the Collège de France (1977–1978)*, by Roland Barthes, and of *In Praise of Blandness: Proceedings from Chinese Thought and Aesthetics*, by François Jullien. *Senses & Society* 3 (1): 103–108.

Harrist, Robert. 2011. Review of *The Great Image Has No Form, or On the Nonobject through Painting*, by François Jullien. *The Art Bulletin* 93 (2): 249–53.

Jirn, Jin Suh. 2015. "A Sort of European Hallucination: On Derrida's 'Chinese Prejudice.'" *Situations* 8 (2): 67–83.

Jullien, François. 1995. *The Propensity of Things: Toward a History of Efficacy in China*. Translated by Janet Lloyd. New York: Zone Books.

———. 1997. "Comment pourrait-on se passer de la 'creation'? Un detour par la pensée chinoise." Interview with François Flahault. *Communications* 64: 191–209.

———. 2004a. *L'Ombre au tableau: Du mal ou du négatif*. Paris: Seuil.

———. 2004b. "Pour un nouveau rôle théorique de l'Europe." Interview with Patrice Bollon. *Revue des Deux Mondes*: 87–96.

———. 2004c. *A Treatise on Efficacy: Between Western and Chinese Thinking*. Translated by Janet Lloyd. Honolulu: University of Hawai'i Press.

———. 2005. *Conférence sur l'efficacité*. Paris : Presses universitaires de France.

———. 2007. *Chemin faisant. Connaître la Chine, relancer la philosophie. Réplique à ****. Paris: Seuil.

———. 2008a. "Eine Dekonstruktion von aussen: Von Griechenland nach China und zurück." In *Kontroverse über China: Sinophilosophie*, edited by Dirk Baecker, François Jullien, Philippe Jousset, et al., 133–59. Berlin: Merve.

———. 2008b. *In Praise of Blandness: Proceeding from Chinese Thought and Aesthetics*. Translated by Paula M. Varsano. New York: Zone Books.

———. 2009a. *The Great Image Has No Form, or On the Nonobject through Painting*. Translated by Jane Marie Todd. Chicago: University of Chicago Press.

———. 2009b. *L'Invention de l'idéal et le destin de l'Europe*. Paris: Seuil.

———. 2009c. "Thinking Between China and Greece: Breaking New Ground: An Interview with Marcel Gauchet." Translated by Simon Porzak. *Qui Parle* 18 (1): 181–210.

———. 2010. *Le Pont des singes: De la diversité à venir. Fécondité culturelle face à identité nationale*. Paris: Galilée.

———. 2012. *L'écart et l'entre: Leçon inaugurale de la Chaire sur l'altérité*. Paris: Galilée.

———. 2015. *The Book of Beginnings*. Translated by Jody Gladding. New Haven: Yale University Press.

———. 2016a. *Il n'y a pas d'identité culturelle; mais nous défendons les ressources d'une culture*. Paris: L'Herne.

———. 2016b. *This Strange Idea of the Beautiful*. Translated by Krzystof Fijalkowski and Michael Richardson. London: Seagull.

———. 2018. "De l'écart à l'inouï—repères I, II, III." In *François Jullien*, edited by Daniel Bougnoux and François L'Yvonnet, 78–88; 119–127; 233–241. Paris: L'Herne.

Kang, Yanbin. 2018. "Late Dickinson: In Praise of Blandness, Agedness, and Oblivion." *Style* 52 (3): 242–67.

Kubin, Wolfgang. 2008. "Wider die Neofiguristen. Warum China wichtig, die Sinolgie aber unbedeutend ist." In *Kontroverse über China: Sinophilosophie*, edited by Dirk Baecker, François Jullien, Philippe Jousset, et al., 65–76. Berlin: Merve.

Lachman, Charles. 2011. Review of *The Great Image Has No Form, or On the Nonobject through Painting*, by François Jullien. *The China Journal* 66: 233–34.

Lin, Esther. 2018. "'Car la Chine, pour absorbante, ne me spécialisera pas, je l'espère.' De l'exotisme de Victor Segalen à l'exotisme de François Jullien." In *François Jullien*, edited by Daniel Bougnoux and François L'Yvonnet, 43–48. Paris: L'Herne, 2018.

Martin, Nicolas, and Antoine Spire. 2011. *Chine, la dissidence de François Jullien. Suivi de: Dialogues avec François Jullien*. Paris: Seuil.

Meighoo, Sean. 2008. "Derrida's Chinese Prejudice." *Cultural Critique* 68: 163–209.

Piorunski, Richard. 1998. "Le détour d'un grec par la Chine: Entretien avec François Jullien." *Ebisu* 18: 147–85.

Potte-Bonneville, Mathieu. 2018. "Versions du platonisme: Deleuze, Foucault, Jullien." In *François Jullien*, edited by Daniel Bougnoux and François L'Yvonnet, 51–58. Paris: L'Herne.

Row, Jess. 2012. "Unmemorabilia." Review of *1Q84*, by Haruki Murakami. *Threepenny Review* 130 (Summer), https://www.threepennyreview.com/samples/row_su12.html.

Said, Edward. 1978. *Orientalism*. New York: Vintage.

Slingerland, Edward. 2019. *Mind and Body in Early China: Beyond Orientalism and the Myth of Holism*. Oxford: Oxford University Press.

Spivak, Gayatri Chakravorty. 1981. "French Feminism in an International Frame." *Yale French Studies* 62: 154–84.

Venuti, Lawrence. 1993. "Translation as Cultural Politics: Regimes of Domestication in English." *Textual Practice* 7 (2): 208–23.

Wang, ShiPu. 2008. Review of *The Impossible Nude: Chinese Art and Western Aesthetics*, by François Jullien. *China Review International* 15 (2): 234–43.

Chapter 1

Chinese Utopias in Contemporary French Thought

> But beware of fascination with China, beware of the East that would save us from the narrowness of European categories, beware of the mysticisms, beware of the East that is the obverse of the West, beware of the irrational East, beware of the gurus' East . . . François Jullien vehemently attacks using China as "the West's safety valve" or as "an instant solution for Europe's theoretical aporia.
>
> —Thierry Zarcone, in conversation with François Jullien[1]

RADICAL CHIC, RADICAL ORIENTALISM

> The Orientalist has a special sibling whom I will, in order to highlight her significance as a kind of representational agency, call the Maoist.
>
> —Rey Chow, *Writing Diaspora*[2]

In *Le pont des singes: De la diversité à venir* (The monkey bridge: on diversity to come), a short book that appears to have been triggered by a visit to Vietnam, François Jullien refers to himself as an "orientalist" (Jullien 2010, 57). Since Jullien is not only a Hellenist but also a sinologist—a specialist of classical China in particular—the designation is technically correct: as an academic who studies China, Jullien *is* very much *an orientalist*. But as Jullien knows very well, that term—"orientalist"—comes with a lot of baggage, and so on the one occasion in his extensive oeuvre where he applies the dubious term to himself (I know of no other instance where he does), it arrives in the context, precisely, of a reflection on orientalism:

En tant qu'orientaliste, je sais ce qu'il faut, au contraire, de patience et de modestie, de décatégorisations et récatégorisations infinies, pour envisager d'entrer dans d'autres cohérences et commencer à *déplier* sa pensée. (Ibid.; emphasis mine)

As an orientalist, I know that what's needed, on the contrary, is patience and modesty, infinite decategorizations and recategorizations, to envisage entering into other coherences and to begin to unwork [*déplier*] one's thought.

As he indicates just before the passage I have quoted here, this is a question of breaking out of "l'hégémonie historique de l'Occident" (the historical hegemony of the occident; ibid.).

In what follows, I would like to hold Jullien's work up to the standard he lays out here—of breaking out of the historical hegemony of the West and into what he enables us to describe as the "other coherence" of China. Part of my interest is in considering Jullien's work as an orientalist and questioning its relationship to orientalism—a project that can hardly be avoided in this context. I will pursue such a consideration in order to lay out the key terms of Jullien's thought as he has developed them throughout his work—but especially in the context of his reflections on the universal (which came late in his career but will be central to this chapter). English-language readers already have access to Jullien's book *On the Universal* (2014a), which captures some of that thinking; but I will be working mostly with three still-untranslated texts: the already-mentioned *Le pont des singes* (Monkey bridge; 2010) but also the lecture *L'écart et l'entre* (Divergence and the in-between; 2012), later published in an expanded form as the short book *Il n'y a pas d'identité culturelle* (There is no cultural identity; 2016a). Starting from what I understand to be the antiorientalist positions that are laid out in that book as well as the lecture, I then return to Jullien's Vietnam book—a sort of travelogue against orientalist travelogues—to critically assess it through the lens of his own antiorientalism.

As a way to mark his own approach as a scholar of China, Jullien often refers critically to "Chinese utopias" in French thought. In *L'écart et l'entre*, he notes that those utopias are numerous, but he does not spell them out. Those familiar with contemporary French theory may see a reference here to the Paris-based avant-garde group of philosophers and writers who created the journal *Tel Quel* (As is) and who had what Jean Chesneaux characterizes as a "love affair" with "Maoist China" in the 1970s (Chesneaux 1987, 21). Ieme van der Poel writes in this context of the "maolâtrie française" (French maolatry; van der Poel 1993, 432) of *Tel Quel* writers Roland Barthes, Julia Kristeva, Marcelin Pleynet, Philippe Sollers, and François Wahl, who together undertook a three-week trip to China in 1974 and reported back about it in their writings (Jacques Lacan was supposed to go but didn't; in an interview, Sollers points out that "the person who was most interested in China was Lacan"; Kao 1981, 34). Across their works, these writers produced a largely "idealized" and "fantasy-like" (ibid., 431, my translation; on 435, van der Poel has "phantasmatic") image of China that has by now been well criticized. (The exception was, perhaps, Wahl, who attacked his colleagues' "sinophilia" but was accused by them of "sinophobia," with antiorientalist tendencies evident in both positions; Hayot 2004, 153.)

There is plenty of scholarship on *Tel Quel*, and my goal is not to review all of it here. Apart from van der Poel, who seeks to understand why China was able to take on "the magical aspect of a modern *Utopia* in the writings of the Telquelians" (van der Poel 1993, 435), United States–based critics Lisa Lowe and Eric Hayot have already explored these Chinese hallucinations (Barthes himself uses the term; Hayot 2004, 154) or dreams, with Hayot dedicating a full third of his book *Chinese Dreams* to *Tel Quel* (he writes of *Tel Quel*'s "dream logic" [ibid., 122] in its approach to China) and Lowe discussing *Tel Quel* as a separate case alongside Kristeva and Barthes in *Critical Terrains* (Lowe 1991). Both Hayot and Lowe refer in this context to Gayatri Chakravorty Spivak's article "French Feminism in an International Frame," which skewered Kristeva's book *About Chinese Women*, a direct result of *Tel Quel*'s China trip (Spivak 1981). Spivak arguably played a leading role in the later debates about *Tel Quel* as well as Western representations of China in general not just due to this review but also due to her critical comments, in her introduction to Jacques Derrida's *Of Grammatology*, about Derrida's use of China in that book (see Chow 2001 and Bohm, Staten, and Chow 2001; see also Meighoo 2008 and Jirn 2015).[3]

Lowe's account in particular can be said to continue Spivak's argument in that it criticizes the orientalist features of Kristeva's, Barthes', and *Tel Quel*'s accounts of China (the ways in which they are "disturbingly reminiscent of [earlier French orientalism's] postures and rhetorics"; Lowe 1991, 137). Those features are all the more damning given the antiorientalism of some of Barthes' work before *Empire of Signs* (his book about Japan) or his writings on China—specifically the entry "Continent perdu" (Lost continent) in *Mythologies*. This "irony" leads Lowe to speak of a "postcolonial form of orientalism" to describe such *orientalist antiorientalist* formations. Lowe criticizes Kristeva and Barthes for "constitut[ing] China as an irreducibly different Other outside Western signification and the coupling of signifier and signified" (ibid., 138). She further criticizes them for construing China as "feminine or maternal" and "disrupt[ing] the 'phallocentric' occidental social system" (139). Lowe's analysis of Barthes is particularly provocative in that it traces the shift in his writing "from the targeting of orientalism as an object of criticism in the late 1950s to the dramatic practice of orientalism as a writing strategy in the mid-1970s" (153) in an attempt to escape the dominant Western point of view:

> Ironically, Barthes' attempt to resolve the dilemma of criticizing Western ideology while escaping the tyranny of binary logic takes a form not unlike that of traditional orientalism: through an invocation of the Orient as a utopian space, Barthes constitutes an imaginary third position. The imagined Orient—as critique of the Occident—becomes an emblem of his "poetics of escape," a desire to transcend semiology and the ideology of the signifier and the signified, to invent a place that exceeds binary structure itself. (154)

Lowe points out that in *Roland Barthes by Roland Barthes* "one of the designations for this space is atopia," which is deemed superior to utopia because utopia "proceeds from meaning and governs it"—whereas Barthes' attempt is precisely to get away from such a space governed by meaning (Lowe 1991, 158).[4] And so a mythical no-place is invented that is called "Japan." As Hayot points out, Barthes is very aware that his Japan is a construction; indeed, he explicitly presents it as such (Hayot 2004, 125). Still, Japan is evoked as

> an imaginary topos of "untranslatable" difference. . . . The imagination of Japan is an occasion to wish, as in a dream, the toppling of the West: the undoing of its systems of language and discourse, its institutions of meanings, its symbolic paternal order. (Lowe 1991, 159)

As such an "antitext to the West, however," Lowe writes, "Japan is ultimately not an 'atopia' but a 'utopia,'" precisely in the sense that Barthes gives to this term: it's the product of an "oppositional desire, still caught within the binary logic he seeks to avoid" (ibid., 159). In short, "Barthes' Japan is a reactive formation," and for that reason, Lowe argues that it fails as an atopia—and succumbs to orientalism.[5]

A similar problem affects Barthes' writings on China: China is, in Barthes' own terms, "hallucinated" in his work—but entirely within Western terms, as the West's opposite. It is "considered exclusively in terms of occidental cultural systems," as Lowe puts it (Lowe 1991, 162). Barthes "does not offer an explanation of how China is subversive within its own autonomous cultural system" (ibid., 162). Rather, it's "invoked according to a logic of opposition" (163). In its blandness, which (as I have discussed in my introduction) Barthes identifies as China's aesthetic trait, it offers "a commentary whose tone would be *no comment*" (Barthes quoted in ibid., 167; emphasis original).[6] "Again," Lowe writes, "as in traditional orientalism, the Western writer's desire for the oriental Other structures the Other as forever separated, unpossessed, and estranged" (ibid., 167). "From this discussion of Kristeva,

Barthes, and *Tel Quel*," Lowe concludes, "we understand that even on the Left the orientalist gaze may reemerge, even when the purpose of its project is to criticize state power and social domination" (189). "The continuing utopian tendency of projecting revolutionary, cultural, or ethnic purity onto other sites, such as the Third World, must be scrutinized and challenged" (ibid.).

Hayot too seeks to understand—in the wake of scholars like Patrick French, Philippe Forest, and Danielle Marx-Scouras—the melding of "the imaginary and the real" (Hayot 2004, 128–29) that we find in *Tel Quel*'s accounts of China. He considers such melding to have been enabled by

> the theoretical ground laid by Foucault (associated with *Tel Quel* early on but no longer involved by the time of the journal's Maoist turn) and Barthes, among others, in which traditional notions of representation and reality gave way to more complicated projections of linguistic systems and dream worlds, blurring the line between actual and imaginary China. (Ibid., 129)

This is very much in line with Edward Said's Foucault-inspired book *Orientalism*, which is interested in the "interchange between the academic and the more or less imaginative meanings of Orientalism" (Said 1978, 3)—between research on the Orient and then also what Said refers to as "a style of thought based upon an ontological and epistemological distinction made between 'the Orient' and (most of the time) 'the Occident,'" which is the starting point for "elaborate theories, epics, novels, social descriptions, and political accounts concerning the Orient, its peoples, customs, 'mind,' destiny, and so on" (ibid., 2). What Said refers to as the "traffic" between the two produces what is, in his view, "the third meaning of Orientalism," "which is something more historically and materially defined than either of the other two": "Orientalism as a Western style for dominating, restructuring, and having authority over the Orient" (3). It's at that point that Said brings up "Michel Foucault's notion of a discourse" (ibid.), noting that he found it useful even if he will also criticize Foucault for not believing enough in "the determining imprint of individual writers upon the otherwise anonymous collective body of texts constituting a discursive formation like Orientalism" (ibid., 23). Overall, one can see here how much Said's own book—which dates from 1978, just four years after *Tel Quel* travels to China—is in line with the work by Foucault to which Hayot alludes.

What Hayot takes issue with, rather, is that for *Tel Quel* "the very theory that supported such a sense of China seemed to be coming from China itself, as if China were justifying, once again in advance, the geo-theoretical conception that made itself possible" (Hayot 2003, 129). "*Tel Quel*'s 'China' was therefore its own cause and its own effect" (ibid.). This is Hayot's way of drawing out the orientalism of *Tel Quel*'s accounts of China: in *Tel Quel*'s perspective, China ultimately becomes no more than a justification for an already-developed theoretical point of view. What Kristeva, Barthes, and *Tel Quel* ultimately find in China is nothing but themselves, to continue Spivak's criticism of Kristeva, and illustrates "the Western intellectual's self-centeredness in the face of the other" (155). They are psychotically hallucinating a version of China to confirm what they already knew—basically, the critical take on the West that they had already developed (129). Hayot partly relies on Rey Chow's *Woman and Chinese Modernity* to emphasize that China is "not the magical utopia Kristeva imagines it to be" (142). Instead, "China is just another place" (ibid.).

If *Tel Quel* may have been one likely referent of those "Chinese utopias" in French thought from which Jullien seeks to distance himself, it's worth pointing out that Kristeva, Barthes, and their colleagues were certainly not the first to fall in love with China.[7] When Chesneaux, in what has become a key text in the field, writes about this love affair, he is writing not only about the 1970s but also the '60s and '50s and traces this contemporary sinophily back to the nineteenth and especially eighteenth centuries. The love affair is complex, as Chesneaux points out, and its contemporary realizations need to be understood within the French context specifically as a "rejection on the part of the French intellectuals of Soviet-styled communism," for example, but also out of an interest in China as "a valuable experiment in Marxist economic theory" (Chesneaux 1987, 21). He goes on to note that

> China also met a basic aspiration among French left-wing intellectuals, which I would describe as political exoticism—that is, the tendency to look for a political homeland and model of reference in distant, exotic countries. At times in Cuba, at one time in Algeria, in Vietnam, then in China; each provided a substitute for the ideal society France was unable to develop at home, especially after the failure of the May '68 movement—which had been so popular with most intellectuals, and not only with students. (Ibid.)

Certainly *Tel Quel* fits the latter bill. However, Chesneaux's overall point is that France's love affair with China extends beyond the journal to what Alex Hughes (commenting on Chesneaux) refers to as "the mid-century moment . . . [that] witnessed a plethora of *voyages en Chine* undertaken by French luminaries in the wake of the Bandung conference of May 1955" (Hughes 2003, 85; emphasis original). Hughes writes,

> That conference spawned the invitation famously proffered to the West by Zhou Enlai [first premier of the People's Republic of China], ventriloquized by the French journalist Robert Guillain, who acted on it in the following terms: "La Chine est ouverte au visiteurs. Venez voir!" (China is open to visitors. Come see for yourself!). (Ibid.)

Hughes adds that Jean-Paul Sartre and Simone de Beauvoir were two of those early visitors. In his article on *Tel Quel*, Ieme van der Poel suggests that it is because Sartre and de Beauvoir had already discovered China in the 1950s that, around the time when *Tel Quel* falls in love with Mao, *Les Temps Modernes* (the journal edited by Sartre and de Beauvoir) "s'intéresse peu à la Chine" (wasn't interested much in China): "Il paraît que pour *Les Temps Modernes*, le culte de la Chine représente une étape du tier-mondisme qui était déjà passée" (it appears that, for *Les Temps Modernes*, the China cult represented a stage of third worldism that had already passed"; van der Poel 1993, 433).

Still, "by and large, Maoist China was very chic in French cultural life of the 1950s and 1960s," Chesneaux writes (Chesneaux 1987, 22). Chesneaux's use of the term "chic" in connection with Mao enables one, with a wink to US novelist and critic Tom Wolfe, to use the phrase "radical chic" to capture *Tel Quel*'s love affair with Mao. Published in *New York Magazine* in 1970, Wolfe's text "Radical Chic" satirizes a party at Leonard Bernstein's where the Black Panthers were the guests of honor (Wolfe 1970). Wolfe's account includes toward the end a rendering of how the Bernsteins, in the aftermath of the party, quickly become the object of criticism: the *New York Times*, which published two noncritical accounts of the party, followed up with an editorial that attacks the Bernsteins' "romanticization" of the Panthers and deems it "an affront to the majority of Black Americans" (ibid.). The party creates, according to the editorial, "one more distortion of the Negro [*sic*] image. Responsible black leadership is not likely to cheer as the Beautiful People [i.e., New York's Park Avenue elite] create a new myth that Black Panther is beautiful" (ibid.). Things got even worse for the Bernsteins when Black Power groups turned out to be voicing "support for the Arabs against Israel" (ibid.), ultimately forcing Bernstein to distance himself from Black Panther politics while he insisted nevertheless that it has a place in democratic culture.

Much in Wolfe's piece, it's worth noting, revolves around the representation of the Black Panthers, who are hailed in Wolfe's satirical account of "Lenny's Party" as "real": "they're real, these Black Panthers . . . who actually put their lives on the line . . . [with] real Afros . . . these are real men" (Wolfe 1970). Wolfe's "Radical Chic" thus stages a problem of representation that's not entirely separate from the orientalist issues that haunt *Tel Quel*'s love affair with Mao: there, too, the issue is, if not so much with the reality of China, with its hallucinatory and dreamlike construction, its psychotic projection, as "real"—*more real* than the West. As Robeson Taj Frazier in his book *The East Is Black* has shown, China furthermore plays an important role in "the black radical imagination" itself, precisely during the same three decades that I've discussed (Frazier's book ranges from the 1950s to the 1970s). This means that the historically and philosophically parallel cases that I've just laid out ("the black panther" and "the dragon of China," to draw from William Worthy's 1967 *Esquire* magazine article; Worthy quoted in Frazier 2015, 109) need to be considered as imbricated into each other as well. Frazier notes early on in his book that orientalism is a real issue in this context (ibid., 64) and in fact uses the phrase "radical orientalism" as part of his discussion (16). He does not consider, however, how, for example, the Black Panthers themselves were exoticized and orientalized in the United States.

Chesneaux's final judgment on *Tel Quel* does not pull any punches:

The whole affair was certainly a strange combination of affectation and naivety, of misinformation and self-complacency, which deserves blame and regret and nothing else. We [French intellectuals] were definitely lacking intellectual rigor, caution, and integrity. Not only did we satisfy ourselves with a rosy picture of China . . . We failed completely to assess properly our responsibility towards French public opinion. (Chesneaux 1987, 23)

When Lisa Lowe quotes *Tel Quel*'s statement from 1971 that in regard to the Chinese Cultural Proletarian Revolution they will do everything "to illuminate it, to analyze it, and to support it" (Lowe 1991, 136), she surely does so to draw out the extent to which they failed (and perhaps also to shed light on her own project, which, while exposing the orientalism of *Tel Quel*, would never purport to speak the truth about China; Said had of course already taught us as much in *Orientalism*). Chesneaux uses the occasion of his text, which is based on the "Morrison Lecture" that he delivered in 1987 in Canberra (it's worth noting Chesneaux himself refers to it as "a kind of unofficial 'Victor Segalen Lecture'"; I will return to the importance of Segalen for the broader context and especially reception of Jullien's work in chapter 4), to express—quite modestly—his regret about this. Noting that "We were certainly wrong in our simplified approach to the complex realities of Chinese politics and Chinese society," he also adds, however, that "we were not necessarily wrong in advocating Maoist analyses and Maoist thinking so as to approach critically what we probably knew better than China—namely, France itself" (ibid., 24). In other words, *Tel Quel*'s project—however flawed—may still have some value beyond its erroneous engagement with China as a critical approach to France.

CHINA AS HETEROTOPIA; OR, WHY JULLIEN IS NOT AN ORIENTALIST

Assuming that we now have a good understanding of what Jullien in his work on China does *not* want to do—he does not want to participate in the tradition of Chinese utopias that is common in French contemporary thought and beyond it—how does Jullien describe his own approach to China? Does it manage to avoid the orientalist trap?

Criticizing the use of China as utopia, Jullien frequently refers to his own understanding of China as a heterotopia, a term he explicitly borrows from Michel Foucault's *Order of Things*. This reference, for which Jullien never provides a footnote, goes back to Foucault's famous preface to *Order of Things*, where he claims that the

> book arose out of a passage in Borges, out of the laughter that shattered, as I read the passage, all the familiar landmarks of my thought—*our* thought, the thought that bears the stamp of our age and our geography—breaking up all the ordered surfaces and all the planes with which we are accustomed to tame the wild profusion of existing things, and continuing long afterwards to disturb and threaten with collapse our age-old distinction between the Same and the Other. (Foucault 1973, xv; emphasis original)

The passage referenced here quotes "a certain Chinese encyclopedia"[8]; in other words, we get here Foucault's take on "China"—and "without so much as a hint," as Zhang Longxi has pointed out, "to suggest that the hilarious passage from that 'Chinese encyclopedia' may have been made up to represent a Western phantasy of the Other and that the illogical way of sorting out animals in that passage can be as alien to the Chinese mind as it is to the Western mind" (Longxi 1988, 110).[9]

"China," by Foucault's acknowledgment (although it's worth noting that this is "China" by way of Borges, an Argentine!), has the capacity not just to shatter Western thought (for surely that is what Foucault means by "our thought") but also to "disturb and threaten with collapse" the oppositional logic of "the Same and the Other" that we've seen is essential to orientalism (orientalism constructs the orient in opposition to the West). Jullien seizes Foucault's "disturbing" and "threatening" characterization of China and aligns it for his purposes.

Disturb and threaten: That is, as Foucault explains later in the preface, what heterotopias do. It's what sets them aside from utopias. Jullien's relationship to China is not a love affair. When looked at carefully, China is much too disturbing and troubling to allow for the exoticization and orientalization that the term "love affair," in Chesneaux, is meant to evoke. In *Order of Things*, Foucault writes that

> Heterotopias are disturbing, probably because they secretly undermine language, because they make it impossible to name this *and* that, because they shatter, or tangle common names, because they destroy "syntax" in advance, and not

only the syntax with which we construct sentences but also that less apparent syntax which causes words and things (next to and also opposite one another) to "hold together." (Foucault 1973, xviii; emphasis original)

The heterotopic collapse, in Foucault's description, is not just at the level of the sentence—or of the relation signifier/signified. It also affects the syntax of words and things, words and their referents (not their signifieds). While this needs to be read negatively first and foremost as a disturbance of and threat to Western thought, it also lays out an implicit, positive image of China as the cause of such threat and disturbance.

How exactly that's supposed to be, Foucault does not make clear: it appears to have something to do with "the wild profusion of existing things"—a weird, vitalist phrase that does not tell us much—and how such wildness challenges the Western order of things, which Foucault suggests is rooted in language. It is, indeed, on the count of language that Foucault in the preface lays out his reference to China just a little bit more. In between the discussion of Borges and his use of the term "heterotopia," Foucault situates China between the consoling utopia of another kind of order (that the passage in Borges lays out, and a heightened order at that, associated with walls—he is thinking of the Great Wall of China, presumably?—that are reflected, Foucault rather flippantly suggests, in the verticality of Chinese writing) and what Foucault characterizes as the more-disturbing heterotopia that would present a fundamental undermining of the attempt to order, including the ordering drive of language itself and the relation between words and things. But this is not based on any serious study of Chinese. It's hard to imagine Jullien agreeing with this characterization of the Chinese language.

Moreover, when one actually looks at Foucault's text "Les hétérotopies" (Heterotopias) in this context, other problematic aspects of the notion emerge. With the notion of heterotopia, Foucault seeks to name places that are "*absolutely* different":

> places that are opposed to all other places, that are destined in a way to be a kind of *counter*-spaces. It's children who know those counter-spaces, those localized utopias, particularly well: it's the back of the garden, of course; or the attic, naturally; or better even, the Indian tent set up in the middle of the attic; or also, it's—on Thursday afternoon—the parents' big bed. It's on this big bed that one discovers the ocean, because one can swim there between the sheets. And this big bed is also the sky, because one can jump there on the mattress springs; it's the forest, because one can hide there; it's the night, because one becomes a ghost between the sheets; and it's pleasure, finally, because, when the parents come back, one is going to be punished. (Foucault 2009, 24; emphasis original)

It's worth asking what remains here of the "disturbing" and "threatening" heterotopia that Jullien finds in the preface to *Order of Things*. If the notion of heterotopia is claimed by Jullien specifically to resist those "Chinese utopias" that succumb to exoticism and orientalism, it's surely also worth asking about the exoticism and orientalism in Foucault's description. The association of heterotopias with children—which seems rich with nostalgia, with gardens and attics and "Indian tents"—seems problematic from this point of view. Later in the same essay Foucault suggests that "the most ancient example of heterotopia would be the garden, the millenarian creation that certainly in the Orient had a magical meaning" (Foucault 2009, 29). Another few pages later, the "hammams of the muslims" are mentioned as another example (ibid., 32). If the essay is, generally speaking, not Foucault's strongest work, the exoticism and orientalism of Foucault's theorization of heterotopias poses some challenges to Jullien's adoption of the term "heterotopia" to name his own strategy; the preface of *Order of Things* is less problematic on this count, but there too questions can be asked.

Let's not focus too much, however, on Jullien's brief mentions of Foucault's heterotopia as a name for his project. What are the terms that Jullien himself develops, and how do they relate to the exoticism and orientalism that Jullien seeks to avoid? Jullien's project is to play out Western thought (specifically, Greek thought) and Chinese thought (specifically, pre-Buddhist, classical Chinese thought) in a divergence with each other, not to argue—as he clarifies in *The Great Image*—that the one is somehow better than the other but to show "how they illuminate each other, each revealing the *unthought* of the other" (Jullien 2009, 40; emphasis original).[10] On that last count, it is important to note that Jullien would not characterize his method as comparative, even if he seems at times committed to comparativism (as critics have noted[11]) and even if the back covers of his books sometimes characterize his work as "comparative philosophy." As he puts it quite simply in *L'écart et l'entre*, "je ne compare pas" (I do not compare; Jullien 2012, 59). Or, if he does, it's "temporairement et sur des segments limités" (temporarily and on limited segments; ibid., 59). Certainly "comparison" does not characterize his overall approach. In *The Book of Beginnings* he writes that, to his mind, "'to compare' is another way of not moving, of not leaving, and therefore of not entering . . . One has remained within one's own overarching categories, beginning from which one orders things; heterotopia [Foucault's term again] and disorientation have not come into play" (Jullien 2015, 13).

Against such a "weak" (as one might perhaps call it[12]) understanding of comparison (which subsumes difference into one term of the comparison and then often universalizes it), Jullien aims for a "European reasoning" that would "*de-* and *re*-categorize itself . . . effectively access an elsewhere, another way of thinking" (Jullien 2015, 14; emphasis original). "Good work on Chinese thought," he writes, "is work that 'disturbs' European thought" (ibid., 12). In a discussion of literary comparison ("as if . . . ") in the *Dao De Jing* (referenced by Jullien as the *Laozi*) in *The Great Image*, Jullien contrasts a mode of comparison that "[aims] to render convincingly, thus allowing us to see better," to one that "aims to make less precise": "instead of focusing on determination and permeating us with its presence, it tends on the contrary to detach us from the order of the 'there is' and to make us return upstream from its actualization" (Jullien 2009, 32). Jullien captures this difference in *This Strange Idea* through the opposition of "variety," which implies essence and refers to "the unitary genus diversifying itself" (Jullien 2016c, 93), and "variance," "in which the essence of the thing dissipates" (ibid.).[13] Whereas the former remains within Western ontology and metaphysics (a claim that I examine in chapter 2), the latter is outside of those. Jullien typically finds it in Chinese thought.

In view of the charge made against Jullien that he generalizes and essentializes both Western and Chinese thought,[14] I should repeat that by "Western thought" Jullien mostly means Greek thought, a notion that refers for him to the tradition of philosophical thinking started by Plato. Jullien's genealogies of Western thought frequently reach back to Plato to reconstruct Western thinking from there. Those reconstructions are hardly unaware of the differences within Western thought: he gives ample attention, for example, to Aristotle's criticism of Platonism (he speaks in this context of the divergence between Aristotle and Plato; Jullien 2016a, 68). But ultimately he seeks to show that certain aspects of Platonism continue in Aristotle and after, all the way to the present day.

By "Chinese thought," as I have already indicated, Jullien mostly means classical Chinese thought. He is focused on Daoism but frequently works across traditions that are generally opposed—Confucianism and Daoism, for example (see Jullien 2004b, 94–95). Ultimately, Chinese thought for him is simply all thought that is expressed in Chinese (Jullien 2012, 41). This is a wide umbrella to be sure, and there is some hopping around within his books and most certainly between books. Jullien also often allows the work of an individual author to stand in for a much larger tradition of thought.[15] All of this makes Jullien vulnerable to the charge of generalization and essentialization, which (as I've already noted) misses the mark in view of his critical project.

No doubt partly in response to criticisms he has received, Jullien has come to lay out some of the key terms of his work—and I'm thinking now of those that relate to the orientalism debate in particular—in some of his recent, shorter books. These include the already-mentioned lecture *L'écart et l'entre*, which he delivered upon his inauguration as Chair of Alterity at the Collège d'études mondiales at the Fondation Maison des Sciences de l'Homme in

Paris on December 8, 2011. It's worth noting, from the get-go, that "alterity" stands in tension with Jullien's declared position. He has often noted that alterity is a philosophical construct and does not capture his approach to China; he does not work on China as "alterity," but his work comes from the *fact*—rather than the philosophical *construction*—of China's *geographical* elsewhere (whereas alterity "se construit," China's elsewhere "se constate"; Jullien 2012, 17). It comes from the fact that for a very long time China did not come into contact with European thought. Jullien's thinking about China is a thinking of "ailleurs" rather than of "altérité"; as such, China marks (as he puts in the lecture's opening pages) an "extériorité," an "outside," to Western thought (ibid., 15). This is what sparked his interest in it.

This also means that, through China, Jullien wanted to discover "notre étrangeté" (Jullien 2012, 17), the West's strangeness. This latter point has to do with something else that Jullien frequently mentions—namely, the fact that he turned to China in order to better understand Greek thought (ibid., 13). The particular disturbance or threat that it brings to Greek thought he describes as a "deconstruction from the outside" (this in opposition to Jacques Derrida's deconstruction, which is always already inside; 15 and 21). As the title of an interview with Thierry Zarcone has it, China operates like a "philosophical tool" for Jullien—in that, through its "detour" (and Chinese thought *is* a thought of the detour for Jullien), he seeks to better understand Western thought. The overall trajectory of Jullien's work seems to confirm this project, since most of his recent books deal with European thinking, which he broached after the detour through China was accomplished. Jullien passes through China to lay bare what he refers to as the West's "unthought"— "notre impensé" (20). By this he means "that *starting from which* we think and that, because of this, we do not think" (ibid.; emphasis original). It refers to the hidden assumptions of Western thought. Chinese thought helps him become alert to those.

Expanding on his rejection of the term "alterity" as a philosophical construct, Jullien also rejects the term "difference" in the context of conversations about "cultural diversity" (Jullien 2012, 24). Instead, he proposes to replace it by the notion of "écart," "divergence" (ibid., 24). Difference, Jullien explains (and here I return to a point I made earlier on), is "un concept identitaire," "an identitarian concept" (ibid.). There can't be such a thing as "cultural identity," because a culture is always a mixed, nonidentitarian formation and it is always a formation in progress; if not, it's a dead culture, similar to a dead language. The only thing proper to culture is that it is constantly transforming and changing (26). (This applies to a notion like culture, but Jullien also applies it to the individual—or, rather, to the subject, whose "ex-istence" is given meaning within this philosophical framework as never coinciding with itself; Jullien 2016a, 57. He even argues that evolution operates in the same way; ibid., 70.) Difference is a concept that orders, he concludes; it stands in opposition to what Foucault envisioned by the term "heterotopia." (An interesting claim, given the presence of the Greek word *heteros*—'ετερος—in "heterotopia"; indeed, this notion of *heteros* will return later in this chapter as well and deserves to be questioned further. Jullien seems to want to retranslate it as a geographical elsewhere rather than as a philosophically construed alterity, as distance rather than as difference, but there are moments in his work where he slips back into the logic of difference and alterity.[16]) All cultures are, in that sense, heterotopic (Jullien 2016a, 48). Part of the problem with difference is that it puts us "in a logic of integration,"[17] "of classification and specification"—"not of discovery" (Jullien 2012, 29). Difference, when it comes to diversity, is "a lazy concept" (ibid.). Instead, Jullien opts for divergence and puts it to work.

Divergence makes us rethink cultures as what Jullien calls "fecundities." Whereas difference establishes a "distinction," divergence establishes a "distance"—a "separation" and a "detachment" (Jullien 2012, 32)—which productively puts that which it separates "into tension" (ibid., 34). As Jullien sees it, this is not a way of ordering but precisely of disordering, of "derangement," which makes "fecundity" appear (35). It's an "exploratory," "inventive," and "adventurous" notion that produces cultural resources (rather than "values" or "roots"; Jullien 2016a, 6 and 64) for "exploration" and "exploitation" (Jullien 2012, 37) by all. This is an approach that goes against cultural "exceptionalism," as Jullien repeatedly points out (Jullien 2016a, 47–62). In this context, Jullien speaks of those resources' "yield" (ibid., 38). There's a "profit" (39) that comes from them. The language, it's worth noting, is both agricultural and economical, a crossover that Jullien has also emphasized elsewhere (see Jullien 2007b).

All of this means that when Jullien speaks of "Chinese thought"

> je ne lui suppose aucune identité, nul essentialisme de principe—faut-il encore le répéter?—mais je désigne seulement la pensée qui s'est exprimée, actualisée, en Chinois. Non que je suppose, là non plus, quelque déterminisme de la langue sur la pensée, mais parce que la langue, elle aussi—ou plutôt d'abord—est ressource. (Jullien 2012, 41)

> I don't assume it has any identity, I don't assume any essentialism in principle—must I repeat myself once more?—but I designate only the thought that was expressed, actualized, in Chinese. Nor does it mean that I assume some linguistic determinism of thought, just that language itself is also—or rather first of all—a resource.

"Babel," he adds, is "the chance of thought"—a quotation to which I will return in chapter 4 (ibid.).

As Jullien points out, his position also takes us out of what he describes as "easy universalism" and "lazy relativism" (Jullien 2012, 44): a universalism that is identity-driven and exports a certain property to the rest of the world, flattening it, rendering it uniform; or a relativism that allows all cultures to exist in their isolated bubbles (ibid.). These points about universalism are further developed in his later text *Il n'y a pas d'identité culturelle*, subtitled "mais nous défendons les ressources d'une culture" (but we defend the resources of a culture). There, as well as in his book *On the Universal* (2014a), he distinguishes between a bad universal—which he characterizes as the general, which renders uniform—and a good, stronger conception of the universal as what has been developed in the context of European thought as an "exigency of thought" (Jullien 2016a, 8). This universal does not name a generality but a necessity: something that cannot be otherwise, in the sense of "the universal laws of nature." (In philosophy, part of the question of course was whether such universality could be found in the realm of morality as well.) Jullien draws out, however, that in spite of the universality of such a strong universal, such a universal is singular, in the sense that it is local, developed within the context of a specific thought (European thought). It derives from European reason. The uniform, by contrast, is not derived from reason but from production (ibid., 11): it's the standard and the stereotype (ibid.), not a necessity but a commodity. The good, strong universal is turned toward the ideal; the bad universal is merely the repetition of the one. It's an "extension of the market" (ibid.). The good universal's political articulation, Jullien argues, is "the common" (12), which—contrary to the uniform—is precisely *not* what is similar. Here we see its connection to divergence, which separates and detaches and thereby constitutes the condition for an "active and intensive" (73) common. It gives new meaning to the term "dialogue" (79).

The universal thus must be conceived, Jullien writes later in this lecture, "in an encounter with universalism" (Jullien 2016a, 27). Unlike the latter,

> L'universel pour lequel il faut militer est, à l'inverse, un universel rebelle, qui n'est jamais comblé; ou disons un universel négatif défaisant le confort de toute positivité arrêtée: non pas totalisateur (saturant), mais au contraire rouvrant du manqué dans toute totalité achevée. Universel régulateur (au sens de l'idée kantienne) qui, parce qu'il n'est jamais satisfait, ne cesse de repousser l'horizon et donne indéfiniment à chercher. (Ibid.)

> The universal for which one must militate is, on the contrary, a rebellious universal, which is never filled; or let's say a negative universal that undoes the comfort of all arrested positivity; not a totalizing (saturating) [universal] but on the contrary one that reopens the lack in all accomplished totality. A regulative universal (in the Kantian sense) that, because it is never satisfied, never ceases to push back the horizon and indefinitely leads to further searching.

This requires, as Jullien puts it, a certain "care" (*souci*) of the universal as "promoting its ideal aspect into a never-obtained ideal, which asks the common not to limit itself too quickly" (Jullien 2016a, 27). A slightly stronger way of putting it is that the universal may require "defending," as the subtitle of Jullien's book has it. But the notion of "defending" requires some explanation here: in Jullien's dictionary, it means to "activate" its resources; it doesn't have, he insists, a fearful and defensive (in that sense) meaning.

Divergence ultimately produces what Jullien calls *l'entre*, "the in-between." Such an "in-between escapes," as he explains, "the determination of 'Being'"—"l'entre échappe à la determination, elle qui fait être" (Jullien 2012, 51). Or, in a pithier formula, "L'*entre* n' 'est' pas" ("the in-between 'is' not," Jullien 2016a, 39; emphasis original). In philosophical terms, it escapes "ontology" (Jullien 2012, 51), an escape that Jullien also associates with Chinese thought (as I explain in chapter 2). He notes at this point that Chinese language-thought did not isolate the notion of "being" in the way that Western thought has. Instead it has developed a notion of "nothingness," which he takes care to explain is not simply the opposite of being: it's a nonontological nothingness (ibid., 52)—the nothingness of the *dao*, of the flow of all things (the nothingness of life between birth and death, for example).

This association of Jullien's overall approach with Chinese language-thought in particular shows that the way in which Jullien theorizes his approach as a sinologist working between China and the West actually has affinities with Chinese thinking. In fact, it's hard not to read it as a rejection of many elements of Western thinking in favor of elements of Chinese thinking (alterity and difference, for example, are replaced by divergence and its associated concepts). At the same time, Jullien also maintains notions of Western/European thought and insists on the resources of Western culture (the notion of the ideal, for example, in his book on Plato). Still, because it was anchored in being (ontology) and focused on metaphysics (on ideal, geometrical forms hiding behind shadow reality, if you follow Plato), Western thought was unable to grasp the in-between that Jullien proposes: it always wanted to go beyond and access the truth of the idea rather than participate in the flow of all things (Jullien 2012, 53). This separates "life," as a metaphysical notion, from "living" (ibid., 57; see also Jullien 2016b). The in-between, rather, makes us "de-ontologize" (Jullien 2012, 56). Some in the Western tradition were attuned to this: the painter Braque, for example, who said—in a quotation Jullien mentions often—"that which is between the apple and the plate should also be painted" (ibid., 56). But by and large, Western thought did not think the in-between.

For Jullien, the (Chinese) in-between becomes a tool for working on both Chinese and Western thought. As a Western thinker, he deconstructs Western thought from the outside, as a sinologist; but as a sinologist, he does not "sinize" himself, which, he notes "disappoints orientalists" (Jullien 2012, 60). Instead, he is on neither side, working between the two. It's this in-between that prevents him from succumbing to those "utopies chinoises" that are so common in France (ibid., 61) and that I discussed in the first section of this chapter. It's at this point that he now also criticizes Foucault's notion of heterotopia (ibid.) and its exoticist and orientalist tendencies: Instead Jullien posits China as perfectly intelligible. It's exterior to the West, but it can perfectly well be understood. This seeks to end phantasmatic constructions of China as some mythological, enigmatic outside to Western comprehension. It's outside to the West, yes, but it's not outside comprehension. There can be, as Foucault says about heterotopias but also seems to deny in his text, a "science" of China's heterotopia. Translation is where the "atopian" (Jullien now shifts to this term, critically reappropriating it from Barthes) work of the in-between is most marked, as a practice that both assimilates and disassimilates (63). It's the logical language for the cultural dialogue that he envisions (Jullien 2016a, 88).

In the final section of his lecture, he also suggests a perhaps-surprising realm of application for his theory of divergence: gender studies (Jullien 2012, 76). Noting gender studies' desire to do away with sexual difference, he considers the potential fecundity of thinking a divergence between the sexes, a divergence even within a single sex itself, to see what resources this might yield. This would entail a shift from a thinking of sexual difference to a thinking of sexual divergence, which surely deserves more explanation. But the suggestion is not developed.

To sum up: By working within a divergence between Western thought and Chinese thought, Jullien is precisely not working within an opposition between the two. Chinese thought is not *different* from Western thought; it does not constitute its *other*. Rather, Chinese thought has a *coherence* of its own that was developed *exterior* to Western thought; the *divergence* between Western thought and Chinese thought that Jullien stages marks that *distance*. Second, Jullien does not essentialize Western thought or Chinese thought. Western thought is thought written in European/Western languages; Chinese thought is thought written in Chinese. (Although he treats the Chinese language as a resource, he makes it explicit that there is no linguistic determinism in his thought.) Neither Western nor Chinese thought adds up to an identity, with a proper core. Instead, cultures are constantly transforming and changing; that is what's proper to cultures, and cultures that don't are dead, like dead languages. (The same is true for subjects; it's what gives meaning to the term "existence.") While he characterizes his concept of China, and of Chinese thought, as "heterotopic"—in contrast to those Chinese utopias in French thought that he rejects—he also points out that by doing this he does not mean to suggest that China is somehow outside of intelligibility. Rather, it can be understood, it has an intelligibility of its own, and it's precisely up to the scholar to work their way into that. Finally, if Jullien has turned to China in this thought, he has done so to better understand the West. His project is not to propose China as a solution to the West's problems, or vice versa; rather, both the West and China present for him cultural resources that can be exploited to yield profits (I will explore Jullien's use of the language of economics in this context in chapter 3). He is critical of both China and the West, and he uses cultural resources from both as well. All of that said, it is worth noticing how much of Jullien's overall framework—his key terms, key ideas—strike one as Chinese, or seem to have been derived precisely from his study of China, and as part of a critical attitude in relation to the West. Jullien's later work, which has marked a return to European thought, has shifted the balance here somewhat, in the sense that he's been dedicating himself almost exclusively in his recent work to Western resources. It seems, then, in spite of what many of his critics have pointed out (often blatantly mischaracterizing his thought), that much of Jullien's work is set up precisely to avoid the traps of exoticism and orientalism that have haunted those Chinese utopias in French thought that he dismisses.

RISK OF ORIENTALISM: *LE PONT DES SINGES*

One of Jullien's harshest critics in this context is Edward Slingerland, a major scholar of early Chinese philosophical thought. Basing himself on five of Jullien's books published between 1995 and 2007, Slingerland—who, like Jullien, writes for both scholarly and popular audiences—attacks Jullien for constructing China as the West's other. Slingerland characterizes Jullien as an orientalist—more specifically, a neo-orientalist (Slingerland 2019, 305): as a representative of what he understands to be the positive, postmodernism-infused version of orientalism that emerged more or less concomitantly with orientalism's exposure (ibid., 2). Calling this kind of neo-orientalism "Hegel with a happy face" (ibid.)—a description that would be hard to maintain when held up against a comprehensive reading of Hegel's role in Jullien's work—he charges not only Jullien with it but also major (Western) sinology scholars, like the late Henry Rosemont Jr. and Roger Ames, as well as some of their colleagues (Zhang Xuezhi; Tan Yijie) working in Chinese (ibid., 2–3; Stathis Gourgouris's development of the practice of self-orientalization could have been a useful reference on this count; Gourgouris 1996). Slingerland presents Edward Said's book *Orientalism* (from 1978) as crucial for the exposure of orientalism both in its negative and positive formations; the positive, postmodernism-infused neo-orientalism with which he charges Jullien has been emerging "since the 1970s or so" (Slingerland 2019, 3).

Slingerland targets specifically the "holistic orientalism" (Slingerland 2019, 2) of Jullien's representations of China, the way in which China is presented in Jullien's work as being beyond oppositions. Importantly, Slingerland is after "the myth of holism," which, he argues, is projected onto China as the other of the "Dualistic West" (ibid., 9). To adopt "a *truly* holistic stance" (ibid.; emphasis original), however, would mean to recognize holism—specifically, weak mind-body holism, some of which (he acknowledges) can be found in early Chinese thought—in the West also as the foundation of *how* human beings *know*. This not only would make the construction of China as the other on this count impossible, it also is more in line with recent scientific discoveries about embodied cognition. Related to this—and this is the more important point that his book lays out at length—is the fact that dualism was certainly not alien to China. Slingerland works hard to uncover it there, against orientalist myths of Chinese holism. Indeed, Slingerland finds that dualism is omnipresent (at the very least in a weak version) in Chinese religious thought. It is strong holism, rather, that is absent. When it comes to Jullien, then, Slingerland would lead one to conclude that he is wrong on both counts: *both* in his description of the West *and* of China.

Slingerland's criticisms include a discussion of Jullien's essentializations and generalizations, familiar from other negative accounts of Jullien's work. Jullien's frequent criticisms of essentializations, present throughout his work but especially in his methodological writings from after 2007 (the date when Slingerland stops reviewing his work), are summarily dismissed as "insincere" (Slingerland 2019, 305) in view of some evidence to the contrary. But Jullien's actual—and frequent, elaborate even—statements against essentialism, and the methodology that he has developed around this in his later work (which, granted, is not yet available in English), are not considered. In other words, and recognizing the evidence that Slingerland brings up, it would have been good to *also* pay careful attention to the framework that Jullien has developed to counter precisely charges such as Slingerland's. (Haun Saussy, one of Jullien's critics on whom Slingerland relies, similarly develops his criticism of Jullien based on a very limited corpus, as I've already noted; see this chapter's note 16.) This would have forced Slingerland to at least explain how it can be so that the title of Jullien's book from 2012, *Il n'y a pas d'identité culturelle* (There is no cultural identity), echoes Slingerland's own view that "it is to our detriment that we start with facile assumptions of radical cultural difference" (Slingerland 2019, 6). Jullien would, I think, agree.

Translation (and it's worth noting Slingerland has translated Confucius's *Analects*) becomes a point of contention in this context: Jean François Billeter's criticism of Jullien's translation of *dao* (道) as "process" is repeated in Slingerland as a sleight of hand that enables Jullien to set up an opposition between a Western thought of being and a Chinese thought of process

(Slingerland 2019, 288). (There is no discussion of Chinese thought's well-established connection to Western process philosophy—see my chapter 4—which seem to suggest that Jullien's translation is not entirely off.[18]) While Slingerland notes, about one of Jullien's generalizations late in his book, that "it is not entirely unreasonable" (ibid., 303), he also indicates that it must be qualified and is "characterized by many exceptions" (ibid.). (This is, indeed, one other meaning that could be given to my own book's title: the fact that Jullien's generalizations overlook the exceptions to the rules they stipulate.) Rosemont and Ames, too, "at times" (305) propose reasonable generalizations (Rosemont especially is both targeted in Slingerland's book and quoted favorably), but then they fall prey to exoticization, something that according to Slingerland troubles Jullien's work as well (he does not discuss Jullien's work on "ex-opticization" on this count and its explicit criticism of exoticism; he would, perhaps, reject it as frivolous). Some of that criticism is tied to Slingerland's criticism of discussions (in Jullien, Rosemont, and Ames, for example) of "the therapeutic usefulness of the Chinese tradition" (292). To turn to the Chinese tradition in the hopes of finding a cure there for what ails the West is orientalist (even if, of course, plenty of work—and especially work for a general audience—that does *not* deal with China also presents itself in this way; don't we, when it comes down to it, often *read* for therapeutic purposes? Indeed, doesn't Slingerland's own study of wu wei in *Trying Not to Try* [Slingerland 2014] fall in the category of books turning to China for therapeutic purposes? As the back cover of my edition puts it, "*Trying Not to Try* is the perfect *antidote* to our striving modern culture"; emphasis mine; by "our" is meant "Western").

Interestingly, when Slingerland ends his acknowledgments by writing, "I hope my work can also help to break down cultural essentialistic [*sic*] views of the Other and allow us to engage more productively and accurately with the worldviews of temporally or geographically distant cultures" (Slingerland 2019, xi), the line weirdly echoes Jullien's explicitly stated position—which is that "alterity" is a philosophical construction and that he is interested instead in the fact of China's geographical "elsewhere." "To engage more productively and accurately with the worldviews of temporally or geographically distinct cultures": now that is precisely what Jullien's strong notion of "dialogue" envisions. It is true that Slingerland and Jullien hardly mean the same thing by this. Slingerland in his book is more interested in uncovering certain things that are shared across cultural worlds (I take his point to be that temporally or geographically distinct cultures aren't always necessarily so different from our own, a point that's become increasingly difficult to make due to postmodernism, which, in its insistence on constructivism, has reinforced cultural difference). Jullien, working outside of the identity/difference dichotomy that he considers central to orientalism, is interested in early

China because of its geographical elsewhere. Influenced by postmodernism (in Slingerland's account), he acknowledges the cultural particularity of some universals and (but this is not covered by Slingerland) seeks to distinguish the cultural resource they mark, arguing for the democratic accessibility of that resource to all. The West has its cultural resources; so does China. They are not the same, even if they are both coherent and can both be explained. Looking at those resources next to each other enables one to tease out the unthought of each tradition—but outside of the logic of identity and difference. This is because neither tradition is self-same: if it were, it would be a dead culture. Therefore, they cannot in any simple way be opposed. They exist in a kind of refuge from each other, as the end of this chapter clarifies. Importantly, and Jullien is quite clear about this in his book *On the Universal* (2014a), this "postmodernism" (if that is what it is) does not draw other kinds of universals—shared universals—into question. Jullien is certainly not against the universal—neither the universal of science nor the aspiration of the universal of human rights, for example, even if he recognizes that the two are different.

Of course, if Jullien has arrived at this position over the years, in those works that Slingerland does not consider, it is in part in response to criticisms he has received, and one would do well to take into account the historical development of Jullien's work on this count. It is rather one-sided, for example, to rely on Billeter's short book against Jullien without considering Jullien's response to it in the form of a longer book. Recognizing, as I have done at length in this chapter, some of the problems that Slingerland as well as other critics of Jullien have uncovered—and acknowledging also (without using this as an excuse) that Jullien writes for a different audience than many of the scholars to whom he is compared; he is obviously *not* a historian like Michael Nylan or Anne Cheng—it also seems that a more-nuanced conversation is needed, one that would seek to be as attentive to Jullien's work and developing thought (which far exceeds what is quoted in Slingerland's book) as it is to the early China that it studies.

Jullien's short little book *Le pont des singes* stands out in this context as a book that is couched in the methodological reflection and terminological work that Jullien is doing in the late phase of his career (its preface and closing sections rehearse much of the thinking and language that I presented above) and because it was triggered by a visit to Vietnam—not China. As a kind of travelogue (though it's not quite that) dedicated in part to his son Guilhem, "voyageur au Vietnam" (traveler to Vietnam), the text is interesting both because it is set in an area of the world that Jullien does not study and because it is proximate to a typical orientalist genre: the travelogue.

Some might wonder whether its title, *Le pont des singes*, echoes René Étiemble's *Ton Yeou-Ki ou le nouveau singe pèlerin* (1958), which is one of the travelogues that Alex Hughes discusses when he is looking at mid-twentieth-century French travel accounts based on trips to China (Hughes 2004). There is no real indication that this is so. Jullien takes his title, in fact, from basic bridges that are construed over the Mekong River with three branches of bamboo. These are called *ponts des singes*, "monkey bridges," because of the agility they require of those who seek to cross them. Jullien writes,

> Qui s'y arrête se prend alors à songer à tout le savoir technicien accumulé, concerté certes mais non pas calculé ni modelisé, pour associer ainsi la souplesse et la résistance et permettre à ses frêles assemblages de supporter l'ébranlement continue des pas de même que les intempéries; à toute l'agilité également acquise dans le corps (mais est-ce seulement de "corps" alors qu'il s'agit?), à cette capacité déployée de la plante des pieds jusqu'à la faculté de vigilance, d'autocontrôle et de réflexe, et qui s'est transmise durant tant de générations, pour pouvoir s'avancer ansi sur ces perches fines, à tout âge, quotidiennement, en un léger balancement—comme en se jouant: l'art de nos équilibristes du cirque, mais sans qu'il y ait spectacle. (Jullien 2010, 21–22)

> Whoever stops there starts to reflect on all the accumulated technical knowledge, concerted but neither calculated nor modeled, to thus associate suppleness and resistance and allow these fragile assemblages to support the continuous shaking produced by human steps and bad weather; about all the agility acquired in the body (but is it only "the body" that we're dealing with here?), about this capacity that's deployed from the placing of one's feet all the way to the faculty of vigilance, of self-control and reflexes, and that is passed on through so many generations, to be able to venture on these narrow perches, at any age, in a light swaying—as if one is playing: it's the art of the tightrope walkers in our circus, but without there being a spectacle.[19]

The passage seems rife with exoticism or orientalism, starting with the word *songer*, which outside of the construction *songer à* means "dreaming." Especially when Jullien goes on to note that at the same time there are plenty of "concrete bridges" that are being built, adding that these introduce a rupture not just practically (they make crossing the bridge a lot easier!) but also mentally: they rupture the particular practical intelligence—which is not just physical, as he points out[20]—that the bamboo bridges require. Note that the concrete bridges are just referred to by the material by which they are made—not by the performance of those who walk across them (human bridges?).

We seem to be all set up, then, for a nostalgic approach that regrets the changes that the concrete bridges bring: if only we could preserve the bridges in bamboo—if only the locals could keep performing for us, Westerners, like monkeys!

But Jullien explicitly rejects such a reading, noting that there is no nostalgia here (the concrete bridges are an improvement, to be sure), even if he also notices a loss. Instead, the scene develops into a criticism of

> ce touriste qui, se déplaçant dans l'espace, voudrait du coup remonter dans le temps et souhaiterait que le monde, un soir, là-bas, lorsqu'il voguait en barque sur un bras du Mékong, lui soit soudain complaisant: qu'il le ramène d'un coup à l'âge de "nos premier parents . . . " Âge d'or des moeurs simples et de la suffisance; qu'il le réconcilie dès lors avec la nature, ailleurs, sait-on, si maltraitée, et fasse enfin pleuvoir sur lui une harmonie réparatrice. (Jullien 2010, 23)

> that tourist who, moving through space, would like to suddenly travel back in time and would like that the world, one evening, over there, when he is floating on a boat on a branch of the Mekong, were pleasant to him: that it would take him back suddenly to the era of "our forefathers . . . " A golden age of simple mores and sufficiency; that the world would reconcile him with a nature that, elsewhere, is as we know treated so badly; and that the world would thereby shower him with a reparative harmony.

This exoticist and orientalist vision is precisely what Jullien does *not* want to propose.

Still, and perhaps echoing Martin Heidegger's thinking about bridges and the worlds they make, Jullien uses the fact of the rupture between the bamboo bridge and the concrete bridge as an occasion to think through the brutality of the global situation it marks. From a mode of intelligence that operates through "integration," one that is "ecological," one has moved to a mode that operates through "effraction": one that is "normative," "modelizing," "beholden to a standard," "calculating," and "*a priori* deciding on solutions" (Jullien 2010, 23–24). What Jullien in his work calls "connivance"—a special kind of knowledge with a wink—has been replaced by Western "knowledge." The shift produces the kind of tourist who is eager to see—and especially to photograph—the old ways. They stop for pictures, fruit, and souvenirs. Thus what Jullien calls "the simulacrum of strangeness organizes itself"—"l'exotisme est arrivé" (exoticism has arrived; ibid., 25).

Of course, for him this is part of a larger criticism of essentialist notions of identity, of individual identity and—more generally—cultural identity. Recall that, for Jullien, there is no such thing as an identity proper, or a cultural identity proper. Rather, and outside of the opposition of identity and difference, he speaks of divergence, which opens up the separation or detachment of the in-between, which in turn is associated with the fecundity of cultural resources (rather than values or roots) that thus become available within cultural identities and identities, resources for all to explore and exploit. If this sounds like an opportunistic capitalist vision (as I discuss in chapters 2 and 3), he insists that it is meant to resist precisely the logic of the market—that the diversity he envisions, and the universal to which it relates, resists precisely the uniformity of the commodity that he characterizes as "utopian" (Jullien 2010, 32) and "exoticist" (ibid.).

Against the kind of tourism that Jullien attacks in *Le pont des singes*, we should cultivate what Jullien calls "connivance," which is the other kind of intelligence that I mentioned before (Jullien also dedicates an entire chapter to it in his book *Living Off Landscape*). It is the centerpiece of the more affirmative part of Jullien's book. But what is it? How is it described? The questions seem particularly pertinent in that Jullien has insisted that the knowledge he finds, for example, in China has an internal coherence, an intelligibility, of its own: it *can* be understood through careful study, and with extreme patience. It is not magical, mystical, or utopian in that sense. With Jullien's theory of connivance, we are arriving at the articulation of such a coherence in the text. The problem is, of course, that Jullien is not dealing with China here; I would say that he is not even dealing with Vietnam. Rather, he is trying to articulate, in an *entirely theoretical* way, the kind of knowledge that is lost when the bamboo bridge is replaced by a bridge of concrete.[21] The risk of exoticism and orientalism is high here.

So, what is connivance according to *Le pont des singes*? Connivance "neutralizes 'value' judgments, which are unavoidably ethnocentric, and takes us out of the hierarchy of what's 'superior' and 'inferior,' 'more' or 'less,' and considers cultural possibilities in an equal way" (Jullien 2010, 34). It introduces a "reflexivity" between cultural possibilities (ibid., 34). Whereas knowledge necessarily brings a rupture, connivance does not presuppose such a cut: "it's discursive, methodical, it knots itself and weaves itself from day to day without a clear goal, without one thinking about it too much, without one thinking that one must think about it" (35). It operates in a global, holistic way—rather than at different levels (which is what knowledge does) (ibid.). Unlike knowledge, connivance does not "abstract" (ibid.). It does not depersonalize, but it relates to the entirety of the person.

At this point, however, Jullien's description of connivance indeed partly goes astray. He notes that connivance's

> sémiologie par suite est secrète, diffuse, ambiguë, oblique; ses codes sont divers et non exclusifs. Ou encore: au lieu d'ériger une extériorité, elle enveloppe dans une complicité et la favorise. Au lieu d'extravertir le rapport, elle le replie sur lui-même et le rend intime: entre des personnes, avec les choses comme avec les bêtes, avec une couleur ou un paysage. *Stimmung*: la connivance n'est donc pas de l'ordre de l'inférieur, vis-à-vis de la connaissance, mais plutôt de l'infra. (Jullien 2010, 36; emphasis original)

semiology is secret, diffuse, ambiguous, oblique; its codes are divert and nonexclusive. Or also: instead of creating an exteriority, it envelops into a complicity and favorizes it. Instead of extraverting the relation, it folds back onto itself and renders intimate: between people, with things as with animals, with a color or a landscape. *Stimmung*: connivance is not of the order of the inferior, in relation to knowledge, but rather of the *infra*.

Identified with the indigenous by Jullien, this form of knowledge is associated with lineage and ancestrality; with nature and the local; with landscape. Linguistically it is associated with dialects; some of the book decries the use of global English and continues Jullien's argument elsewhere for translation as the linguistic equivalent of his approach. Strangely, given his use of the term "indigenous" (to which I will return in chapter 4), he notes that it "demeure donc en deça du politique"—"it remains beyond the political" (ibid., 37).

Critical readers may pick up here on some orientalist elements, familiar to us, for example, from Lisa Lowe's discussion of Kristeva and Barthes—namely, the association of connivance when it comes to semiotics with "secrecy, the diffuse, ambiguity, the oblique"; later on, there is also the association with nature, the local, landscape. Indeed, Jullien's description sounds almost mystical.[22] In these passages, it seems to me that Jullien sounds like an orientalist,[23] possibly because he is working in a purely theoretical fashion rather than building his theory from concrete examples taken from Vietnamese culture—although one would have to note that even such examples would not *necessarily* save one from orientalism or exoticism. While much of what's here is arguably informed by Jullien's work on China, one has to ask whether he would tolerate someone associating Chinese knowledge with "secrecy" or the other exoticist and orientalist tropes that we find in these passages. My guess is that he would not.

When Jullien, four years later, dedicates an entire chapter to connivance in *Living Off Landscape*, it is in a book about Chinese landscape painting. There the notion is developed very concretely in the context of a coherent thought about Chinese landscapes, and all of a sudden none of the mysticism remains. In fact, one understands here that what Jullien with the notion of connivance is after is much closer to what he calls "l'impensé," referenced in the book's subtitle specifically as "the un-thought-of reason"—"l'impensé de la raison." Connivance, Jullien now succinctly and with some caution notes,

> stakes a rightful claim **opposite** knowledge. It recovers what knowledge has ended up repressing, though not quite abolishing, and from this **opposite** position demonstrates the coherence of what has been repressed. . . . Knowledge has evolved into speculative knowledge (i.e., knowledge for its own sake) and in so doing has, via science, foresworn any need to adapt to the world of its

birth. In becoming it [*sic*] own end knowledge has **disengaged from the vital**. It therefore now confers on us the strictly correlative task of reconsidering the relation that reason has covered up but that still maintains our tacit understanding with things, though it now operate [*sic*] in the shadows. This "understanding," however, escapes our awareness. It remains implicit, lying beneath the relational work undertaken by reason. We will prove unable to elucidate it unless we compel reason to retrace its steps, go back into its history, in order to explore what it has **separated** itself from: not things it has historically **fought against** (obscurantism **opposing** the Enlightenment) but things that, in the righteous and mighty battle to impose itself, reason could only allow to **escape**—what now lies dormant in our *un-known*, and thus **escapes** our intelligence. If *knowledge*, as we know, stands in **opposition** to ignorance, what stands in **contradiction** to knowledge is *connivance*. They stand **on equal footing but also back-to-back**. The Latin *connivere* means to come to an understanding "with a wink." (Jullien 2018, 105–106; bold emphases mine)

J'appellerai *connivence* cette autre relation au monde qui, s'instaurant de plein droit **en vis-à-vis de** [in relation to] la connaissance, en récupère ce que celle-ci a fini par enfouir, mais n'a pu pour autant abolir, et qui, **face à elle** [before], fera valoir sa cohérence. (Façon aussi de se démarquer de l'insuffisant « co-naissance » claudélien et de tout ce qui s'y recèle de mysticisme revanchard.) Car que, se développant en savoir spéculatif, c'est-à-dire en savoir pour le savoir, la connaissance se soit détachée, *via* la science, du besoin d'adaptation au monde dont elle est née et, se prenant elle-même pour fin, se soit **débranchée du vital** nous confère désormais cette tâche strictement corrélative : celle de revenir sur ce rapport recouvert par la raison et qui, dès lors opérant dans l'ombre, ne nous en maintient pas moins dans une entente tacite avec les choses—mais "entente" que nous ne pensons pas. "Entente" restant donc implicite, en deçà du travail relationnel auquel se livre elle-même la raison, et que nous ne pourrons éclairer qu'en conduisant celle-ci à retourner sur ses pas, à remonter dans son histoire, pour explorer ce dont elle s'est **écartée** : non pas ce **contre** quoi elle s'est héroïquement **battue** (l'obscurantisme **face aux** Lumières), mais ce que, dans son juste et puissant combat pour s'imposer, elle a dû laisser **échapper**—et qui repose désormais dans notre *insu*, donc **échappe** à notre intelligence. Si le **contraire** [the contrary] de la *connaissance* est l'ignorance, comme on sait, son **contradictoire** [what contradicts it] est la *connivence* s'instaurant **à parité** avec elle en même temps qu'elles **se tournent le dos**. *Connivere*, dit le latin : s'entendre "en clignant des yeux." (Jullien 2014b, 212; bold emphases mine)

At stake here in this passage—and we need to consider the French original to fully assess this—is the language of opposition. Note that the English quotation starts out by using the language of opposition, which we know is problematic in the context of orientalism, which all too often construes the orient as simply the opposite of the West. In the French, however, that's not quite what we get: Jullien puts *vis-à-vis*, which means "in relation to," and *face à*, which means "before," "in the face of," and is a more correct, less orientalist way of rendering the divergence that Jullien envisions here. In the English, this language of opposition then shifts to the terms "disengaged" and "separated" (the same terms appear in the French); these are more in line with Jullien's use of the term *écart*, or "divergence," and he uses them explicitly elsewhere to describe the distance that divergence produces. At this point, in fact, the language of "opposition"—in French, again, we get *face aux*, "before"—is used to describe something different: the relation between the Enlightenment and obscurantism. And so Jullien is really insisting here that the relation of connivance to knowledge is *not* one of opposition, or *not* opposition *in this way*; he insists that connivance precisely is not obscurantism. Connivance, then, ends up being something, in both the English and the French, that *escapes*—which is not at all the same as what is *opposed*. *Opposition* operates entirely within the logic of identity and difference; that which opposes is tied to that to which it is opposed. The only instance where the English "opposed" is allowed in the above paragraph is in the parenthesis about the Enlightenment's relation to obscurantism. *Escape* names another logic of disengagement or separation. Indeed, Jullien ends by using the language of opposition (in French, *le contraire*, "the contrary") once again, but to describe the relation of knowledge to ignorance. Connivance is now said to "contradict" knowledge, which is not a very happy term in this context either unless its contrast to the opposition of "contrary" is noted. Connivance and knowledge stand "on equal footing but also back-to-back"—at the same level, but turned away from each other. This is not exactly a relation of opposition. Rather, I think this description—"equal footing but also back-to-back"—names precisely the topology of divergence, and it's strange not to see that language from Jullien's late work being used here in association with connivance.[24]

My point, of course, is that this long, final passage corrects some of the exoticism and orientalism of the descriptions of connivance in *Le pont des singes* (not all: I also bolded the notion of the vital, which is associated with connivance here in the same orientalist way that it is associated with the heterotopia of China in Foucault's *Order of Things*). Because it seeks to break out of the logic of opposition, of an oppositional construction of connivance in relation to knowledge, there is another space that opens up here outside of the Orient/Occident divide. This is perhaps most obvious in *Living Off Landscape*, which deals with a painterly genre—landscape—that can be found in *both* the West *and* the Far East. In short, if landscape is associated with the special form of knowledge called "connivance," connivance too names a kind of knowledge that can be found both in the West and the Far East. By theorizing it, Jullien hardly exoticizes or orientalizes, hardly opposes the Orient as "other" to the West as "same." Rather, connivance and the unthought that it names need to be conceived as a typical example of what Jullien in the two other texts that I analyzed here—*L'écart et l'entre* and *Il n'y a pas d'identité culturelle*—calls a "déconstruction du dehors," a "deconstruction from the outside." While the deconstructive efficacy of connivance may open up through a divergence between the West and the Far East, its traces can also already be found within these traditions, as forgotten markers of what each of them have left unthought.

NOTES

1. Zarcone 2003, 20.
2. Chow 1993, 10.
3. I won't engage Derrida's use of China in *Of Grammatology* here since many others have already commented on it.
4. It's worth noting that Jullien also uses this term (Jullien 2012, 63), precisely when he is critically negotiating his own use of the term "heterotopia" to describe his approach to China. I will return to this later.
5. The charge is, in my view, justified, although Jan Walsh Hokenson's discussion of Barthes in *Japan, France, and East-West Aesthetics* can bring some nuance to it. Hokenson discusses in the book the long-standing "idiosyncratic French practice of *japonisme*" (Hokenson 2004, 20) and situates Barthes' book on Japan within it. Although Hokenson does "not seek to deny that orientalism, in Said's sense of the term, is often latent in *japoniste* texts" (ibid., 26), she also indicates that to criticize *japonisme*, or Barthes' book in particular, "for not truly understanding Japanese culture, for writing a mere guidebook to enigmas because he sees the country solely 'in terms of "difference"' from the West" (ibid., 20), is misguided. It does not recognize that "French writers themselves have insisted on the constructed, reflexive nature of their *japonisme*" (ibid.): Hokenson thus mentions *japonistes* who explicitly never wanted to set foot in Japan—who never traveled there and, "pointedly, never [wish] to do so" (ibid.). The point of *japonisme* is precisely that it uses Japan as an imaginative construction to reflect on France: "French *japonisme*," Hokenson writes, "is primarily about France, about problems in the French practice of occidental arts and letters, and only secondarily about Japan, imagined source of proposed solutions" (ibid., 21). Later, in a brilliant section on Barthes, she writes, "Far from falling prey to orientalism, Barthes shows how it works" (361). For other, equally more-nuanced, approaches to Barthes' Japan book, see Knight 1997 and Genova 2016.
6. Jullien's book on Chinese wisdom, *Un sage est sans idée*, ends with the words "No comment" (Jullien 1998, 232), which seem to mark his proximity to Barthes. Shu-bao Dong, in a discussion of Jullien's *Procès ou création*, goes so far as to state that Jullien "consciously saw himself as the heir to the French contemporary philosophers Foucault, Deleuze, and Barthes" (Dong 2018, 747)—though there is no footnote reference, and I don't know of any place where Jullien quite puts it this way (even if, of course, he references work by all of those thinkers).

Certainly Jullien's use of Barthes in, for example, his discussion of the Chinese aesthetic of the bland is highly critical. To me it seems that this is the mode of engagement throughout: adopting certain terms or ideas from philosophers like Foucault, Deleuze, or Barthes and then critically reworking them through an in-depth engagement with Chinese thought. Something similar could be said about Jullien's notion of "the unheard-of," *l'inouï*, which (as, for example, Charles Forsdick has noted) appears, for example, in Barthes' book on Japan as well to characterize the Japanese "symbolic system" (Barthes quoted in Forsdick 2006, 70). Barthes uses this in a work of *japonisme*; Jullien critically turns it into a key term in his in-depth study of China.

7. When he writes of Chinese utopias in French thought, Jullien himself definitely has this longer history in mind of a sinophilia that is renewed, as he puts it, through Maoism (Jullien 2008, 135).

8. Here is the passage from Borges, as quoted in *The Order of Things*, which divides animals into "(a) belonging to the Emperor, (b) embalmed, (c) tame, (d) suckling pigs, (e) sirens, (f) fabulous, (g) stray dogs, (h) included in the present classification, (i) frenzied, (j) innumerable, (k) drawn with a very fine camelhair brush, (l) et cetera, (m) having just broken the water pitcher, (n) that from a long way off look like flies" (Foucault 1973, xv).

9. Jullien has, it's worth noting, made the same point, even if he doesn't explicitly reference Foucault in this instance: "Trop souvent on prête aux Chinois une sorte de gentil désordre, n'est-ce pas? Non! Il y a des systématisations extrêmement fines, rigoureuses, complexes" (All too often one attributes to the Chinese a sort of gentle disorder, right? Wrong! There are extremely fine, rigorous, and complex systematizations [in Chinese thought]; Piorunski 1998, 153). Longxi's entire discussion of the use of Borges in Foucault is worth reading and includes an engagement with Said's *Orientalism*.

10. The reciprocity here is important. When Hokenson briefly discusses Jullien, she appears to inscribe him in "this endeavor to use an Asian tradition to rethink the bases of occidental aesthetics, [which] began in France around 1860" (Hokenson 2004, 33); but this only covers half of Jullien's project, which also mobilizes the Western tradition to rethink the bases of Chinese aesthetics. This is why the strategy of Jullien's work does not match that of the *japonistes*.

11. See Weber 2014.

12. By distinguishing here between "weak" and "strong" modes of comparative work, I do not mean to suggest that Jullien presents some form of "strong" thought, even if Jullien himself in defenses of his work has characterized the thought of his opponents as "weak." As Ralph Weber points out (Weber 2014, 235), Jullien's response to Swiss sinologist Jean-François Billeter ends with a chapter titled "Requiem pour une pensée faible" (Requiem for a weak thought; Jullien 2007a). In view of Jullien's criticism of Western metaphysics in particular, it would in fact be worthwhile to precisely consider Jullien's work within what, after Italian philosopher Gianni Vattimo, has come to be called *pensiero debole*, or "weak thought," and its relations not only to postmodernism but also to Christianity and communism. Jullien himself comments on this distinction between Vattimo's "weak thought" and what he calls Billeter's "weak thought" (ibid., 133).

13. In *The Book of Beginnings*, Jullien suggests that such a method "produces a parity. That is what, first of all, puts the cultures on an equal footing on principle and stops ethnocentrically hierarchizing them" (Jullien 2015, 123). Clearly there is an ethical and political point to his method.

14. See Billeter 2006.

15. This is of course a charge that applies to many thinkers and to a certain extent to all theoretical thinkers, including—to just give one relevant example in this context—Edward Said.

16. In an appreciative but critical discussion of Jullien, Haun Saussy has exposed Jullien's aspiration to approach China as "elsewhere" not only as a project that—through the polarities between which it operates—in fact approaches China as "alterity" but also as an alterity that is a reverse image of the self, as an "own other" (Saussy 2001, 111). Strangely, however, Saussy's discussion of Jullien does not review the key terms of Jullien's philosophical system and, most importantly in this context, its explicit project of returning to European thought through the detour of China, in order to exploit the cultural resources of each tradition.

17. In his use of the term "integration," Jullien is not consistent, as it appears in *Le pont des singes* with a positive connotation (Jullien 2010, 23).

18. As a nonspecialist reader, I can attest to the different readings that different translations of the term *dao* produce. When one is used to Jullien's rendering of *dao* as "process," for example, translations of *dao* as the "way" (in Ames and Hall 2003, for example) or also as "course" (in Ziporyn; Zhuangzi 2009) certainly change one's interpretation of the text and the thought that it conveys.

But this is a very standard issue when one is working with translations; I don't see this as something for which Jullien (or any of the other translators) should be faulted. Things get interesting precisely when working between different translations—and also between translations and commentaries. Jullien's choice to translate *dao* as "process," for example, with its concomitant push of classical Chinese thought in the direction of process philosophy, comes with a criticism of the philosophical notion of the "event," as I will discuss in chapter 2. But when Ames and Rosemont characterize classical Chinese as a language in the "Philosophical and Linguistic Background" that they provide for their translation of Confucius's *Analects*, they characterize Chinese precisely as "an eventual language" (Confucius 1998, 20, as translated by Ames and Rosemont). Whereas the West experiences "a world of *things*," Chinese thought "experiences a world of *events*" (ibid., 21; emphasis original). Jullien would likely oppose "event" (West) to "process" (China) on this count, or "thing" (West) to "relation (China). As I see it, however, these are not issues that ought to be settled: thought happens precisely in between these different renderings and the interpretations they enable. After all, all words are inadequate when it comes to the *dao*.

19. I thank Olivia C. Harrison for her help with the translation of this passage.

20. An appropriate name for such intelligence could be *mètis*, the "cunning intelligence," as discussed by Marcel Detienne and Jean-Pierre Vernant in their landmark book about this neglected form of intelligence in the Greek world (Detienne and Vernant 1991). As I discuss in chapter 3, this book is an important reference for Jullien; it

plays an important role in his work on efficacy as an element within the Greek world that has connections to China.

21. Detienne and Vernant articulate such a knowledge in their book *Cunning Intelligence in Greek Culture and Society* (1991); but note that they do not articulate it in a purely theoretical fashion. Rather, their book strikes one as extremely valuable precisely because it is so rooted in the close reading of Greek myths and Greek literature—literary and philosophical—at large. One does not walk away from *Cunning Intelligence* with the sense that a clear concept was construed or a theoretical model was created; rather, the book navigates a whole lot of sources that all contribute to a loose understanding—as the authors themselves point out—of what the Greeks called *mètis*.

22. One never gets this sense from Detienne and Vernant's book on metis, perhaps in part because it is continuously, and excessively, based in concrete examples.

23. There are other places in his work where this is the case as well: see Wang 2008, 236. Xing Wang has in this context associated Jullien with "neo-orientalism," or "humble orientalism": "This type of orientalism is different from its predecessor, as it embraces and accepts cultural differences as such and tries to neutrally represent different cultures in Western social discourse and intellectual framework [*sic*]. However, it is still a power relation, an imposition of adjusted Western cultural categories onto the East" (Wang 2018, 5). I don't think the latter applies to Jullien.

24. This paragraph invites a consideration of the place of Hegel's dialectics in Jullien's work. While Jullien emphatically resists Hegel's racism, specifically when it comes to the orient, he also dedicates extensive reflection to Hegel's dialectics throughout his work, and in particular in his book *L'ombre au tableau* (Jullien 2004a). While dialectics is presented there as progress in relation to the logic of the theodicy, which Jullien also discusses at length, its work on the negative still stands at a distance from the Far Eastern processual thought of silent transformations that Jullien is interested in. In other words, Hegel's dialectic does not allow us to think the processuality of Chinese thought. *L'ombre au tableau* remains untranslated into English, but an excerpt in English from the beginning of the book was published in *Critical Inquiry* (Jullien 2005). It's not only because of the risk of orientalism but also due to Jullien's extensive engagement with Hegel that one should be extremely cautious to render any relationality in Jullien's work in the language of oppositionality. The risks are high.

REFERENCES

Ames, Roger, and David Hall. 2003. *Dao De Jing: A Philosophical Translation*. Translated by Roger Ames and David Hall. New York: Ballantine.

Billeter, Jean-François. 2006. *Contre François Jullien*. Paris: Allia.

Bohm, Arnd, Henry Staten, and Rey Chow. 2001. "Derrida and Chinese Writing." *PMLA* 116 (3): 657–60.

Chesneaux, Jean. 1987. "China in the Eyes of French Intellectuals." *Journal of the Hong Kong Branch of the Royal Asiatic Society* 27: 11–29.

Chow, Rey. 1993. *Writing Diaspora: Tactics of Intervention in Contemporary Cultural Studies*. Bloomington: Indiana University Press.
———. 2001. "How (the) Inscrutable Chinese Led to Globalized Theory." *PMLA* 116 (1): 69–74.
Confucius. 1998. *The Analects of Confucius: A Philosophical Translation*. Translated by Roger Ames and Henry Rosemont Jr. New York: Ballantine.
Detienne, Marcel, and Jean-Pierre Vernant. 1991. *Cunning Intelligence in Greek Culture and Society*. Translated by Janet Lloyd. Chicago: University of Chicago Press.
Dong, Shu-bao. 2018. "Detour and Access, Deleuze and Guattari's Researches on Chinese Immanent Becoming." *Journal of Literature and Art Studies* 8 (5): 739–49.
Étiemble, René. 1958. *Ton Yeou-Ki ou le nouveau singe pèlerin*. [France]: Gallimard.
Forsdick, Charles. 2006. "'(In)connaissance de l'Asie': Barthes and Bouvier, China and Japan." *Modern and Contemporary France* 14 (1): 63–77.
Foucault, Michel. 1973. *The Order of Things: An Archaeology of the Human Sciences*. New York: Vintage.
———. 2009. *Le corps utopique, les hétérotopies*. Paris: Lignes.
Frazier, Robeson Taj. 2015. *The East Is Black: Cold War China and the Black Radical Imagination*. Durham: Duke University Press.
Genova, Pamela A. 2016. "Beyond Orientalism? Roland Barthes' Imagistic Structures of Japan." *Romance Studies* 34 (3–4): 152–62.
Gourgouris, Stathis. 1996. *Dream Nation: Enlightenment, Colonization, and the Institution of Modern Greece*. Stanford: Stanford University Press.
Hayot, Eric. 2004. *Chinese Dreams: Pound, Brecht, Tel Quel*. Ann Arbor: University of Michigan Press.
Hokenson, Jan Walsh. 2004. *Japan, France, and East-West Aesthetics: French Literature, 1867–2000*. Teaneck: Fairleigh Dickinson University Press.
Hughes, Alex. 2003. "The Seer (Un)Seen: Michel Leiris' China." *French Forum* 28 (3): 85–100.
———. 2004. "Looking and Feeding in the People's Republic of China." *French Cultural Studies* 15 (1): 21–33.
Jirn, Jin Suh. 2015. "A Sort of European Hallucination: On Derrida's 'Chinese Prejudice.'" *Situations* 8 (2): 67–83.
Jullien, François. 1998. *Un sage est sans idée, Ou: L'autre de la philosophie*. Paris: Seuil.
———. 2004a. *L'ombre au tableau: Du mal ou du négatif*. Paris: Seuil.
———. 2004b. *A Treatise on Efficacy: Between Western and Chinese Thinking*. Trans. Janet Lloyd. Honolulu: University of Hawai'i Press.
———. 2005. "The Shadow of the Picture: Of Evil or the Negative." Translated by Gila Walker. *Critical Inquiry* 32 (1): 130–50.
———. 2007a. *Chemin faisant. Connaître la Chine, relancer la philosophie; Réplique à ****. Paris: Seuil.
———. 2007b. *Vital Nourishment: Departing from Happiness*. Trans. Arthur Goldhammer. New York: Zone Books.
———. 2008. "Eine Dekonstruktion von aussen: Von Griechenland nach China und zurück." In Dirk Baecker, François Jullien, Philippe Jousset, et al., 133–59, *Kontroverse über China: Sinophilosophie*. Berlin: Merve.

———. 2009. *The Great Image Has No Form, or On the Nonobject through Painting*. Translated by Jane Marie Todd. Chicago: University of Chicago Press.

———. 2010. *Le pont des singes: De la diversité à venir. Fécondité culturelle face à identité nationale*. Paris: Galilée.

———. 2011. *The Silent Transformations*. Translated by Krzystof Fijalkowski and Michael Richardson. London: Seagull.

———. 2012. *L'écart et l'entre: Leçon inaugurale de la Chaire sur l'altérité*. Paris: Galilée.

———. 2014a. *On the Universal, the Uniform, the Common and Dialogue between Cultures*. Translated by Michael Richardson and Krzysztof Fijalkowski. Cambridge: Polity.

———. 2014b. *Vivre de paysage, ou l'impensé de la raison*. Paris: Gallimard.

———. 2015. *The Book of Beginnings*. Translated by Jody Gladding. New Haven: Yale University Press.

———. 2016a. *Il n'y a pas d'identité culturelle; Mais nous défendons les ressources d'une culture*. Paris: L'Herne.

———. 2016b. *The Philosophy of Living*. Translated by Krzystof Fijalkowski and Michael Richardson. London: Seagull.

———. 2016c. *This Strange Idea of the Beautiful*. Translated by Krzystof Fijalkowski and Michael Richardson. London: Seagull.

———. 2018. *Living Off Landscape or the Unthought-of in Reason*. Translated by Pedro Rodriguez. London: Rowman & Littlefield.

Kao, Shuhsi. 1981. "Paradise Lost? An Interview with Philippe Sollers." *SubStance* 10 30 (1): 31–50.

Knight, Diana. 1997. *Barthes and Utopia: Space, Travel, Writing*. Oxford: Clarendon Press.

Longxi, Zhang. 1988. "The Myth of the Other: China in the Eyes of the West." *Critical Inquiry* 15 (1): 108–31.

Lowe, Lisa. 1991. *Critical Terrains: French and British Orientalisms*. Ithaca: Cornell University Press.

Meighoo, Sean. 2008. "Derrida's Chinese Prejudice." *Cultural Critique* 68: 163–209.

Piorunski, Richard. 1998. "Le détour d'un grec par la Chine. Entretien avec François Jullien." *Ebisu* 18: 147–85.

Said, Edward. 1978. *Orientalism*. New York: Vintage.

Saussy, Haun. 2001. *Great Walls of Discourse and Other Adventures in Cultural China*. Cambridge: Harvard University Press.

Slingerland, Edward. 2014. *Trying Not to Try: Ancient China, Modern Science, and the Power of Spontaneity*. New York: Broadway Books.

———. 2019. *Mind and Body in Early China: Beyond Orientalism and the Myth of Holism*. Oxford: Oxford University Press.

Spivak, Gayatri Chakravorty. 1981. "French Feminism in an International Frame." *Yale French Studies* 62: 154–84.

van der Poel, Ieme. 1993. "*Tel Quel* et la Chine: L'Orient comme mythe de l'intellectuel occidental." *History of European Ideas* 16 (4–6): 431–39.

Wang, ShiPu. 2008. Review of *The Impossible Nude: Chinese Art and Western Aesthetics*, by François Jullien. *China Review International* 15 (2): 234–43.

Wang, Xing. 2018. "Rethinking Material Religion in the East: Orientalism and Religious Material Culture in Contemporary Western Academia." *Religions* 9 (62): 1–13.

Weber, Ralph. 2014. "What about the Billeter-Jullien Debate? And What Was It About? A Response to Thorsten Botz-Bornstein." *Philosophy East & West* 64 (1): 228–37.

Wolfe, Tom. 1970. "Radical Chic." *New York Magazine*, July 8. http://nymag.com/news/features/46170/.

Zarcone, Thierry. 2003. "China as Philosophical Tool: François Jullien in Conversation with Thierry Zarcone." *Diogenes* 50 (4): 15–21.

Zhuangzi. 2009. *Zhuangzi: The Essential Writings*. Translated by Brook Ziporyn. Indianapolis: Hackett.

Chapter 2

In Between Landscape and the Nude

> Tell me what your definition of the beautiful is, and I will tell you what your philosophy is.
>
> —François Jullien, *This Strange Idea of the Beautiful*[1]

AESTHETIC DIVERGENCE

In *Living Off Landscape or the Unthought-of in Reason*, François Jullien returns for the length of a short book to a topic that had already occupied him elsewhere: landscape. His book *The Great Image Has No Form or On the Nonobject through Painting* was already largely about Chinese landscape painting (specifically, the so-called "ink and wash" painting of the Southern "literati" school), even if it included just one chapter title that mentions landscapes (chapter 9, "The Spirit of a Landscape"). There are discussions of landscape in his books *This Strange Idea of the Beautiful* and *The Propensity of Things: Toward a History of Efficacy in China*, as well. Indeed, Jullien's earlier *In Praise of Blandness*, which was based on "a subchapter of [his] doctoral thesis" (Jullien 2008, 24),[2] published as *Procès ou création: Une introduction à la pensée des lettrés chinois* (Process or creation: an introduction to the thought of the Chinese literati), already included a chapter on "The Landscape of the Bland" and suggests that the interest in landscape has been present throughout his by now extensive oeuvre.

To be clear, landscape is not the only theme that ties Jullien's work together: the line "the great image has no form" (大象無形; Ames and Hall 2003, 140[3]) for example, which Jullien takes from the *Dao De Jing* or the

Laozi—literally, the "book" (*jing*, 经) of how to obtain "virtue" (*de*, 德) by following the "*dao*" (道); a short book attributed to the philosopher Laozi, or "old master" (*lao zi*, [老子]), and in spite of its mere five thousand words the foundational text for the Daoist school—returns in Jullien's *The Impossible Nude: Chinese Art and Western Aesthetics*, a book about the absence of the nude in Chinese painting. It resonates in all his works on aesthetics. Far from being restricted to just his book on the topic, the nude (in its turn) is also discussed in detail in *This Strange Idea*. In fact, one gets the impression, upon reviewing Jullien's oeuvre, that in terms of its aesthetic interests, it can be situated in between landscape and the nude and furthermore that there is a relation between this in-between and Jullien's overall thought—that Jullien's overall thought could be approached through the lens of this aesthetic in-between, which could thus come to stand in for the two kinds of thought between which he operates (Western thought and Chinese thought).

Within this optic, however, one would have to note that the landscape, which would operate within this point of view as the realization[4] of Chinese thought (as will become clear), is also very much present on the Western side. There is a well-established tradition of landscape painting in the West, obviously. Jullien's claim about the nude, however, is bolder: he suggests that the nude, at least in the way he theorizes it, is absent in Chinese art history (this does not mean, I should add, that there are no nude bodies in Chinese art; it's simply that they aren't rendered in the way they are in the Western tradition and haven't quite taken up the same central importance as in Western art). Still, the latter seems to set up a dubious opposition between the West and China, one that carries the risk of exoticism and orientalism (as I have discussed in the previous chapter) and moves away from the "deconstruction from the outside" that Jullien claims to pursue in his work. As I've explained in chapter 1, Jullien's work between the West and China is precisely not about creating oppositions but about staging a divergence that opens up an in-between where the fecundity of cultural resources can be exploited by all. If the nude is perhaps most at risk of exoticization and orientalization, it's worth noting that Jullien situates it on the side of the West, as if to preempt such a move; on the other hand, it's not as if landscape is any less susceptible to exoticism and orientalism. He notes, however, that there is landscape on both the Western and the Chinese side; the surprise, if anything, is that according to Jullien there is no nude in the orient—that the nude is (deliberately) wrested away here from its common orientalization. In fact, and from the opposite point of view, one could argue that Jullien *occidentalizes* the nude: that he turns it into the key aesthetic figure of the West. If such essentialization seems problematic, one should point out that as part of this move, Jullien precisely turns the nude into a figure of essentialization, making essentialization one of the key features of Western thought. If there is occidentalism here, it's a *critical occidentalism* that is yet to receive its theoretical articulation. The final issue, then, seems to be that we are left with the suggestion that there is *no* essentialization in Chinese thought, whereas the landscape's de-essentializing and de-ontologizing effect can be found in *both* the West and China.

In this chapter, I take a closer look at Jullien's extensive work on aesthetics to consider how his approaches to both the landscape and the nude—his working in the divergence between the landscape and the nude, exploiting the cultural resources that are laid bare by such an in-between—provide insights into the key philosophical stakes of his work, specifically the divergence between Western thought and Chinese thought. From a philosophical point of view, much of Jullien's work on landscape targets, I show, Western metaphysics and ontology, specifically what I intend to characterize as their exceptionalist tenets. In his work *The Nude*, Jullien theorizes the Western nude precisely as the realization of such exceptionalism, and he explains its absence in Chinese art history from this perspective as logical given Chinese art history's philosophical background. Chinese thought, then, could be characterized as unexceptional, a term that appears in Jullien's work but is eclipsed by the more dominant overall characterization "the bland," applied to Chinese aesthetics in his book *In Praise of Blandness*, which Jullien critically reappropriates from Roland Barthes' writings about China (Barthes 1982). Finally, and in anticipation of the next chapter, I will consider some political and economic aspects of what I call Jullien's "unexceptional" thought.

LANDSCAPE VERSUS METAPHYSICS AND ONTOLOGY

Living Off Landscape is fairly typical of the overall methodology in Jullien's work. In Europe, Jullien writes in his discussion of landscape that "it is through composition that we . . . com-prehend" (Jullien 2018a, 19). We think such a logic is universal "because compositional logic is embedded in our language":

> Its fundamental schema, as the Greeks themselves observed, is the structure of the alphabet (letters, as units, come to compose syllables, words, phrases, and speech), and it has ruled over all knowledge. It has ruled over geometry (from point to line, surface, and volume) as well as anatomy (each part of the body, broken down as far as it will go, revealing its function at ever larger scales of the whole). Such was the method of the mind itself, from Plato to Descartes. "Analysis" divides into constituent parts, and "synthesis" reassembles from these a coherent whole. (Ibid., 19)

Jullien develops the point about anatomy further in his book *The Impossible Nude*, this time in a discussion of nudes rather than landscapes. "To Leonardo [da Vinci]," he writes,

> as throughout the whole of classical painting in Europe, the human body is a physical body subject to rigorous principles of muscular tension, balance, and counterpoise. It is both governed internally by the causality of forces and perceived externally according to the laws of optics. It follows that in order to depict this body, which he always initially considers as naked, the painter must first draw its blueprint, and using it as a case study he must dissect the composition of forces, analyze movements in terms of thrust and traction, evaluate the points of exertion, and determine the bearing points. At once geometrician and physicist, he builds axes, deduces centers of gravity and support, makes his calculations in terms of angles, determines proportions, and draws up equations. (Jullien 2007b, 56)

"In China," by contrast—and here Jullien relies in part on work by Western sinologists and scientists Manfred Porkert and Joseph Needham—"the human body is perceived in quite a different way":

> Anatomy has been of very little interest to the Chinese, who hardly explored the field. They pay less attention to the identity and specificity of morphological components (organs, muscles, tendons, ligaments, and so on) than to the quality of the exchanges between "outside" and "inside," which ensure the vitality of the body as a whole. This explains why they see no problem in the unclothed body being summarily represented as a sack: it is a receptacle pierced with orifices. As such, however, it is the container for infinitely subtle energies, whose diffusion it is important to keep track of. (Ibid., 59)[5]

Clearly, the nude and the landscape merge in Jullien's oeuvre as aesthetic sites where his philosophical concerns are articulated. While Jullien still uses the word "anatomy" in *Living Off Landscape* to characterize a different, Chinese sense of landscape (see Jullien 2018a, 55; "anatomy" is there in the English, but the original French has *membrure* [Jullien 2014, 117], which should really have been rendered as "frame"),[6] the term is emphatically associated with a Western approach to landscape and the human body, one that is rooted, according to Jullien, in the compositional structure of Western languages.

Indeed, if the Western mathematical, anatomical, and analytical approach to landscape is characterized by the part-whole relation, by the primacy of visual perception, and dominated by the subject-object relation (as Jullien summarizes it early on in *Living Off Landscape*), there is (by contrast) landscape in Chinese thought when the common type of perception, reconnaissance, and observation, in which the eyes are agents, allows itself to be overwhelmed by the other type, in which the eye no longer seeks for identification or information but instead allows itself to be "absorbed." . . . The gaze gives us occasion to pry into the relations of things, to immerse ourselves in the tension-setting network of oppositions-correlations. "Subject-hood" is thereby undone simultaneously (proportionately) as initiative and as monopoly. Moreover, we can now gaze for more than an instant, or more than whatever time we need to complete an observation. Truth be told, the eye thus used has no reason to stop "roaming," from one thing to another—or rather *between* them—as it is bandied about by their polarities and loses itself in their profusion. (Jullien 2018a, 14)

While one might quibble with the translator's use of the word "gaze" here[7]—Jullien makes it clear that he prefers "contemplation" over "gaze" in chapter 11 of *The Great Image*; the passage draws out well the Chinese apprehension of landscape as "a play of correlations . . . the entire world in its vibrancy: not a world that beckons from Elsewhere but a world perceived in the to-and-fro of its respiration. This same tension of *living* is what Chinese painting captures in landscape" (ibid., 26; emphasis original). Jullien arrives at this conclusion in part through a close reading of a fifth-century landscape poem by Xie Lingyun.

The last quotation goes back to the Chinese understanding of landscape as process that I already mentioned earlier. "In China, where thought finds no support in identity or Being . . . it is 'constancy' that undergirds the ordered engendering of things and thus regulates the world's process" (Jullien 2018a, 28). As will already be clear, there is a vital dimension to this, as illustrated by "China's very first pictorial theories (Xie He, in the fifth century)" (ibid., 29):

> It is not the depiction of a character, not a face . . . that best conveys the *animating tension* from which life springs, or that sustains life. For nothing unitary, nothing isolated, can succeed in this. Such a depiction would reduce to outer traits, and traits, not being *held in tension* by a polarity-forming *other*, ossify at the surface. They are doomed to fixity. To reverse our formulation, it is only by correlation, by the opposition/association of factors, by communication between these factors, and through an exchange between them that we can accede to life. Mountains and waters are no more subject to imposed form than rocks and clouds. But if we trace their twists and turns, follow the sinuous contours in their ceaseless transformation and pairing, as far as the eye can see, the privileged expression—the *site*—of an unquenchable *vitality* will come into view. (Ibid., 30)

Landscape in Chinese reads as "mountain(s)-water(s)" (*shanshui*, 山水; Jullien 2018a, 15); the Chinese painter, as Jullien writes in *The Impossible*

Nude, "considers the rock alive" (Jullien 2007b, 70). While Jullien is sometimes accused of reducing Chinese thought to immanence,[8] it becomes clear in passages such as this (written in reference to the work of Zong Bing) that it is, rather, "internal transcendence" (Jullien 2018a, 99) that he is after:

> Landscape is indeed made of "physicality" but in such a way that it is aspirated into a spiritual dimension. This is why landscape is essentially a form of soaring, an impulse, and a going forth; this is why it is alert rather than inert. The physical and the spiritual are distinct, but we are always going from one to the other, and doing so via the landscape. (Ibid., 59)

A crucial term in such an understanding of landscape is tension, which, in the Western aesthetic tradition, is "underdeveloped because kept under the reign of *kallos*, το καλλος, 'beauty'" (Jullien 2018a, 77). It is not so much Western "knowledge" that can claim to understand this but what Jullien in the closing pages of his book calls "connivance," from the Latin *connivere*—"understanding with a wink" (ibid., 105). Chinese thought enables Western thought's capacity for knowledge to "[shift (invert)] into *connivance*" (ibid., 107).

Much of what is in *Living Off Landscape* also appears in Jullien's much longer and more detailed study, *The Great Image*, which can be read as the umbrella work on aesthetics under which not only *Living Off Landscape* but also *The Impossible Nude* and *This Strange Idea* can be placed. It is here that one begins to clearly understand something that was already present in *Living Off Landscape*—namely, that the central counts on which Western thought and Chinese thought diverge are ontology and metaphysics. As such, this is nothing new: other French theorists had already pointed this out. But none with the amount of evidence and primary research that Jullien brings to this case.

Ontology refers to the logic of being, which understands the world in terms of unitary essence and identity. Even if variety within such a logic is possible, it is the variety of what Jullien calls "comparison," which merely confirms unitary essence and identity. The Chinese mode of "comprehension of things stands apart from ontology" (Jullien 2018a, 32), Jullien writes in *Living Off Landscape*. It can "be understood only by correlation" (32), by which Jullien means the relations between everything. (He frequently points out, for example, that "thing" in Chinese is rendered as "east-west" [*dong xi*, 东西; Jullien 2016, 35], that is, as a correlation rather than as being.) Chinese thought explores thinking as de-ontology. Driving such thought is not the Platonic question of the "What is it?"—the celebrated *ti esti* (τ['εστ[) that is at the core of the Platonic dialogues (Jullien 2009, 7). Dong Yuan's paintings are praised instead, Jullien writes in *The Great Image*, for their "as-if-there-were-as-if-there-were-not" quality (ibid., 3). The Western principle of noncontradiction has no reign here: "there is thus no self-identical entity to erect into an essence or from which to constitute an object" (ibid.). In fact, Jullien clarifies that in *The Great Image*, his "object is the nonobject: [that which] is too hazy-indistinct-diffuse-evanescent-con-fused to keep still and isolated" (ibid., xv). Chinese thought escapes not only subjectification but also objectification (10). It is interested not just in mountains but also in mountains in clouds, haze, penumbra; waters; mist, fog. The human form is only interesting when it is moving, which is why it is shown with undulating garments (Jullien 2007b, 36, 61). Chinese thought is interested in floating and melting. "To melt," Jullien writes in *This Strange Idea*, "thus speaks of the transition where the physical (the opaque) dissolves and opens out, makes itself indistinct and becomes expansive. And opens itself up to the imperceptible and the unlimited—to 'melt' is the antidualist word par excellence" (Jullien 2016, 60). In *Vital Nourishment*, Jullien writes in his extended analysis of the *Zhuangzi*, chapters 3 and 19:

> To float is the ability to avoid getting locked in any one position or tending in any particular direction. It means to be in constant motion, susceptible to the ebb and flow of respiration, without incurring expense or risking resistance of any kind. The word "float" negates all thought of a destination and therefore cancels out any idea of finality. (Jullien 2007c, 114)

Importantly, Jullien adds that this is not "the vagueness of hesitation, ambivalence, or drift (or the adventurous intoxication of the unguided, as Rimbaud would have it). Boats that float easily at anchor in a bay undulate with the waves and can animate a landscape" (ibid.).

Unlike Western thought, Chinese thought is not a philosophy of presence (Jullien 2009, 6). Jullien contrasts philosophies of presence to philosophies of what he calls "pregnancy" (also rendered as "fecundity"), which he illustrates with a reference to the painting of Shen Zhou:

> that modality which does not isolate but which passes through, "transpires," "transmits." It is of the order of the "between," like the resonance—and lets emanate by means of decanting; which does not focus but disperses, which does not immobilize but allows to communicate, and above all, literally, which is swollen with (pregnant with), which therefore obstructs the great antinomy of presence and absence (from which the tragic is born), consequently distrusting clarity and the definite (in which respect it is rebellious toward the idea) and does not let dis-cern. Consequently, it is against the *distinct* character that makes beauty. (Jullien 2016, 128)

Related to Chinese thought's position outside ontology is the fact that it did not develop a theology (Jullien 2009, 6, 7). It completely "[sidestepped] or even [bypassed] Being" (ibid., 7), but it felt no need to fill in this absence with god. Ontology is quite simply set aside. Interested in the foundation-fount of all things, their ground and source, it sought to paint the "Without-form" (ibid., 18). Such a "Without-form" "cannot enjoy an ontological status"; because it is without form, "it does not give rise to the determination of essence, or *eidos* [ε[δος; ADB]" (ibid., 19). "At the same time," Jullien adds, "it cannot be considered *chaos* [χαος, ADB]" (ibid.). There is certainly coherence here, but it is not the coherence of ontology. The Daoist "Without-form" therefore should not be understood simply as a negative; "it is not of the order of nonbeing or nothingness" (ibid., 21). In that, it differs from the nothingness of Buddhism, which arrives in China from India and is still ontological (Jullien 2012, 52). It is, quite the contrary, the ground or source from where "'there is' can come about by becoming distinct—just as a line can ap-pear, a form ex-ist" (Jullien 2009, 21). Hence Jullien's interest in the first stroke that opens up a canvas. Any ontologically determining discourse "on" the *dao* or the way should be avoided (ibid., 32). As per the *Dao De Jing*: "Each utterance does not picture but *de*-picts. The *de*- here signifies not completion but the reverse: effacement, undoing" (33).

Apart from the fact that Jullien considers this perspective to lie at the origin of the Western split between philosophy (determining) and literature (indistinct), he also points out the challenges it poses to Chinese painting, which is nonmimetic through and through. For how to paint within this kind of thought? How to paint the *dao*? "It is not," Jullien writes, following authors like Li Rihua and Bu Yantu,

> that [painters] gave up the ink and brush but that they used a wash so diluted, so close to the dry-pale end of the spectrum, that it approximates the white of the paper. It is so dim that it almost fades away altogether. Hence the painter pictures while de-picting: in using that "inkless ink" and that "brushless brush," that ink grown pale and that barely painting brush, he paints between form and without-form and renders the evanescence of the foundational. (Jullien 2009, 35)

If ontology "rests essentially on a gesture of assigning," Chinese painting is interested in, for example, "the wind" (present throughout Chinese thought, across different schools), which is unassignable (ibid., 41). Hence the importance of the sketch in Chinese painting.[9] Jullien discusses Pablo Picasso in this context as a painter who is caught up in the Western paradigm but nevertheless reveals some affinity with Chinese thought (59).[10] Why do painters send their finished work to the museum "for boring display" (61) while they hold on to their sketches? Might this not be reason enough to "leave behind the ontological fold in order to conceive of the sketch as full-fledged work while no longer crediting the determined form with a fullness of being" (66)?

It is the moment prior to actualization or individuation that is important for Chinese thought.

In both *The Great Image* and *Living Off Landscape*, the other name (in addition to ontology) that is most frequently given to Western thought is metaphysics. Consider Jullien's definition of it in *This Strange Idea*:

> If things are judged beautiful [in the Western tradition], it is because there exists "the beautiful" that renders them beautiful. In "the beautiful" as substantive, what is beautiful is no longer seen as related to anything other but is withdrawn into what becomes its substance. . . . From what "is beautiful" to "the beautiful"—(European) philosophy was born from this added article and is promoted in its displacement. (Jullien 2016, 9)

China, however, "projects no metaphysical 'beyond,' because it does not split the world (in the Platonic way) such that the intelligible (Being) in-forms the sensible, and such that the sensible amounts to a mere reflection of the intelligible" (Jullien 2018a, 31). Again and again, we are reminded that in Chinese thought there is no metaphysical split (see ibid., 71). Chinese thought sets metaphysics aside (see Jullien 2009, 13). Consider what the metaphysical notion of the beautiful "obliterates": "process," "vital interactions" (Jullien 2016, 35). It replaces those by an "Elsewhere" (ibid., 43), a metaphysically instigated "Ideal" (47). By focusing on the process of things, Chinese thought follows a completely different path: immanent, certainly, but not without spirituality. Metaphysics is the reason why, as Jullien puts it at the very beginning of *Silent Transformations*, "all that tirelessly occurs in front of us, that functions in such an effective way and is also obvious, remains unseen" (Jullien 2011, 1). "Subject" needs to be replaced by "process" (ibid., 6); "aging" is not something that happens to us but the process that we are (7). Jullien does not shy away from suggesting that we have merely invented the metaphysical notion of "time"—as something that for example our bodies are in—because our thought was unable to account for the silent transformations that *are* the body (99, 101).[11] We need to pass from the metaphysical and the ontological to the "taoique," as the translators somewhat awkwardly copy the French (34; why not "taoic," as the translator of *The Great Image* suggests [Jullien 2009, 23]?). This is another way of saying that "the ageing has always already started" (Jullien 2011, 57). (Who past the age of twenty-five could deny this wisdom?) In the West, it is literature—and Jullien mentions the novel in particular[12]—that has been the closest to this perspective, in particular in its split from philosophy. In China, Jullien suggests, this split does not exist.

In parallel to his association of ontology with theology, Jullien underlines the theological dimension of metaphysics—for example, in the chapter "The

Cult of the Beautiful" (Jullien 2016, 218). In the West, the beautiful is sacralized, and works of art collectively share, in Jullien's words, the "charter of exception" (ibid., 219). However, he is "unaware of any functional equivalent in China or in other countries of the far east" (ibid.). There works of art are not "erected as totalitarian symbols of beauty" (ibid.). In the West, the veneration of art has come close to the veneration of the "divine," and art has become the object of a "cult" (ibid.). Jullien characterizes this as the cult of "exceptional beauty" (220). The beautiful has become isolated and promoted as "the only divine thing left which does not compromise, but is compatible with, science and even very ably counterbalances it, and into which the religious consequently can flow back without difficulty" (221). The museum is "the modern temple" (221); "it offers the immense, even unique, advantage of a profane sacred" (ibid.). The beautiful "is the final messianism left to us" (ibid.).[13]

The unthought-of ontology, then, is the *dao*. Metaphysics posits a split and venerates what lies beyond that split but leaves process unseen. In his work *Silent Transformations*, Jullien associates both ontology and metaphysics with philosophies of the event. It is here that we find most explicitly what I consider to be Jullien's argument against exceptionalist philosophies of "'sudden' shattering" (Jullien 2011, 62), the "resonant thunderclaps of Revolutions" (ibid., 65), "spectacular bombshells, shocks and political aftereffects" (67), "rupture" (95). In a chapter titled "Mythology of the Event," Jullien takes on the Western philosophical notion of the event as a representation of "exceptional . . . irruption [and] upheaval" (116), arguing that it is a "fictive or mythological representation" (ibid.). Instead, and coming from Chinese thought, Jullien theorizes the event as "a matter of emergence" (126). Where Western philosophy finds the "incomparable, nonintegratable event" (122), Chinese thought offers "a silent maturation of the negative" (121) that, when "conditions are ripe for it" (119), leads the event to emerge.

Singling out Alain Badiou's thought as an example of how "the event still continues to fertilize philosophy today" (Jullien 2011, 122), Jullien considers the "characteristic of Chinese thought" to be "precisely to dissolve the event" (ibid., 126). Thus the event enters into an "equality with others, without privileging one moment or excepting it in relation to all moments" (126–27). Chinese thought, as he puts it, "absorb[s] the prestige of the event" (127). In Jullien's Chinese thought the "brutality of the 'event' [only] amazes us, because we have not known how to distinguish the silent transformation which has imperceptibly led to it" (129–30). Chinese thought does not know rupture. If Jullien mobilizes such thought, it is against what he characterizes as the "reign," the "dictatorship" (130) even, of the event, which has discreetly infiltrated all communication. In *The Book of Beginnings*, Jullien makes it abundantly clear that he considers the event to be a theological notion, associated with the god of creation, an act that is conceived of as "a break-in," an "intervention" (Jullien 2015, 41). "The order of Creation," he writes, is "affirmed by rupture and something like a break-in," and for that reason

> it must necessarily detach itself from an earlier disorder, a mumbo-jumbo of the unformed. It could not otherwise make an event that could be announced. With all this in mind, we can more easily take measure of what, in contrast, makes the processive order so original on the Chinese side: it is not brought from Beyond, not introduced, but neither is it progressive; rather, it is deployed in an internal mode, *sua sponte*, which could be called "natural." (Ibid., 43)

Here it becomes clear that "the silent transformation" is another way for Jullien to refer to what he elsewhere calls "the propensity of things" (Jullien 1995), in short, his thinking of efficacy—and, more precisely, efficiency (see Jullien 2004, 120–36)—in Chinese thought (I will discuss this at length in chapter 3). Efficacy comes about not so much through action but by letting things come to maturity in the way one desires, by applying oneself upstream from the action. It is a slow, much more time-based process than the Western notion of efficacy. At the end of his book on wisdom, Jullien captures this process, and more broadly the way of the *dao*, with the simple French expression *Ça va* (Jullien 1998, 208–9, 232). It is in such flat, ordinary, indeed unexceptional linguistic formulas, Jullien suggests, that the *dao* circulates.[14]

THE NUDE; OR, TOWARD THE UNEXCEPTIONAL FAR EAST

If landscape is the best aesthetic site to understand Chinese thought, Jullien presents the nude as a comparable site for Western thought. For Jullien "the nude is a paradigm of what the 'West' consists of in cultural terms and brings to light the stances that originally underpinned our philosophy" (Jullien 2007b, vii). He mentions, immediately following, "the question of essence, of the 'thing itself'" (ibid., vii), which takes us back to the previous discussions of ontology and metaphysics. If the nude is interesting to Jullien, it is because it does not allow us to imagine a beyond. "Part of the real stops there," he writes. "After the nude there is nothing more. . . . It is the end, *the very point of contact*" (2; emphasis original). As such it "always has the impact of an immutable revelation: the 'everything is there,' 'this is it,' with no horizon or receding perspective, no beyond. All the rest is merely allusive. . . . There is nothing to be decoded in it, the nude is no longer a sign, the unsurpassable is simply there, before our eyes" (3). The nude "surg[es] out"; it is "stunning"; Jullien characterizes it as an "event, offered like a miracle for contemplation" (36). He contrasts it on these counts to nakedness, which always "implies a diminished state" (4). The nude, on the other hand, "tends toward the Ideal and serves as the 'image' (*eikon*) for the Idea" (7). In that sense, it "turns toward the 'divine'" (7)—not at all toward the bland, the oblique, and the discreet that, under the header of "blandness," is characteristic of Chinese thought.[15]

Given that until the seventeenth century the male nude dominated European painting, Jullien asks whether Adam, perhaps, was considered to be closer to this Idea, this ideal Form, than Eve. Overall, however, he is not interested in such questions, even if they could open a new, gender-focused approach to his thought.[16] What intrigues him more is how European art's fixation on the nude mirrors European philosophy's fixation on the true (Jullien 2007b, 13). In philosophical terms, Jullien is interested in the "metaphysical experience of the nude" (ibid., 22), the way in which it "*exposes* Being more completely"—and he adds to this, anticipating his work in *This Strange Idea*, that "this is where its 'beauty' lies" (23; emphasis original). Given this philosophical status of the nude, the close relation between the nude and Western philosophy, it comes as no surprise that the nude would be lacking in China, a "vast cultural space that has never been penetrated by the nude" (30). As a philosopher, Jullien is interested in a transcendental question: What are the conditions of possibility in the West that made the nude possible? What are those conditions such that the nude, in China, has remained impossible? By now, we are familiar with those conditions from the other works by Jullien that I have discussed.

The Impossible Nude is in part so valuable, however, because it answers important questions related to both ontology and metaphysics *for the Western philosophical tradition*. Those questions pertain to the notion of "form," which is having a bit of a moment in contemporary thought.[17] Consider Byung-Chul Han's short little book *Shanzhai: Deconstruction In Chinese*. When Han discusses Western ontology and metaphysics, he characterizes Western thought as "monomorphic," adding the Greek term *monoeides* to mark Western thought's preference for the Platonic Idea or *eidos*, "Form" (Han 2017, 11). But this rendering of "monomorphic," which is already a Greek term that falls apart into the words "mono" (μονος) and "morphic" (μορφη), or "single" and "form," *as* the Greek *monoeides*, *mono* and *eides*, which also translate as "single" and "form" surely seems odd—unless the Greek words *morphe* and *eidos* mean exactly the same thing? Han does not give this any further discussion. But it is on this count that Jullien shows himself to be the more interesting thinker, since he rises to the challenge of the divergence that these questions open up.[18]

In what are some of the more striking pages in contemporary Western philosophical thought, Jullien—here wearing his Hellenist hat—writes the following:

> For *form*, Plotinus uses two words in conjunction with each other and often goes so far as to suggest that they can be synonymous: *eidos*, which is the idea-form—intelligible form, with ontological status, and *morphe*, which designates the contour that circumscribes matter. . . . A similar ambiguity is to be found in the language of Saint Augustine: *forma* is used to mean (1) the model form (Intelligence, the Divine Word), (2) the external form that is the contour, and also (3) form perceived as the source of beauty. This should also be read the opposite way around: beneath the "plastic," visible form, we keep sensing the informing, ontological, model form. (Jullien 2007b, 65)

It is through the lens of this ambiguity that Jullien then looks at the nude:

> Now it is out of this very ambivalence that the possibility of the nude is conceived: the Nude is the embodiment of our quest for the model, archetypal, "primary form" to be reached through the sensible form. For the nude is not just one form among others: it is the form par excellence (the Nude). It is the essential form that appears with the sensible, just as, in reverse, it is the sensible form rejoining the idea-form. In fact, through the Nude, we have tried unceasingly to find a hypostasis of Form. . . . And it is even the Nude which, because it is the most sensible—immediate to the senses, uncovered: laid bare—brings the two poles of plastic form (modeled relief and contour) and idea-form most directly into communication, within it-self. The plastic form uncovers the idea-form, and the last veil finally falls away; the idea-form ennobles the plastic form: we are in the very presence of the Idea, of the model and archetype. (Jullien 2007b, 65–67)

This eventually leads Jullien back to his critical concern with metaphysics:

> Hence the elevating tension of the nude: the tension is imparted by our metaphysical dualism. It gives rise to the transcendence summoned up by the nude—the vertigo of the extreme to which it leads: our awed amazement (*thambos*) [θαμβος] at the nude (the ecstasy). At the same time, it melts (dissolves/resolves) this dualism into the sole unmediated possibility of perception—that which is *laid bare*: this explains the characteristic sense of satisfaction, concurrent and soothing, that we experience when we look at the nude. (Jullien 2007b, 67)

The identification of *morphe* (form as contour) with *eidos* (form as idea) that we found in Han is, Jullien reveals, common at least since Plotinus. However, when trying to understand the unique place of the nude in the Western art-historical tradition (and its unique absence in China), one must remain attuned to the difference between *morphe* and *eidos* and the way in which *eidos* continues to stir underneath *morphe*.

While the nude is hylemorphic in the sense that it combines matter (*ule*; ʽυλη) with plastic form (*morphe*), the nude at the same time participates in ideal form (*eidos*), and its significance in Western art history comes from there—from its proximity, as a plastic form, to the ideal Form (and beauty). Pushing back against the identification of *morphe* and *eidos*, as Jullien points out Martin Heidegger among others has done (Jullien 2007b, 67), one senses "another possibility for thought," one that would sidestep the ideal Form entirely. Jullien finds this other possibility in China, which "did not conceive of any intelligible form beyond the realm of the sensible, nor any immutable form that is an essence" (ibid.). Again, China does not have metaphysics; it doesn't have being—only process. The Chinese term that translates as "form" is, Jullien points out, the notion of *xing* (形), which "designates an ongoing actualization of cosmic energy-breath" (ibid.). Form in China thus needs to be understood as "formation" (ibid., 68). As Jullien recalls, "the great image has no form" (77). These arguments are repeated in *This Strange Idea* (Jullien 2016, 75), where Jullien underlines once more that in Chinese thought "No form stabilizes, no *eidos* is isolated" (ibid., 85). What we find here, according to Jullien, since Plotinus, is a subtle fusion of Aristotelian ontology (the hylemorphic position) with the Platonic theory of ideal Form, which in fact made possible Western theories of art as allowing Form to appear through sensible matter/form. Thus Plotinus redeemed art from the discredit cast upon it by Plato, as Jullien points out (Jullien 2007b, 91).

As I see it, this is the precise fusion that underlies, for example, the work of Italian philosopher Giorgio Agamben, which takes as its starting point the Greek split between *zoe* (ζωη) and *bios* (βιoς), the simple fact of living common to humans, animals and gods, and ethical and political forms of life (Agamben 1998). In particular in the conclusion of Agamben's *Homo Sacer* trilogy, which begins with this split, it becomes clear that what Agamben is targeting is the biopolitics of Aristotelian ontology: the hylemorphism of "life" that underlies the entire Western political tradition. To overcome the hylemorphic split, however, Agamben proposes the enigmatic notion of form-of-life,[19] rendered in *The Use of Bodies* as *eidos tou biou* (ειδος του βιoυ; Agamben 2015), a form—and I think we can say, given his use of the Greek *eidos*, an ideal Form—in which no *zoe* nor *bios* could easily be separated. In other words, Agamben recovers, from underneath the (Aristotelian) hylemorphic split that structures Western politics, a Platonic notion of ideal Form, something that he had been interested in since his earliest writings (as the essays on Plato in the collection *Potentialities* evidence; Agamben 1999).

Can it still be a surprise, at this point, that Agamben has written about the nude, and has characterized it—positively—in precisely the terms that Jullien suggests, as having the "impact of an immutable revelation: the 'everything is there,' 'this is it,' with no horizon or receding perspective, no beyond" (Jullien 2007b, 3)? But how are we to read this characterization?

In an article titled "Nudity," which starts with a discussion of a performance by Vanessa Beecroft, Agamben criticizes how in Western thought "nudity" has always been marked by a "weighty theological legacy" (Agamben 2011, 65). It is due to this legacy that nudity has always only been what he describes as "the obscure and ungraspable presupposition of clothing," something that only appears when "clothes . . . are taken off" (ibid.). Nudity, within such a theological optic, is nothing but the "shadow" of clothing (ibid.). Agamben's project in his text is to "completely liberate nudity from the patterns of thought that permit us to conceive of it solely in a privative and instantaneous manner," and therefore the focus of such a project will have to be "to comprehend and neutralize the apparatus that produced this separation" (66) between nudity and clothing. He considers such a project to be realized in Beecroft's performance, in which "a hundred nude women (though in truth, they were wearing transparent pantyhose [and in some instances also shoes, as he points out later]) stood, immobile and indifferent, exposed to the gaze of the visitors who, after having waited on a long line, entered into a vast space on the museum's ground floor" (55). There are obviously naked—or sort of naked—bodies here, but Agamben's perhaps surprising conclusion at first is that in Beecroft's performance, nudity did not take place: instead, everything was marked by that theological legacy that renders nudity into a presupposition of clothing.

And yet Agamben finds in the performance something that might also neutralize this legacy, and more broadly the separation between nudity and clothing, and that is the indifferent and expressionless faces of the women in the performance. He argues, toward the end of his text, that these faces practice a "nihilism of beauty" (Agamben 2011, 88) that shatters this theological machine. It is the beautiful face that marks this machine's limit and causes it to stop by "exhibiting its nudity with a smile" and saying, "You wanted to see my secret? You wanted to clarify my envelopment? Then look right at it, if you can. Look at this absolute, unforgivable absence of secrets!" (ibid., 90). Nudity can in this sense quite simply be summed up as "*Haecce*! there is nothing other than this" (ibid.).[20] Agamben goes on to describe the effect of such a stop as a disenchantment that is both "miserable" and "sublime" due to how it moves "beyond all mystery and all meaning" (ibid.). There is no mystery to dispel, no meaning to uncover, no secret to be revealed. In nudity, all there is, is the beautiful face. It is, in this way, the beautiful face that frees nudity from its theological weight and lets it be, quite simply, naked.[21]

It is worth noting that there are important differences between how Agamben and Jullien characterize this nudity: whereas Jullien associates it with an event, Agamben seeks to move away from such an association (he associates the theological understanding of nudity with the "event" [Agamben 2011, 90] of denudation). Perhaps most importantly, Agamben's "there is nothing other than this" differs from Jullien's "everything is there," in that it marks, precisely, a reduction of beauty to appearance (ibid., 88) that Agamben seeks to celebrate against a metaphysical model of nudity. But while Agamben may find a defusing of theology and metaphysics here, his language reveals—and it is Jullien who enables us to see this—that this is hardly the ultimate defusing of Western thought, which continues its life in these quotations, precisely as Jullien suggests, as "aesthetics" (which steps in to fill theology's gap). In the nude, or rather the *beautiful* face of the nude, Agamben encounters the stop that, as per Jullien's reading, the nude in the Western tradition presents. But whereas Agamben stops at this stop, so to speak, by accepting how it defuses the theological apparatus in which the nude is caught up, Jullien considers the hidden tensions of this stop, the ways in which in this stop, one hears *eidos* stir underneath *morphe*. Indeed, if Agamben finds in the beautiful face of the nude and the stop it poses to theology the form-of-life or *eidos tou biou* that he praises elsewhere, it is clear that *eidos* or the ideal Form is able to realize itself aesthetically for him in the beautiful face of the nude. If Agamben's teacher Heidegger opened up the possibility of a thought that would not identify *morphe* with *eidos*, and if Jullien considered taking the path of *morphe* rather than *eidos*, Agamben ultimately goes the other way here, back to Plato, and thus becomes the apogee of Western thought.

Jullien notices many of the same things as Agamben does but considers these in the context of the divergence between Western thought and Chinese thought. This leads him somewhere else, outside metaphysics and ontology. It leads away from an aesthetic of "the beautiful," outside of essence and Being. This leads away from the nude; or at the very least it would lead to a very different kind of nude. Try to conceive, he writes in *The Impossible Nude*,

> of a "form" that would be seen only—as is the case in China—as the temporary actualization of the ongoing evolution proper to all living things. Think, therefore, of a body that is only the concretion (by individuation, and hence fleetingly perceptible) of the invisible underlying mass of energy in ceaseless deployment—actualization and resorption—as it forms the universe: the consistency on which the nude hinged disappears immediately, leaving no essence to be immobilized. My body comes into the world, grows, ages, and decays. It is constant prey to the transformation that brought it into existence, even though the process is so seamless that it is imperceptible to the eye. The body

presents no durable (and much less any definitive) state that might characterize it—the state immobilized by the nude—and I am aware only of different phases. (Jullien 2007b, 33)

If it is difficult—indeed, impossible—to imagine such a nude, we know where this description leads Jullien: to landscape and the "Without-form."

All of this also means that, while Agamben has become known as a thinker who criticizes political exceptionalism, his thought in "Nudity" ultimately remains caught up in the exceptionalism it contests. Jullien, by contrast,[22] operates in what one might by now also characterize as *the unexceptional Far East*.[23]

UNEXCEPTIONALISM, POLITICS, AND ECONOMICS

Given all of the previous, I would like to start thinking about Jullien's thought—a little provocatively—as "unexceptional."[24] Specifically, and here is where the slight provocation reaches its target, I would like to present Jullien's thought as going against the exceptionalism that, in my view—and I think Jullien provides ample evidence for this—typically constitutes Western thought. I am thinking, for example, of the notion of the event, which has thrived in contemporary thought as a name for such exceptionalism. Consider, for example, the already-mentioned work of Alain Badiou, whose math-based philosophy Jullien in an uncharacteristic gesture explicitly targets in his book *Silent Transformations* (Jullien 2011, 122). The thought of the event is a thought of the break, the rupture, of radical caesura—of the miracle, which Jullien frequently mentions. This is also the thought of the subject, the author, the artist, the genius, the sovereign, and the creator. They create, decide, invent, act. As will be clear, such exceptionalism is political as well as aesthetic. As I have discussed, it is philosophical—ontological and metaphysical—as well as theological. If Jullien in all of his work operates within the divergence between Western thought and Chinese thought, I want to suggest that he thereby illuminates Western exceptionalism and shows how Chinese thought is unexceptional.

It might seem in all of this that Jullien *prefers* Chinese thought over Western thought, even if he also says he does not want to present one as better than the other. The risk of such a preference is that China becomes, in Jullien's work, another figure of the exception, that China comes to constitute yet another exception—and there are some instances in his work (for example in his book on the nude) where this risk becomes real, and where Jullien writes about China as an exception (see Jullien 2007b, 55). However, this goes against the grain of his overall project, which undermines the exceptionalism that saturates Western thought, and seeks to promote the unexceptional under the name of what Jullien calls "the bland."

It is worth noting that Jullien's book *A Treatise on Efficacy: Between Western and Chinese Thinking* (originally from 1996, which is five years after *In Praise of Blandness* was published) ends with a chapter titled "In Praise of Facility," in whose opening paragraph the "unexceptional" is praised as a key feature of Chinese thought:

> The image of what constantly flows past our feet—water forever closely embracing every hollow in the terrain, conforming to its shape so as to move onward—is totally unexceptional, yet its repercussions at a theoretical level are endless. And the more unexceptional the image, the more endless its implications are. Chinese thought has always drawn inspiration from this image to find words for the hardest thing of all to express: the evident "facility" of what which is ceaselessly realized in an unremarkable and unnoticed fashion. As if to interpret the message more clearly, Chinese thought projected this onto the sky, giving it the emblematic form of the body of a dragon, whose shape is almost impossible to make out, so quickly does it change, coiling and uncoiling as the clouds dictate. (Jullien 2004, 184)

As such, it is associated in the paragraph with "the evident 'facility' of that which is ceaselessly realized in an unremarkable and unnoticed fashion" (ibid.). There is a close connection, then, between the facility that is praised in this chapter and the unexceptional, and between the unexceptional and the blandness that Jullien praises as "Chinese."

By calling Jullien's thought unexceptional, I want to draw out the unexceptionalizing tendency that Chinese thought can bring to Western thought, which Jullien shows to be exceptionalist through and through. In the context of my discussion of Jullien's thought on aesthetics, I am using the exceptionalism/unexceptionalism pairing as one name for the divergence that Jullien stages between Chinese thought and Western thought. Undoing exceptionalism in Western thought—specifically, unexceptionalizing or de-exceptionalizing[25] Western thought, as Jullien might put it—can lead us away from some of the more problematic exceptionalisms that have constituted it. The ultimate goal here, as I already stated in my introduction, is not so much to oppose the West and China on this count as two identities, one of which could be discarded in favor of the other (there obviously is unexceptionalism in the West just as there is exceptionalism in China); rather, it is to play out each thought's respective resources in their divergence with each other so as to see what their in-between might yield.[26]

While the terms "exception" or "exceptional" can be found throughout Jullien's oeuvre, and the idea of the exception saturates his presentations of Western thought, Jullien does not use the term "unexceptional" as a key term to criticize Western thought. Instead, he opts for the "bland." It is a good choice, in that "bland" cannot immediately be read in opposition to the exception—and indeed thinking outside of oppositions is one of the things that Chinese thought invites one to do. The bland names a neutral subtlety and discreetness; "'rare' are those who can 'gain awareness of it': it presents no telltale identifying marks, boasts no remarkable 'flavor,' and blends in with the normal state of things" (Jullien 2008, 50). Or, as Confucius puts it, negatively, "Attempting to live differently from others [or, according to another interpretation: attempting to penetrate the mysteries of the most obscure], along with trying to accomplish miracles so that future generations have a reason to speak of one—now, here are things that I myself will assiduously avoid!" (ibid.)[27] The gentleman "prefers to remain in the shadows" (ibid., 51); "the strongest presence is conveyed in the greatest reserve" (52). As such, the bland is the "flavor of sagehood . . . because blandness is the most basic and authentic of flavors: that of the 'root' of things" (53). From there, "all true efficacy" (49) matures.

However, it is worth noting that each of these various descriptions of blandness includes within itself two tendencies: while it is bland, blandness is also the most basic and authentic of flavors; while it is conveyed with the greatest reserve, it also reveals the strongest presence; et cetera. On each count, a "negative" limit is combined with a "positive" limit, thus preventing a dull reading of the bland as merely bland—as merely negative. What sets the bland apart is that within its negation, within its withdrawal and restraint, it allows a positive, a presence and affirmation, to arise. This is a blandness, then, that must indeed be *praised* as the title of Jullien's famous book has it—in spite of the title's already-noted ironies.

Sharpening Jullien's engagement with Western thought as a criticism of Western thought's exceptionalism, I want to propose the term "unexceptional"—next to the bland—to mark the way in which Chinese thought diverges from Western thought. Note that by using this term I do not slip into the easy opposition of the exception to the norm, which arguably coconstitutes the notion of the exception. Instead, I am interested in un- or de-exceptionalizing the exception—in using China as a cultural resource to de-exceptionalize Western thought. This means, as the very term unexceptional reveals, that I still hold on to a (Western?) trace of the exceptional within this move. This is because, on the one hand, I consider the exceptional a cultural resource of the West and, on the other, there is obviously exceptionalism in China as well, as the notion of the bland illustrates. A trace of exceptionalism is clearly present in Jullien's understanding of the bland: "most basic and authentic of flavors," "strongest presence," et cetera—all terms of exception. These traces do not fit the word "bland"; they are, in fact, *why* the bland ought to be *praised*. They show, I think, that within the divergence between Chinese and Western thought that Jullien sets up, Jullien is not moving into Chinese thought entirely, if by that one would understand a moving away from the exception entirely. Instead, the exception's verticality is continued in an entirely different way: through its unexceptionalization. Similarly, Jullien does not move away from Western thought entirely. He insists, on various occasions in his work, that he has not been "sinized" by his research. And neither does he "Westernize" Chinese thought. Instead, his approach is about divergence. Indeed, it's in the pairing of the exceptional/unexceptional that we can see divergence—rather than difference—at work.

The disadvantage of the term "unexceptional" is that it unavoidably gives priority to the West, since we start with a Western exception that is unexceptionalized by way of China. But Jullien too starts with the West—as a "Greek"—and takes "a detour" via China, which came second, to better be able to read Greek. With the notion of bland, however, Jullien is able to break out of such a prioritizing of the West, something that seems particularly important because it is the bland that, in Chinese thought, *comes first*: it is out of the bland that, in China, the exceptional emerges. In China there is first the bland and then the exceptional; in the West, thoroughly saturated with exceptionalism, Chinese thought can bring an unexceptionalizing tendency due to the priority China gives to the bland.

It will be clear then that, while Western thought and Chinese thought diverge on the count of the exceptional, it would be difficult to fully *oppose* Chinese thought to Western thought in this way. After all, traces of the exceptional continue in Chinese thought. The difference is, however, that they emerge from the bland. One needs to let go of the facile opposition of Chinese thought to Western thought to trace instead the more complicated ways in which they relate. When Chinese thought prefers floating, for example, Jullien knows very well the kind of reading this may immediately provoke: an appraisal of being adrift, aimless, in ambiguity. But he adds right away (in *Vital Nourishment* where this example is being discussed) that this is not what is meant by floating: "Boats that float easily at anchor in a bay undulate with the waves and can animate a landscape" (Jullien 2007c, 114). In short, there is an anchoring to this floating that generates a vibrancy in the landscape—that turns *the* landscape into *landscape*.[28] Again, different elements are combined in order to avoid precisely the facile opposition to which an easy embrace of floating might lead.

This is very important in view of the charge that Jullien would be reducing Chinese thought to immanence. While it is true that part of Jullien's criticism of Western thought's exceptionalism involves the breaking down of transcendence, one has to acknowledge that this breaking down maintains what Jullien calls "internal transcendence" as, for example, the just-mentioned vibrancy of landscape. Everything goes back to the processes of nature rather than to the stable eternity of the divine; but there is transcendence on both counts.[29] Chinese thought, as Jullien presents it, is hardly an entirely immanent thought.[30]

If I've mostly stuck to aesthetics and philosophy in this chapter, I should note—in anticipation of both my next chapter and conclusion—that I consider Jullien's unexceptional thought to be important today perhaps especially from a political point of view, in a time when a certain kind of political exceptionalism has been on the rise as part of a revival of the political right and a nationalist politics of sovereignty. I make this connection partly in view of the fact that, while Chinese thought may be unexceptional, certainly ancient and classical China did not lack in sovereignty. In *Propensity of Things*, Jullien points out that in ancient and classical China, "no form of political regime other than royalty was imaginable" (Jullien 1995, 44). The theory of efficacy, which Jullien exposes both in *Propensity of Things* and *Treatise on Efficacy*, and according to which one exercises authority most effectively, most totally, not through "Western" interventionism but through "Chinese" acting upstream—in other words, not through the moment of the decision but through a slow process of manipulation—leads in Jullien's description to "a totalitarianism reminiscent of our own times" (ibid., 47), which operates through both punishment and surveillance (49). He explicitly evokes Michel Foucault on this count, both the paradigm of the "town quarantined because of the plague" and "Jeremy Bentham's famous panopticon" (55). Some in fact saw this panoptical sovereign exercise of total authority as "a perfect extension to the *Dao*" (52), since the sovereign does not need to act to exert total control over a situation. In *Treatise on Efficacy*, this "acting-without-action" is characterized as "a kind of laissez-faire" (Jullien 2004, 91). This may be a particular risk that the unexceptional holds, the downside of a thought that "[reduces] to the utmost all forms of rebellion and discontinuity" (Jullien 1995, 245). At the same time, unexceptionality does not seem to be immune to sovereignty, even if in some of its aspects it may critically work against it.

While Jullien is clearly a thinker of the political, whose *Treatise on Efficacy* could feature on any syllabus of contemporary political thought, he has been criticized for not paying enough attention to politics. It is not so much that politics is absent from his works; Jullien often arrives at it in the final chapters of his books, and it certainly comes up often and at length in interviews with him. But I don't think one could say that politics drives his work. (He has also asked whether Western readers expect politics to drive his work *because* he writes about China.)[31] *Silent Transformations* stands out in his oeuvre as a book where politics does come up more frequently, and in which "current events" appear into his critical thinking about the philosophical category of "the event." Strangely, however, the events in question are mostly

Western events (the September 11 terrorist attacks, for example; Jullien 2011, 120). But Chinese politics remains largely absent in the book's pages. As a reader, I would have liked to see more reflection on how Jullien's analysis of ancient and classical Chinese thought relates to, say, communist China and its development into a capitalist/neoliberal nation-state today.[32]

One such political reflection arrives at the very end of *Silent Transformations*, where Jullien characterizes Deng Xiaoping as "the 'silent transformer' of China." Deng's silent transformation worked so well, Jullien writes, "that China, we note retrospectively today, has been able to reverse completely its social and economic system by continuous transition, leaving the regime and the Party in place but profoundly transformed" (Jullien 2011, 153). "Compare this," he adds parenthetically, "with the USSR becoming Russia again as it passed through so many successive ruptures" (ibid., 153). A little further down, the slow expansion of the Chinese quarter in Paris is compared to "the tactic of enveloping in the game of Go"[33] (and contrasted to "the frontality of the game of chess"): whoever appreciates the difference "will easily understand its importance by learning not to destroy the adversary but to control as much territory as possible by constructing networks while extending out from them through an entanglement which increasingly tightens its influence" (153–154; these examples as well as the 9/11 reference are repeated in Jullien 2005).

Let's pause for a moment to ask what purpose these passages serve. On the surface, they illustrate the process of silent transformation that is central to the book from which they are quoted, and that is explained in various other volumes in Jullien's oeuvre as well (most notably *Treatise on Efficacy*, but also *Propensity of Things*). It seems odd, however, that Deng Xiaoping—associated with China's neoliberalization—is treated as what appears to be a neutral example, taken from politics and economics, of what Jullien understands by silent transformation. If anything, Jullien appears to praise the way in which Deng has wielded power: the Olympic games of 2008 represented, he writes, how China since Deng has made "good use of all the conditions or rivalries favorable to it and without any great events" (Jullien 2011, 153).

Perhaps part of the point is something that appears elsewhere in Jullien's work—namely, that Jullien in his analysis of Chinese thought operates beyond good and evil, so to speak, that he is not making a moral assessment of such thought. Indeed, Chinese thought at times does not appear to bother with moral assessments, as Jullien presents it: good and evil are merely tendencies that relieve each other; the important thing is not to get stuck in either one. This might not apply to Confucianism, but one does get that sense from the *Zhuangzi*, which Jullien is analyzing in *Vital Nourishment*. "Ultimately, it matters little whether the action is 'good' or 'evil,'" he writes in *Vital Nourishment*. "The important thing is not to become so attached to a position as to remain trapped by it" (Jullien 2007c, 31). The key here is "respiration": "a continual incitation not to dwell in either of two opposite positions—inhalation or exhalation" (ibid., 31).

If it seems difficult to speak about contemporary Chinese politics and economics in this way, Jullien's Paris example appears strange for the opposite reason: because there, clearly, some kind of moral assessment works its way back in. How else to read the image that Jullien offers not of the West's hegemony in the process of globalization but precisely of China—the Chinese quarter in Paris—confronting the rest of Paris as an "adversary," out for control, territory, and influence? The Chinese presence in Paris is characterized as a form of strategic warfare.[34]

Is Jullien welcoming this Chinese expansion? Is he critical of it, as his language seems to suggest? If indeed there is a moral assessment, does it reflect back on his discussion of Deng, which seems strangely neutral? Clearly in the Paris example Jullien is not merely explaining Chinese thought, as he claims to be. It reads like a warning for the yellow peril. In *Book of Beginnings*, on the other hand, the author claims to "enjoy the names of the Chinese restaurants in my neighborhood" (Jullien 2015, 119). This time he smiles at how their Chinese names are rendered in French. The Chinese *Xin cheng*, "New—flourishing" or "in full bloom," appears as Delicious Monge (for the Rue Monge on which the restaurant is located); *Qian heng*, "initiatory capacity—expansion," is simply rendered as Chez Tonny. On this count, Jullien criticizes the lack of encounter between China and the West—the Westernization of the Chinese restaurant names. This seems closer to what he argues throughout his work, and stands in contrast to the Paris quarter example from *Vital Nourishment*.

Going back to my discussion in chapter 1 of Gayatri Chakravorty Spivak's review of Kristeva (Kristeva 1977), and the "more or less vaguely articulated conviction" she finds in "Derrida, Lyotard, Deleuze, and the like" that working within the divergence between West and East could tell us something about "the morphology of capital" (Spivak 1981, 157), I would like to ask some further questions about economics as well. The topic is largely absent from Jullien's oeuvre, even if he occasionally characterizes Chinese thought—for example, the strategy of silent transformation, as discussed above—as extremely economical (because it seeks to operate through minimal losses). It is interesting to note, however, that his book *Conférence sur l'efficacité* (Lecture on efficacy) appears to be a lecture for managers; Jullien mentions having accompanied French companies in China to assist them with negotiations and help them understand Chinese strategies of negotiation (Piorunski 1998, 173). Jean-François Billeter has drawn attention to this in one of the more useful sections of his book *Contre François Jullien* (Billeter 2006, 67–69). Jullien's most explicitly economic book, in my view, is *Vital*

58 *Chapter 2*

Nourishment, but it does not speak about economics in any direct way. It is a book about life—or, more precisely, living (Jullien prefers the process of living over the metaphysical notion of life)—and specifically about hygiene and longevity. It is, if one wants to use a term most often associated with Foucault, a *biopolitical* book. Whenever we are talking biopolitics, however, economics is never far away (as Foucault taught us; Foucault 1990 and 2008).[35]

Jullien's starting point for *Vital Nourishment* is "a very common expression [in Chinese]: 'to feed one's life'" (Jullien 2007c, 8). In the book, he is interested in "the ability to 'feed life' . . . to maintain one's capacity to evolve by refining and decanting what is vital in oneself, so as to develop that vitality to the full" (ibid., 8–9). Feeding one's life is about learning "to deploy, preserve, and develop the capacity for life with which we are all endowed" (14). The question is, of course, what it might mean to feed one's life, and Jullien takes up this issue in full cognizance of the fact that it is "a major and growing concern among Westerners today, a concern that is in a sense converting many of them" (20). He writes,

> In a dechristianizing world that no longer defers happiness to the hereafter, and which is by the same token less and less inclined to sacrifice in the name of a higher cause (be it revolution, fatherland, or what have you), we are in fact left, once we have rid ourselves of all these projections and associated hopes, with nothing other than the need to manage and maintain "that" which, if nothing else, at least cannot be suspected of being an illusion: namely, the *life capital* that is imparted to each individual being and that, stripped of all ideological guises, is said to be indubitable and therefore authentic "self." (Ibid., 20)

Jullien notes all of the pseudophilosophy that on this count has appeared in the West, often with reference to Chinese thought. It is also in order to save Western thought from "casually abandon[ing] the ideals it has constructed and plung[ing] into a socially disastrous irrationalism"—that is, in order to save it from such pseudophilosophy—that Jullien embarks upon *Vital Nourishment*, and he notes that this is a "political as well as philosophical point" (ibid., 21). Here his focus (and one might want to note that it is a salvational one) appears to be the West rather than China.

"Stripped of all ideological guises": let me return to that phrase in the last block quotation. Jullien had already said at the outset of his book that by focusing on "the question of living by way of vital potential or capital . . . ineluctable distortions of ideology are kept to a minimum" (Jullien 2007c, 8). Is this so? Much of *Vital Nourishment* echoes and develops further familiar themes of Jullien's thought: an interest in the subtle (ibid., 24), immanence and transformation (27), the middle way and the alternation between tendencies (rather than the mathematical middle) (30), or the refusal to theologize

(35). But all of that now gets rephrased as part of a project to manage and maintain one's life capital. Importantly, such a project is not about thinking "how 'to live more'" (36). Those who do so "[deplete] the source of life within [themselves]" (ibid.). Indeed, it is not about clinging to life at all. Instead, "we 'abandon' our lives, we 'eliminate' ('kill') all concern for our own lives, and then we no longer die. . . . In order to live fully (completely), we must not cling to life" (ibid.). We must be "guided solely by incitement, freed from all febrile stimuli and in contact with a more intimate source of energy" (48). The duality of body and soul is dissolved in Chinese thought, which dissolves in fact the very notions of "body" and "soul." This goes back to Jullien's discussions elsewhere of ontology: Chinese thought "has no world of concrete essences. It possesses neither an individuating soul nor an opposing concept of matter (no *ule*, which Aristotle treats as the matter of the body)" (ibid., 69). This doesn't mean Chinese thought does not have "materialization" (as process) "by way of continuous concretion (under the yin factor), as well as 'animation,' which dispels its opacity and unfolds it (under the factor yang). Like the external world, I am shaped and kept alive by this tension between self-compensating opposites" (ibid.). Once again, the emphasis is on breath and flow—on floating.

All of this said, it is interesting to see Jullien later describe the management and regulation of one's life capital as the "enterprise" of a "vital potential" that can "produce a larger or smaller yield in the agricultural or financial sense" (Jullien 2007c, 121; see also Jullien 2005). In what appears to be a discussion of the thought of Xi Kang,[36] a thinker from the period of the *Zhuangzi*,

> a good field is said to yield ten *hu* per *mou* of land, but if one cultivates the land more intensely by dividing it into smaller parcels for the sake of better irrigation, a yield ten times greater can be achieved. Similarly, market transactions can be made to yield many times the usual profit. Though such extraordinary results may be surprising, they are not fantastic hopes but straightforward consequences of the art of management. Why shouldn't we manage our vital potential as we would any other form of *capital*, since we know that capital is something we are bound to squander unless we learn what it takes to make it productive? (Jullien 2007c, 121–22; emphasis original)

"Feeding one's life," this passage concludes, "is nothing other than this art of management" (ibid., 122).

To feed one's life means, then, to become the entrepreneur—agricultural or financial, no matter—of oneself, in order to achieve "extraordinary results": "many times the usual profit"! To manage oneself, one's vital potential, is similar to managing any other form of capital. If the passage I just quoted sounds neoliberal, here we get to the core of the issue, which is really that we must become *capitalists* of *ourselves* (which is not a bad description of the human condition under neoliberalism). Contrary to the Western approach to health, which Jullien associates with rule (the rule of absolute health, for example, versus the to-be-governed-reality of relative health), the Chinese approach focuses on management and regulation. But make no mistake: while the verticality of rule is thus removed in favor of process and transformation, *the verticality of extraordinary profit remains*: in other words, the exceptionalism of rule is eclipsed here by the exceptionalism of profit. Sovereignty, if I may put it this way, gives way to capitalism (and, ultimately, neoliberalism).

I find it difficult to see, first of all, how these remarks from later in *Vital Nourishment* are to be read with those from earlier in the book, saying, for example, that "he who clings to life and is always thinking about how 'to live more' depletes the source of life within himself" (Jullien 2007c, 36). The logic of capital—now isn't that precisely about how to turn money into money that is worth *more* (via the intermediary of the commodity)? Isn't the very condensation of this Karl Marx's celebrated formula of capital (M-C-M'), shortened in the first volume of *Capital* to M-M', the formula to capture interest-bearing capital (Marx 1990)? How can feeding one's life be *both* about managing capital in the agricultural or financial way *and not* about "thinking about how 'to live more'"? Granted, in Marx the "more" is tied to a labor theory of value that locates the accumulation of surplus-value (*Mehr-wert*, as Marx writes; literally, "more-value") in the exploitation of human life/labor potential. In Jullien, on the other hand, the entire project is about feeding human life potential—but still, feeding it in an attempt to make it yield more.

More what? Importantly, there is no finality to the discourse. Jullien does not have a product in sight. The "more," by contrast, pertains to an openness for change, transformation, process. It is a decommodifying "more," one focused on "processive actualization or formation" (Jullien 2007c, 71). In the closing pages of his book, Jullien characterizes it as tied to "a common definalization of existence based solely on managing the way we care for ourselves" (ibid., 159). "Art today demonstrates," he closes, "how this can be done" (160).

Indeed, art probably does. But with that said, it seems clear that the discourse, including the role of art and aesthetics in all of this, demands more critical analysis. One wants to see the relations to capitalism spelled out; one wants to see the relations to neoliberalism spelled out. Jullien might think his discourse is "stripped of all ideological guises" and that the "ineluctable distortions of ideology are kept to a minimum"; but it seems to me any critical reader will want to hear more about how, exactly, Jullien situates *Vital*

Nourishment in relation to the current economic situation *in both the West and China*. None of that works its way into his book.

From such a vantage point, much of what Jullien has to say in *Vital Nourishment* would appear in a more dubious light, one that might in fact reflect outward also to some of his other works, which remain curiously silent on politics and economics. If this is in part to unexceptionalize a political and economic discourse focused on events, and to foreground instead a Chinese thought of silent transformations, one wonders, in the end, whether such a thought, focusing on gradual process as Jullien claims it does, would not ultimately overlook actual politics and economics that, though they may have arrived silently, nevertheless still require our moral assessment—even if such assessment might condense them into "events" and Westernize them as a consequence?[37] To work within the divergence between Western and Chinese thinking may then mean, as the trajectory of Jullien's entire career allows us to understand, to pursue the divergence in that direction—from the West *to* China—as well.

NOTES

1. Jullien 2016, 17.

2. The reference is to Jullien's French research doctorate in Far East studies, which he obtained in 1983, after already having received his French university doctorate in 1978.

3. Note that Ames and Hall translate this line as "The greatest image has no shape" (Ames and Hall 2003, 141).

4. I avoid here terms like "image," "symbol," or "allegory" because I do not think Jullien uses the nude and the landscape in this way. Instead, these painterly *topoi* realize something as paintings—and not as images, symbols, or allegories—through the material operation of their works—of what Jullien understands to be Western thought and Chinese thought. It's very important in this context, I think, to steer clear from any hint of representationalism, or separations between a painting and what it images, symbolizes, or allegorizes. With both the landscape and the nude, Jullien's point will be that they realize, in their works, the thought he finds in them. In other words, they do not merely "stand for" that thought.

5. Anatomy is tied to mathematics and the mathematical model, which Jullien associated with Western thought. "I know of no great Chinese thinkers who were inspired by mathematics" (Jullien 2009, 37), Jullien writes in a footnote in *The Great Image*. In his book *Vital Nourishment: Departing from Happiness* (2007c), Jullien shows how the Western distinction between absolute (perfect mathematical) health and relative health is derived from this (see ibid., 25).

6. For more on this, see Jullien 1995, 99.

7. The translation of the passage is in fact problematic: when Jullien has the word "gaze," the translator renders it as "eye." This takes away the entire point of

the passage, which is to move away from the notion of the gaze—to accomplish a "conversion of the gaze," a "conversion du regard" (Jullien 2014, 38), as Jullien quite literally writes—toward something else. Instead, when the something else arrives in the passage, the translator finally enters "gaze" into the translation, thus suggesting it might actually name the conversion of the eye that Jullien aspires to. But one gathers from this passage, as well as Jullien's other work, that this is not so.

8. See Jullien 2015, 2.

9. There is a connection here with what Edward Said has theorized as "late style" (Said 2006). In his discussion of the sketch, Jullien associates the sketch with "the latest works attributed to the old masters," which he deems to be of special interest in this context:

> After completing so many finished works that brought them renown, these masters declare their freedom and cast aside perfection and workshop norms. Now doing as they like, they paint only to paint—that is, to put the powers of painting to work once again, wishing each time that these powers will be even more radical. They do not paint to paint well, with everything that "well" implies in terms of the intolerable stricture imposed by diligent work. Having reached the pinnacle of his art, the painter confines himself to blotches or inventive, inchoative brushstrokes, ridding himself of all the extras: he will be careless about filling in. (Jullien 2009, 62).

This late style thus comes close to the sketch. One might relabel Said's late style in this context as "Chinese." As I will explore in chapter 4, Jullien's affinities with postcolonial thought extend far beyond this connection.

10. He also mentions Georges Braque as being close to Chinese thought (Jullien 2012, 56, 72).

11. On this, see also his still-untranslated book *Du "temps": Éléments d'une philosophie de vivre* (2001).

12. "More generally, the novel, as a characteristic genre of the modern age and one which we recognize as fundamentally new, finds its function and legitimacy in narrating silent transformations. Indeed, I believe this may be its real object, notably when dealing with those great sweeping and multilayered historical transformations that set in play so many vectors and factors of the social and that cannot be contained by any single date or episode" (Jullien 2011, 63).

On this count, I don't find Jullien's thought consistent. In *Book of Beginnings*, for example, he writes that in Chinese thought "we will not find the least element of narration. We therefore find neither crime nor punishment: there is no tragedy to fear or salvation (a way out) to hope for. There is (are) neither agent(s) nor story(ies)" (Jullien 2015, 63). This characterization is then associated with postmodernism and the disappearance of "great narratives" (ibid., 63), and it is suggested China never had those great narratives in the first place. Clearly Jullien's characterization of "the novel" as "Chinese" elsewhere would have to be nuanced in view of the passages just quoted. Another example: in *In Praise of Blandness*, Jullien follows Barthes, "this lover of rhetoric," in his characterization of (bland) China as "Prose" (Jullien 2008, 28). But in *Book of Beginnings*, Jullien suggests the stylistic equivalent to the Chinese thought of processivity is "pure parataxis that absolutely nothing coordinates" (Jullien 2015, 100). More transparent is his claim in *A Treatise on Efficacy* that "China produced no epic" (Jullien 2004, 59) due to its lack of a Western theory of action. I would like to come back to these various claims elsewhere.

13. Here one should point out that Jullien's discussion does not come with any overview of attempts within Western art to go against this, even if occasional cases are mentioned. In the same way that he appears to overlook "Chinese" modes of thinking within Western philosophy, he overlooks "Chinese" practices of art within Western art.

14. At least to this reader, it seems clear that Jullien is arguing against event-based, theological philosophies in these pages of *The Silent Transformations*. Yet in his books *De l'Intime* and *Ressources du Christianisme*, he also appears to praise the event as a resource of Western and specifically Christian thought. In *De l'Intime*, the intimate is positively associated with the event and the miracle (Jullien 2013, 44); Saul's conversion on the road to Damascus is mentioned as an example of the sudden break that the irruption of the intimate brings (ibid., 76). (I single out this example due to its centrality in Badiou's event-based philosophy; Badiou 2003.) Jullien's recent *Ressources du Christianisme* continues this thinking. Most notably, in *De l'Intime* Jullien uses the language of "silent transformation and transition" (Jullien 2013, 77) to mark the process that precedes the event of the intimate, indicating that it is perhaps not so much a question here of fully undoing the exceptional through the unexceptional but of drawing out how every exception is ultimately only the result of a silent process of transformation that precedes it. Jullien is not so much operating within the opposition of the exceptional to the unexceptional but in the divergence between the exceptional and the unexceptional.

15. This paragraph, with minor modifications, already appeared in Boever 2019.

16. One reason why Jullien may have avoided this approach overall may be the comparison, made by Pierre Ryckmans, a.k.a. Simon Leys, in the aftermath of Billeter's attack on Jullien, of China's alterity to sexual difference (Jullien 2007a, 44). Jullien strongly disagrees with this comparison and frequently notes that he is not interested in China's "alterity." Instead, he starts from China's "elsewhere." Jullien notes that whereas "elsewhere" is a geographical fact, China's "alterity" is a philosophical construction. I nevertheless offer here some questions that are difficult to avoid in Jullien's discussion of the nude.

Is Western metaphysics first and foremost masculinist? Does the rise of Eve in the history of the nude mark her incorporation into this masculinist metaphysics? Has "man" fallen out of the ideal Form only to let "woman" take its place? More critically, might this substitution have produced a change within the masculinist model of metaphysics? Has there been an unworking of the masculinist model of metaphysics from the side of the feminine? Might such an unworking put one on the track of Chinese thought, perhaps even on the track of Chinese landscape painting, as a feminine counterpart to the masculinist model of the nude in which, in the West, both "men" and "women" are caught up? (What are the problems of such an approach, which would "feminize" China in relation to the West?) Finally, and taking up the central theoretical concern of this article, if the masculinist model is one of exceptionalism (in which women have progressively become caught up), is unexceptionalism associated with the feminine?

I ask those questions partly in anticipation of my conclusion in this book, and in view of Bonnie Honig's work on exceptionalism, and specifically the call for "countersovereignty" that it contains (Honig 2013, 2, 10, and elsewhere). The latter Honig characterizes as bringing a break or interruption to "many theorists' fascination with rupture over the everyday, powerlessness over sovereignty, and heroic martyrdom over the seemingly dull work of maintenance, repair, and planning for possible futures" (Honig 2013, 2). Honig is defining an exceptionalism here: she is talking about a break or interruption with the notion of countersovereignty, but it is an exceptionalism of the everyday, maintenance, repair, planning. In an interview with Diego Rossello, Honig has associated this other exceptionalism with "second-wave feminism," which, she notes, "was particularly critical of the register of the extraordinary for being masculinist and heroic" (Rossello 2015, 701). Honig has also worked with queer models of countersovereignty in this context (Honig 2014); and the latter may help to move this particular conversation beyond the masculine/feminine opposition that (problematically) structures the questions I derived here from Jullien.

17. See, for example, Levine 2015.

18. This paragraph as well as the following up to the section break already appeared (with minor modifications) in Boever 2019.

19. I have commented on this in Boever 2016.

20. Note that Agamben characterizes this here as a "matheme."

21. Agamben had made this point previously in Agamben 2007. Even before then, this argument about the face can also be found in Agamben 2000.

22. The contrast is less marked in Jullien's books on Christianity: Jullien 2013 and 2018b. Similarly, but for wholly different reasons, the contrast is less marked in some of Agamben's other texts. There the contraction of *zoe* and *bios* into an *eidos tou biou* is accomplished without a continued attachment to beauty. Eske Møllgaard has argued for example that in *The Coming Community* Agamben defends an unorthodox kind of transcendence that needs to be opposed to the one of Plato's ideal Forms. This would be the idiosyncratic transcendence of "the very 'taking-place of the entities,' their 'being irreparably in the world,' the very fact 'that the world is, that something can appear'" (Agamben quoted in Møllgaard 2005, 5). Note, however, that there is no mention of beauty here. Møllgaard furthermore argues that this is the sense of transcendence that can be found in the *Zhuangzi*, and Jullien's work on the *Zhuangzi* also features in Møllgaard's text. Elsewhere Møllgaard has put Agamben's sense of transcendence in dialogue with both the *Zhuangzi*'s understanding of the *dao* and Heidegger's notion of "releasement" (*Gelassenheit*; Møllgaard 2006, 54). The relation of Agamben to Jullien warrants a much longer discussion that would need to consider Jullien's book on Plato (Jullien 2017) and what Mathieu Potte-Bonneville has called Jullien's "anti-platonisme fécond" (productive antiplatonism; Potte-Bonneville 2018, 52). The relation of *eidos* to *telos* would need to be considered here as well, especially in view of the emphasis Agamben has placed on a philosophy of "means without end" (Agamben 2000).

23. By this phrase, "the unexceptional Far East," I am partly trying to draw out the peculiar fact that the name "Far East" itself carries connotations of "exceptionality" in French: *l'Extrême Orient*, the "extreme" Orient. Jullien's work on Chinese thought targets this peculiarity.

24. I propose and develop this notion here partly in a silent conversation with scholars like Emily Apter 2017 and Gourgouris 2013.

25. *The Great Image* is presented as "An Essay in De-ontology," and in the preface Jullien associates deontology with "de-picting, de-representing" (Jullien 2009, xvii).

26. As I've explained in my introduction and chapter 1, Jullien has written most clearly about this methodological point in his most recent works. My sense is that he has focused on clarifying it in response to the charge that he operates within an opposition between Western and Chinese thought and construes China as the absolute other, either to embrace it over the West or to reject it. But Jullien insists this is not so: his is not a thought of identity and difference but of resources and divergence. Nevertheless, it is not always easy to avoid the suggestion of opposition in his thinking.

27. As I have pointed out earlier, Jullien is able to positively reference Confucius in his largely Daoist-based thought because he is interested in the connections between Confucianism and Daoism, which are generally opposed.

28. The lack of the definite article here is important. Jullien uses the definite article with the nude, paradigmatic of the West, but *not* with landscape, paradigmatic of the East. Indeed, one of his main criticisms of Western renderings of Chinese texts is the addition of definite articles in the translations. Chinese thought, as he makes clear, prefers the indefinite.

29. Note here that in *De l'Intime*, "anchoring" is associated with Christian thought; Jullien 2013, 73.

30. The same argument can be made about Jullien's "materialism." On the question whether the Chinese are "materialists" or not, see Jullien 1995, 248–53. It's with respect to the term "immanence" that Jullien's relation to Deleuze and Guattari is often negotiated. In my view, Shu-bao Dong situates Jullien too close to Deleuze and Guattari here (Dong 2018); Peng Yu strikes closer to the mark with a more-nuanced reading of immanence in Daoist thought—one that fits better with Jullien's own understanding of the notion (Yu 2016).

31. On this point and the previous, see Piorunski 1998 and Martin and Spire 2011.

32. See also Billeter 2006.

33. Some might consider this an orientalist trope.

34. It is probably worth noting that Jullien's work has been cited in the field of comparative military studies (it has played a role in strategic studies in particular). I will discuss this in detail in chapter 3.

35. I would argue the same about *Treatise on Efficacy* and *Propensity of Things*.

36. The passage is not footnoted.

37. It is worth noting on this count the rather strange turn Jullien takes at the very end of his *Treatise on Efficacy*, where he observes that "there is a price to pay" for the consistent adherence to Chinese thought. In what is to my knowledge a unique moment in his writing, he draws out what Chinese thought "kills": "under the heading of 'subject,' the infinite possibilities of subjectivity; passion, of course; and the pleasure derived from exerting ourselves; but above all relation to 'others' who really are *others* (and who are there to be discovered not simply 'others' defined as our polar partners/adversaries)" (Jullien 2004, 197; emphasis original).

REFERENCES

Agamben, Giorgio. 1998. *Homo Sacer: Sovereign Power and Bare Life*. Translated by Daniel Heller-Roazen. Stanford: Stanford University Press.
———. 1999. *Potentialities: Collected Essays in Philosophy*. Translated by Daniel Heller-Roazen. Stanford: Stanford University Press.
———. 2000. "The Face." In *Means Without End: Notes on Politics*, translated by Vincenzo Binetti and Cesare Casarino, 91–100. Minneapolis: University of Minnesota Press.
———. 2007. *Profanations*. Translated by Jeff Fort. New York: Zone Books.
———. 2011. "Nudity." In *Nudities*, translated by David Kishik and Stefan Pedatella, 55–90. Stanford: Stanford University Press.
———. 2015. *The Use of Bodies*. Translated by Adam Kotsko. Stanford: Stanford University Press.
Ames, Roger, and David Hall, trans. 2003. *Dao De Jing: "Making This Life Significant": A Philosophical Translation*. New York: Ballantine Books.
Apter, Emily. 2017. *Unexceptional Politics: On Obstruction, Impasse, and the Impolitic*. New York: Verso.
Badiou, Alain. 2003. *Saint Paul: The Foundation of Universalism*. Translated by Ray Brassier. Stanford: Stanford University Press.
Barthes, Roland. 1982. *Empire of Signs*. Translated by Richard Howard. New York: Hill and Wang.
Billeter, Jean-François. 2006. *Contre François Jullien*. Paris: Allia.
Boever, Arne De. 2016. *Plastic Sovereignties: Agamben and the Politics of Aesthetics*. Edinburgh: Edinburgh University Press.
———. 2019. *Against Aesthetic Exceptionalism*. Minneapolis: University of Minnesota Press.
Dong, Shu-bao. 2018. "Detour and Access, Deleuze and Guattari's Researches on Chinese Immanent Becoming." *Journal of Literature and Art Studies* 8 (5): 739–49.
Foucault, Michel. 1990. *History of Sexuality: Volume 1*. Translated by Robert Hurley. New York: Vintage.
———. 2008. *The Birth of Biopolitics: Lectures at the Collège de France*. Translated by Graham Burchell, edited by Michel Senellart. New York: Palgrave.
Gourgouris, Stathis. 2013. "The Question Is: Society Must Be Defended Against Whom? Or What?" *New Philosopher*, May 25. http://www.newphilosopher.com/articles/the-question-is-society-defended-against-whom-or-what-in-the-name-of-what/.
Han, Byung-Chul. 2017. *Shanzhai: Deconstruction in Chinese*. Translated by Philippa Hurd. Boston: MIT Press.
Honig, Bonnie. 2013. *Antigone, Interrupted*. Cambridge: Cambridge University Press.
———. 2014. "Three Models of Emergency Politics." *boundary 2* 41 (2): 45–70.
Jullien, François. 1995. *The Propensity of Things: Toward a History of Efficacy in China*. Translated by Janet Lloyd. New York: Zone Books.
———. 1998. *Un sage est sans idée, Ou: L'autre de la philosophie*. Paris: Seuil.

———. 2001. *Du "temps": Éléments d'une philosophie de vivre*. Paris: Grasset.
———. 2004. *A Treatise on Efficacy: Between Western and Chinese Thinking*. Translated by Janet Lloyd. Honolulu: University of Hawai'i Press.
———. 2005. *Conférence sur l'efficacité*. Paris: PUF.
———. 2007a. *Chemin faisant. Connaître la Chine, relancer la philosophie. Réplique à ****. Paris: Seuil.
———. 2007b. *The Impossible Nude: Chinese Art and Western Aesthetics*. Translated by Maev de la Guardia. Chicago: The University of Chicago Press.
———. 2007c. *Vital Nourishment: Departing from Happiness*. Translated by Arthur Goldhammer. New York: Zone Books.
———. 2008. *In Praise of Blandness: Proceeding from Chinese Thought and Aesthetics*. Translated by Paula M. Varsano. New York: Zone Books.
———. 2009. *The Great Image Has No Form, or On the Nonobject through Painting*. Translated by Jane Marie Todd. Chicago: University of Chicago Press.
———. 2011. *The Silent Transformations*. Translated by Krzystof Fijalkowski and Michael Richardson. London: Seagull.
———. 2012. *L'écart et l'entre: Leçon inaugurale de la Chaire sur l'altérité*. Paris: Galilée.
———. 2013. *De l'Intime: Loin du bruyant amour*. Paris: Grasset.
———. 2014. *Vivre de paysage, ou l'impensé de la raison*. Paris: Gallimard.
———. 2015. *The Book of Beginnings*. Translated by Jody Gladding. New Haven: Yale University Press.
———. 2016. *This Strange Idea of the Beautiful*. Translated by Krzystof Fijalkowski and Michael Richardson. London: Seagull.
———. 2017. *L'Invention de l'idéal et le destin de l'Europe*. Paris: Gallimard.
———. 2018a. *Living Off Landscape or the Unthought-of in Reason*. Translated by Pedro Rodriguez. London: Rowman & Littlefield.
———. 2018b. *Ressources du christianisme*. Paris: L'Herne.
Kristeva, Julia. 1977. *About Chinese Women*. Translated by Anita Barrows. London: Marion Boyars.
Levine, Caroline. 2015. *Forms: Whole, Rhythm, Hierarchy, Network*. Princeton: Princeton University Press.
Martin, Nicolas, and Antoine Spire. 2011. *Chine, la dissidence de François Jullien. Suivi de: Dialogues avec François Jullien*. Paris: Seuil.
Marx, Karl. 1990. *Capital: Volume 1*. Translated by Ben Fowkes. London: Penguin.
Møllgaard, Eske. 2005. "Zhuangzi's Notion of Transcendental Life." *Asian Philosophy* 15 (1): 1–18.
———. 2006. "Dialogue and Impromptu Words." *Social Identities* 12 (1): 43–58.
Piorunski, Richard. 1998. "Le détour d'un grec par la Chine. Entretien avec François Jullien." *Ebisu* 18: 147–85.
Potte-Bonneville, Mathieu. 2018. "Versions du platonisme: Deleuze, Foucault, Jullien." In *François Jullien*, edited by Daniel Bougnoux and François L'Yvonnet, 51–58. Paris: L'Herne.
Rossello, Diego. 2015. "Ordinary Emergences in Democratic Theory: An Interview with Bonnie Honig." *Philosophy Today* 59 (4): 699–710.

Said, Edward. 2006. *On Late Style: Music and Literature Against the Grain*. New York: Pantheon.
Spivak, Gayatri Chakravorty. 1981. "French Feminism in an International Frame." *Yale French Studies* 62: 154–84.
Yu, Peng. 2016. "Zones of Indeterminacy: Art, Body, and Politics in Daoist Thought." *Theory, Culture, and Society* 33 (1): 93–114.

Chapter 3

In Management as in War

My prime purpose has been the pleasure of following up an idea.

—François Jullien, *The Propensity of Things*[1]

PHILOSOPHY AND BUSINESS IN CHINA

In an interview with Richard Piorunski that was published in the journal *Ebisu* in 1998, François Jullien states the following:

> Moi j'ai accompagné des entreprises françaises en Chine pour négocier. Il y a des stratégies, des stratégies chinoises classiques, anciennes, auxquelles les Chinois ne renoncent pas. Par exemple, dans mon travail sur l'efficacité j'oppose manipulation à persuasion. Quand les hommes d'affaires européens vont en Chine, souvent ils veulent persuader les Chinois. On me dit: "Mais comment les persuader de . . . ?" Là, vous retrouvez d'un coup toute la Grèce, l'orateur . . . Déjà en Homère les personnages veulent se persuader les uns les autres. Et ça aboutit à des institutions politiques comme l'agora ou le tribunal, l'assemblée. La démocratie repose sur une chose: la persuasion. Alors qu'en Chine ce n'est pas le problème: on manipule. C'est-à-dire qu'on aménage les conditions telles que vous passiez par où l'on veut que vous passiez. (Piorunski 1998, 173)

> I've accompanied French businesses in China to help them negotiate. There are strategies, ancient, classical Chinese strategies, to which the Chinese will stick. For example, in my work on efficacy I have opposed manipulation to persuasion. When European business leaders go to China, often they want to persuade the Chinese. They tell me: "But how can we persuade them of . . . ?" There you have in a nutshell the Greek approach, that of the orator . . . Already in Homer,

certain characters want to persuade others. And that culminates in political institutions like the agora or the tribunal, the assembly. Democracy rests on one thing alone: persuasion. Whereas in China this is not the problem: there, one manipulates. That is to say one manages the conditions in such a way that you will follow the path that they want you to follow.

My goal in this chapter is to unpack this paragraph, starting from its opening statement, which presents us with a philosopher who accompanies French business leaders on their negotiating trips to China. *How did Jullien get here?* I would like to both lay out this trajectory, a project that has descriptive and explanatory value in itself (in a historical—and more precisely genealogical—way), and also critically assess it, since the genealogical approach will provide me with a good vantage point to critique some economicopolitical aspects of Jullien's work. As my title indicates, throughout I will be moving between economics and politics as it is at that very crossroads that Jullien's work on efficacy, which he gives central importance in the quotation with which I started, takes place. I hope to show that such a project provides us with sharp insights into the West's present economicopolitical juncture. In other words, while Jullien is a sinologist, and develops his thinking on efficacy through a sustained engagement with various Chinese sources, I am not and do not. But I have benefited from his work in my attempts to better understand the specificity of the contemporary Western condition.

That said, I don't think that my project is, in the end, all that different from Jullien's. Note for example that the interview from which I have quoted is titled "Le détour d'un grec par la Chine"—A Greek thinker's detour via China. The title echoes something that Jullien has written and said in multiple other contexts: namely, that he turned to China, the Chinese language, and Chinese thought in order to improve his understanding of Greece, Greek thought, and his reading of Greek. This is especially clear in his most recent books, which explore "the stakes of European thought in regard to Chinese thought" (Jullien 2009, 184). If this seems to place China in a subservient position by marking it as merely a "detour," nothing could be further from the truth. Jullien has spent extensive time living in mainland China (studying in both Beijing and Shanghai) and Hong Kong (in an administrative role, establishing a connection between French sinologists and the Far East) as well as Japan (at the Maison Franco-Japonaise), and his work demonstrates that he has a deep knowledge of the Chinese language. I already noted that Jullien will often mobilize translation in his work as a strategy to counter the Westernization (through translation) of Chinese texts. In his view, the latter is precisely what the translator should *not* do (Martin and Spire 2011, 187–88).

Jullien's countertranslations (as one might call them) seek to instead reopen a divergence (*écart*) between China and the West that allows ancient and classical Chinese thought to remain in what he specifically calls the fact of their "elsewhere" rather than their philosophically constructed "alterity."[2] There is an indifference in Chinese thought to Europe that interests him. If Jullien turned to China in order to better understand Western thought (and not Sanskrit or Arabic, for example), it is because it provided the elsewhere he needed for such a project. In the same interview with Piorunski, Jullien characterizes it as a "methodological," "ex-optic" (Piorunski 1998, 171) rather than "exotic" project (ibid., 148). As he also often puts it, he pursues a deconstruction "from the outside" (*déconstruction du dehors*; 135), the Chinese outside. Jacques Derrida's project is different from Jullien's because it deconstructs *from within*, the Western within. Ultimately, Derrida remains too much with the Judeo-Christian tradition; his thought does not offer an outside. Arabic and Islam, too, remain within this frame. Jullien himself has characterized his position between Western and Chinese thought as that of a Nietzschean "dancer" or tightrope walker (142).

Jullien's overall approach has led to the charge that Jullien "instrumentalizes" China not so much in the service of Western thinking but for his own thought in particular (an interview with Thierry Zarcone that was published in English is titled "China as Philosophical Tool"; Zarcone 2003). His translations have been criticized. As I've already noted, his method—which often focuses on a single literary or philosophical figure and then goes on to enlarge what he finds in their work to apply to "Chinese thought," "the Chinese," or "China" as a whole—has been said to erase difference. While Jullien's work appears to demonstrate a more than superficial knowledge of the Chinese language, his books—like many of the books by his French colleagues, I might add—generally lack footnotes and do not demonstrate a deep scholarly knowledge of the critical field in which they intervene (he has many books on Chinese aesthetics, for example, but he almost never engages any of the recognized authorities in this well-developed field; he almost never references secondary sources). He has been criticized bitterly by Swiss sinologist Jean-François Billeter—in a polemical 122-page book titled *Contre François Jullien* (Against François Jullien; Billeter 2006)—for what Billeter understands to be his highly reductive approach to China. Fifteen philosophers responded to what has become known as the "Billeter-Jullien debate" with passionate defenses of Jullien's work in *Oser construire: Pour François Jullien* (Dare to build: for François Jullien; Allouch, Badiou, Chartier, et al. 2007).[3] Indeed, Jullien himself responded to Billeter in in some 150 pages of his own, titled *Chemin faisant. Connaître la Chine, relancer la philosophie* (Step-by-step: getting to know China, relaunching philosophy; Jullien 2007), which—in a stinging gesture—elides Billeter's name from its subtitle (it's replaced by ***) and mentions Jullien's Swiss antagonist by name only once (Jullien uses the initials JFB thereafter). In the meantime, conferences have been organized about Jullien's work not just in France or in Europe but also in China and Taiwan. Of his more than thirty books, about half have been translated into English (and in many other languages), even if he has remained fairly unknown in the United States. By the time the monumental *Cahier de l'Herne* about Jullien's work was published in 2018 (Bougnoux and L'Yvonnet 2018), the Billeter debate seemed to have been largely forgotten: it operates in the affirmative, even celebratory, mode and pays tribute to a great philosopher's lifework. In his contribution to the volume, historian, philosopher, and sociologist Marcel Gauchet remarks that Jullien may be one of the last of his kind: an experimental thinker whose work the structures of the contemporary university risk to make impossible (Gauchet 2018).

I am not going to spend more time here assessing Jullien's work as a sinologist. I have discussed in chapter 1 how I consider his heterotopic (troubling, disruptive) understanding of China to stand apart from what Jullien himself critically refers to as those "Chinese utopias" (Jullien 2005, 11) in contemporary French thought. In the context of French theory, the first reference that comes to mind in this context is probably the journal *Tel Quel* and the stimulating criticism that it received from scholars like, for example, Gayatri Chakravorty Spivak (her article "French Feminism in an International Frame" [Spivak 1981] is a biting critique of Julia Kristeva's book *About Chinese Women*). Lisa Lowe (Lowe 1991) and Eric Hayot (Hayot 2004) have both built on Spivak's work in this context. But this fascination with, even idolization of, China in France in the 1970s goes back to the 1950s and 1960s, as Alex Hughes, for example, has pointed out, and "a plethora of *voyages en Chine* [voyages into China] undertaken by French luminaries in the wake of the Bandung conference of May 1955" (Hughes 2003, 85).

I leave those debates aside here because my project in this chapter does not stand or fall with whether Jullien is a bona fide sinologist. Rather, I am pursuing an issue that is internal to Jullien's work: a consideration of how the idea of efficacy has developed in its pages. As I already indicated, I propose to do so from a specific location—namely, Jullien's presence in China as a negotiating advisor to French businesses. Overall, the direction of my inquiry reverses that of anthropologist Aihwa Ong's chapter "Reengineering the Chinese Soul in Shanghai?" in her book *Neoliberalism as Exception*. If Ong is interested in how neoliberal "management ideas and practices" are introduced to "Asian sites" (Ong 2006, 219)—in other words, and more specifically, in the "transfer of Western business knowledge and practices to Shanghai" (ibid., 220)—I follow Jullien here in considering how those management ideas and practices to a certain extent are already present in Chinese thought, which has in fact been shaping Western business knowledge and practices. This reversal is not meant to contradict Ong's work, which draws out the frictions within the process she describes, the ways in which Chinese subjects need to be reengineered to function within Western management models. Rather, it seeks to lay bare the flipside, if you will, of that process—namely, the ways in which Western working subjects are reengineered to fit the influence of Chinese thought on Western management.

A TRILOGY ON EFFICACY; OR, "MANAGERS 'À LA SUN ZI'"

I bet on sure things. Sun Tzu: "Every battle is won before it is fought." Think about it.

—Gordon Gekko, *Wall Street*[4]

As Jullien indicates in the quotation with which I began, his presence in China at the side of negotiating French businesses is due to his work on efficacy. This work extends over three volumes. There was, first, the book *The Propensity of Things*, which (as per its subtitle) proposed to work "Toward a History of Efficacy in China" (Jullien 1995). This was followed by the much shorter *Treatise on Efficacy: Between Western and Chinese Thinking*, which explicitly continued the thinking of the earlier book. (Both of those titles have been translated into English.) Finally, there is Jullien's still-untranslated *Conférence sur l'efficacité* (Lecture on efficacy), which is even shorter and also more informal in tone, closer to the mode of oral delivery. The title of the book's German translation is more revealing about the origin of this particular work: *Vortrag vor Managern über Wirksamkeit und Effizienz in China und im Westen*—in other words: "Lecture for managers on efficacy and efficiency in China and the West." What began as a historical, and densely academic, project in *Propensity of Things* about the notion of potentiality (*shi*, 勢) in Chinese thinking evidently morphed over time into a much less dense, much less formal lecture for business leaders (managers) about efficacy and efficiency. (In another interview, Jullien indicates that he has "learned" from exposing his thought on efficacy to business leaders; Martin and Spire, 2011, 214). The book in the middle, *Treatise on Efficacy*, is about "warfare, power, and speech" (Jullien 2004, ix). But its opening question already anticipates the later *Conférence sur l'efficacité*: "What do we mean," Jullien asks there, "when we say that something has 'potential'—not 'a potential for' but an absolute potential—for example [he writes] a market with a potential, a developing business with a potential?" (ibid., vii). *Treatise* might be a book about war, but the theory of war it develops is framed as an inquiry into economic potential, into the potential of a business. Clearly, whatever Jullien will have to say in the book about war is presented as applying to business as well. *In management as in war*, one might say. But what would be the content of such a parallel construction? And what light might it shed on the West's economicopolitical present?[5]

I propose to use as my lens the relatively unknown *Conférence sur l'efficacité* and include references to both *Treatise* and *Propensity*, which have already received discussion elsewhere. To start, it's important to note that *Conférence sur l'efficacité* reads like an informal summary of *Treatise*—in other words, that it's very much a lecture on war. But this is perhaps not its key concern. If it comes to naming the precise connection between military theory and management theory, it is not so much the notion of "war" as of "strategy" that is most relevant. Indeed, at its most philosophical, *Conférence sur l'efficacité* seeks to open a divergence between European and Chinese strategies for bringing something about—strategies for efficacy, as the title of both *Treatise* and *Conférence sur l'efficacité* suggest. If I'm speaking about war here, Jullien points out to his audience, it's because it leads me "à une question dont je pense qu'elle vous concerne plus directement dans la gestion des affaires et le management: celle de l'efficacité" (to a question that I think concerns you more directly in business and management: that of efficacy; Jullien 2005, 15). At this level, the central question of both *Treatise* and *Conférence sur l'efficacité* is not essentially related to war at all; rather, it's because theories of efficacy have been developed mostly in theories of war that Jullien turns to those to lay out his thinking about efficacy. His main concern is efficacy, not war, even if already in *Propensity* he starts out with a discussion of military strategy (Jullien 1995, 25). "Warfare," he writes, explaining the link between war and efficacy,

> has often seemed the domain of the unpredictable and of chance (or fatality) par excellence. However, from early on, Chinese thinkers believed that they could detect in warfare's unfolding a purely internal necessity that could be logically foreseen and, accordingly, perfectly managed. This radical concept betrays the effort that must have accompanied its elaboration; as a result, Chinese strategic thought stands as a perfect example of how one can manage reality, and provides us with a general theory of efficacy. (Ibid., 25)

Let's try to unpack this passage.

After some preliminary remarks that lay out his method and address, indirectly, criticisms that have been leveled at his work (he restates, for example, his heterotopic understanding of China and contrasts it with those "Chinese utopias" so common in French thought [Jullien 2005, 11]; he warns against exotic approaches to China and opposes them to his own methodological approach [ibid., 15]; et cetera), Jullien arrives in his *Conférence sur l'efficacité* at the divergence that is central to his work on efficacy: between the Western approach to efficacy, which constructs a model, plan, or ideal form (*eidos*, to use the Platonic term) to achieve a goal (*telos*; (τελος)). Once that's done, the subject acts according to this plan, seeking to achieve the set goal. In *Treatise*, Jullien gives three examples: "a revolutionary designs the model of the city that must be built; a soldier sets out the plan of war to be followed; an economist decides on the growth curve to target; and all of them, whatever their respective roles, operate in a similar way" (Jullien 2004, 3). These are, Jullien allows us to explain with reference to Plato, geometrical models. "To be a good general, he writes, one must be a good geometer" ("Pour être un bon general . . . il faut être un bon geomètre"; Jullien 2005, 17). He argues that the Western thought of war demonstrates this logic, all the way up to Carl von Clausewitz, who appears in both *Conférence sur l'efficacité* and *Treatise* as a kind of hinge figure. This is because the late eighteenth-, early nineteenth-century Prussian general and military theorist both presents us with Western warfare-by-modelization, if you will, and realizes its limits—namely, the fact that no war will match the model, plan, or ideal form—the geometry—that has been set for it. "The ideal, up in the sky, is inaccessible" (Jullien 2004, 5). Jullien points out that this kind of objection to Plato already starts with Aristotle, who is much more attuned to what escapes the model (Jullien 2005, 17). Already with Aristotle then, but this becomes particularly visible in Clausewitz, there is a gap that opens up between the theory and the practice of warfare—"to think about warfare is to think about the extent to which it is bound to betray the ideal concept of it" (Jullien 2004, 11)—and it's this gap that opens up a point of contact with the Chinese theory of warfare.

Note, however, that if this opens up a view on China in Jullien's writing, this gap is internal to the Western tradition itself. Indeed, both in *Conférence sur l'efficacité* (Jullien 2005, 18–21) and in *Treatise* (Jullien 2004, 7, 104) Jullien recalls Marcel Detienne and Jean-Pierre Vernant's magisterial book *Cunning Intelligence in Greek Culture and Society* (Detienne and Vernant 1991, originally from 1974; it was translated by Janet Lloyd, who, it's worth noting, also translated Jullien's *Treatise* and *Propensity*), which deals with the form of practical intelligence called *mètis* (μητ|ς), associated with the mythical Titaness Metis, daughter of Oceanos and the first great spouse of Zeus (Zeus will in fact eat her, an act by which he incorporates her special kind of intelligence into his sovereignty forever).[6] However, such a practical intelligence, which stands apart from the theoretical (geometrical) knowledge of ideal Forms ("*mètis* foils any attempt to stabilize its identity on the basis provided by Being or God, to which Greek thought is devoted"; Jullien 2004, 9), was never theorized in the Western tradition, even if some of Western literature's major figures—Odysseus, for example—practice it marvelously.

When Jullien comes to describe Odysseus in this context, he calls him a "surfer," with a nod to the contemporary associations of this term (presumably, he is thinking of the way we manage the world wide Web): "D'Ulysse, je dirais qu'il surfe. Lui qui, durant tant d'années, est emporté au gré des flots et survit accroché à son radeau" (About Ulysses, I'd say he surfs. For so many years, he's taken along by the waves and survives by attaching himself to his raft; Jullien 2005, 20). For Jullien, Ullyses, who is *polumètis* (πολυμητ[ς), full of *metis*, thus becomes the figure of an opportunism that, he emphasizes, is not to be valued morally but needs to be reconceived strategically, as a practical form of intelligence that stands apart from its traditional, idealist understandings. It's in Clausewitz, Jullien argues, that the need for this kind of intelligence rises to the surface again, because Clausewitz is so attuned to the gap between theoretical and practical war, and theorizes what he calls the "friction" (ibid., 26) between the model and the reality of it. Modeling war is like walking on land, he suggests, whereas waging war is like walking in water (27). The battle of Austerlitz, with its famous "fog" marking the "circumstances" that make Napoleon's victory impossible (28), is his main example. In the end, war does not happen the way we model it. This is the cross that the Western theory of war has to bear. "Probability theory," in Jullien's view, is one of the ways in which the West dealt with this situation (Jullien 2004, 42); Chinese strategy, on the other hand, "has always avoided" "the kind of gamble accompanied by risk and danger" (ibid., 82).

But Jullien uses this realization, which comes from a gap within the Western theory of war, to jump to the Chinese theories of war by Sun Zi (fifth century BC) and Sun Bin (descendant of Sun Zi; Sun Bin's manuscript has largely gone lost, but parts of it—written on bamboo slips—were recovered/unearthed in China in 1972; Jullien relies on this in *Propensity*, Jullien 1995, 27). Jullien points out, when he begins to discuss these authors, that "beaucoup de managers aujourd'hui s'inspirent de ces auteurs, sans trop les comprendre (la traduction en est en premier lieu responsable), en Europe aussi bien qu'au Japon. Ce sont de managers 'à la Sun Zi'" (today many managers take inspiration from these authors without understanding them well [the translation is first and foremost responsible for that], both in Europe and in Japan. Those are managers 'à la Sun Zi'" [Jullien 2005, 29]; in other words, they are managers that take inspiration from ancient Chinese theories of war).[7]

Jullien, however, proposes to take the strategic thought that's developed in those treatises back "des mains des gourous" (out of the hands of the gurus; ibid., 29) and "return it to philosophy" ("pour la rendre à la philosophie"; ibid.). Chinese strategy, Jullien explains, starts from the potential of a situation (30), from the *shi* of a situation as he discussed it in *Propensity*. "Instead of imposing our plan upon the world, we could rely on the potential inherent in the situation" (Jullien 2004, 16). This potential could be moral—for example, the motivation of soldiers—or topographical—for example, how the land is laid out (19). What happens in war—the efficacy achieved in war—needs to be understood as the actualization of that potential, as the natural outcome of the situation (Jullien 2005, 32). Most important when going to war is not to make a model, plan, or ideal Form but to evaluate the situation and its potential (ibid., 33): a good general will understand the potential of a situation to such an extent that, when they engage in war, the outcome of the war is entirely predetermined—the situation could not allow it develop otherwise (35). "We should rely on the way that a process unfolds in order to attain the hoped-for result; rather than think of drawing up plans, we should learn to make the most of what is implied by the situation and whatever promise is held out by its evolution" (Jullien 2004, 16–17).

As Jullien explains, because the Chinese theory of warfare focuses on evaluating the potential of the situation rather than making a model, there is zero uncertainty about the outcome it anticipates (the outcome is "unswerving," "inevitable," determined before the battle, etc.; ibid., 42). Whereas in the West, war is haunted by the language of chance, necessitating a plea to the gods through sacrifice, for example, to try to obtain a desirable outcome, Jullien points out that Sun Zi's *Art of War* explicitly forbids this, because nothing in warfare should be exterior to the logic of a situation (Jullien 2005, 35). It's about a certain kind of attunement with reality that enables one to allow reality to follow its path, its course, its *dao*, but to one's advantage in war. Chinese warfare is not warfare-by-modelization but warfare-by-regulation, and the *dao* is what regulates all things. In *Propensity* this is rendered as follows:

> Whereas tragic man clashes irrevocably against superior powers, resisting all surrender (*eikein* [ε[κε[ν] is the crucial word in Sophoclean drama), the Chinese strategist prides himself on his ability to manage all the factors in play, for he knows how to go along with the logic behind them and adapt to it. The former *fatally* discovers, all too late, his "destiny"; the latter knows how to anticipate the propensity at work so that he has it at his own disposal. (Jullien 1995, 35; emphasis original)

It's the "head-on clash" of Western fighting versus the preference for the crossbow—associated with propensity or *shi*—on the Chinese side (ibid., 35–36). In the Chinese model, "warfare" needs to be conceived of as "'automatic' rather than in terms of probability" (37). In the third part of *Propensity*, Jullien demonstrates how the Chinese model conceives of history along the same lines.

If the Western model is *telos*-oriented and governed by a means-ends logic, Jullien points out that such an architecture cannot be found on the Chinese side (where we have set-up and efficacy), even if that does not mean it is illogical.[8] Rather, efficacy is achieved by allowing the consequences of a situation to come to fruition or maturation. Interestingly, this leads in both *Conférence sur l'efficacité* and *Treatise* into a "praise of facility": "la grande stratégie," Jullien writes, "est sans coup d'éclat, la grande victoire ne se voit pas" (the great strategy does not ring out, the great victory remains unseen; Jullien 2005, 41). He continues by noting that we can reflect on this both in politics "comme dans le domaine de l'entreprise et du management" (as in business and management; ibid., 41). The great manager, he suggests, the truly effective one, is one who remains in the shadows, who is not discussed, about whom one hears very little, almost nothing (this is not a "great man" view of history, or at least it defines "greatness" in a very different way [ibid., 50–53][9]; this founds Jullien's claim, made here as well as elsewhere, that China has not known the "great man" genre of the epic [ibid., 52]). There is no heroism associated with generals; there is no glory in managing a business. It has nothing sensationalist to it: effective victories remain unseen (ibid., 42), and they ought, in fact, to be easy. Indeed, they merely realize to a business' advantage the logic that already lay contained in nature. A manager does not so much "do" or "act"; they don't "force" (ibid., 45). Instead they let come to fruition or maturation. ("All action is *naïve*," Jullien writes in *Treatise*; Jullien 2004, 55.) Or, in *Propensity*, "Efficacy does not depend on personality" (Jullien 1995, 39). Thus, in China, "no one would ever dream of erecting a statue to the best of generals. For he will have gotten the situation to evolve in the desired direction so successfully, gradually intervening well in advance, that he will have made the victory seem so 'easy' that it does not occur to anyone to praise him for it" (Jullien 2004, 58). "Victory was a foregone conclusion" (ibid., 58). As Jullien points out, this is not an exceptionalist model (59; 77).

The example that comes up here again and again, and to which I will return later, is taken from agriculture and can be found in Mencius. One cannot pull on plants to make them grow. But neither should one do nothing and think they will grow by themselves. Instead, one must act discreetly to help their growth come along (Jullien 2005, 45). Neither voluntarism nor passivity, as Jullien puts it (ibid., 45); one allows the propensity of things to fully realize itself (ibid., 46). The strategy of management, then, is a strategy of (natural) growth: rather than a premodeled strategy of forced progress, it is a strategy of process developed through the evaluation of a situation. It's about helping along what's already coming by itself ("aider ce qui vient tout seul," ibid., 47)—"to *assist* whatever happens *naturally*" (Jullien 2004, 90; emphasis original). This is also characterized as a logic of "unfolding" (ibid., 23).

Jullien notes some political consequences. Whereas crisis can occur in the Chinese model, and is fully part of its logic, revolution is "unthinkable" (Jullien 1995, 238) within it—it is not the way of the *dao*. In the Chinese model, "all forms of rebellion and discontinuity" are "reduced" in favor of "eternal transition" (ibid., 245). Opposition can only occur as part of "a regenerative alternative within the framework of a regulatory logic of alternation, simply a link in the chain of successive developments" (ibid.).

To overstate the case somewhat, one might describe this as a theory of "nonaction" (Jullien 2005, 53), as Jullien does in both *Conférence sur l'efficacité* and *Treatise* (Jullien 2004, 84–103). It would be more precise, however, to substitute "action" by "transformation" in this context: the Chinese general—like the Chinese sage, in fact—does not so much "act" as "transform," seeks to discreetly "transform" their adversary rather than confront them head-on. After all, the Chinese model, as Jullien points out, still "leaves plenty of room for human initiative" (Jullien 1995, 203). Nevertheless, if "action" in Jullien's summary is "of the moment," "local," and "subject-related," "transformation" is "global," "durational" (Braudel's "longue durée" gets an appreciative mention here), and "discreet"—it does not *necessarily* refer back to a subject (Jullien 2005, 56). While such transformation is efficacious, it takes place "silently" (ibid., 58), unnoticed.[10] The strategy of transformation breaks with the Western mythology of "the event" (58–62), which is closely related to Christianity in Jullien's analysis (it's associated with creation, for example). It's the Vietnam War, and specifically the strategy of the Vietnamese, that illustrates this best. To win without battle: instead, there is "a process of progressive erosion, of making the adversary lose countenance" (61), which Jullien associates with "psychological warfare" (61). In the West, warfare amounts to destruction. But in the Chinese theory of warfare, losses ought to be avoided, and on both sides: in war, it's preferable to leave the troops intact (62; Jullien 2004, 47). He associates this with deconstruction rather than destruction (Jullien 2004, 48). As Jullien also puts it in *Treatise*, "nothing could be more economical" (ibid., 48).

Indeed, we should not forget that Jullien is offering all of this theory of Chinese warfare in the context of a "Lecture for Managers." Management is a little like psychological warfare, he appears to be saying; you're trying to decountenance your adversary not through action but silent transformation. That's what management is about. At this point in his *Conférence sur l'efficacité* he arrives, in fact, at a section—unique in his oeuvre as far as I can tell; much else that's in the text appears in modified form in his many other books—about contracts. He apologizes for speaking about something as lowly as contracts but points out that his audience will probably be interested. Speaking from his experience accompanying French businesses in China, Jullien observes,

> Or, j'ai eu l'occasion de remarquer que, en Chine, le contrat signé n'arrêtait pas pour autant l'évolution: le contrat demeurait en transformation. Des

infléchissements très minimes d'abord lui étaient portés; ou de légères contradictions surgissaient du sein même de la situation, qui laissaient paraître peu à peu une fissure—puis une faille, puis une brèche, puis un fossé . . . —entre le texte signé et l'évolution ultérieure du chantier; bref, une déstabilisation s'instaurait qui faisait osciller progressivement tous les repères jusqu'à conduire les signataires européens, à peine un an plus tard, à ne plus oser eux-mêmes invoquer, pour se protéger, le contrat signé. Le procès des choses de lui-même, graduellement, avait modifié la donnée. (Jullien 2005, 66)

Now, I've had the occasion to see that, in China, the signed contract does not end the evolution [of the negotiations]: the contract remains in transformation. At first very minimal changes were brought to it; or small contradictions emerged at the very heart of the situation, which slowly but surely made a fissure appear—then a crack, a gap, a wide breach even . . . —between the signed text and the later evolution of the work; in short, a destabilization would put itself into place that progressively makes oscillate everything in the contract that one could fall back on so that its European signatories, not even a year later, themselves no longer dared to evoke the original signed contract, in order to protect themselves. The process of things had itself, gradually, modified the given situation. [I have benefited for my translation from Janet Lloyd's translation of Jullien 2004, 69, where some of the same language is used.]

This leads to the interesting conclusion that in China, a contract may be superfluous:

Quand on dit "vieux amis" aujourd'hui encore, en Chine, entre partenaires, on peut entendre, sous la politesse de la formule, le bénéfice du capital qui, sans même qu'on s'en rende compte, au fil des jours, imperceptiblement a crû et est devenu solide, et même intangible . . . il n'est plus alors besoin de la "glue" des contrats . . . pour se lier. (Jullien 2005, 67–68)

Today still, when one says "old friends" in China between business partners, one can hear underneath the politeness of the formula the benefit of capital that, without fully realizing it even, has grown over the course of time and become solid, intangible even . . . to a point that one no longer needs the "glue" of contracts to be bound [to a business partner].

All of this makes Jullien opt for an interesting shift in both *Conférence sur l'efficacité* and *Treatise*—a shift that's reflected in the German translation of *Conférence sur l'efficacité*, which tellingly (but unlike Jullien's own French title) hovers between "Wirksamkeit" and "Effizienz"—from "efficacy" to "efficiency," with "efficiency" naming the discreet, indirect way in which silent transformations take place, outside of the logic of the event, allowing things to grow progressively through a process of maturation (for there is still progress in this process, even if it is not Western progress; Jullien 2005, 75).

This means that on the Chinese side Jullien's thought is truly a thought of efficiency, not efficacy, which remains associated with the Western framework.

There's much else I could say about Jullien's *Conférence sur l'efficacité*, but let me continue to allow the quotation with which I opened this chapter to guide my selection of topics and terms: there Jullien speaks about the difference between persuasion and manipulation, which so far hasn't been given any attention here. Persuasion is, as the quotation indicates, associated with the Greek model, with Homer, for example, and with the persuasive force of argument. Manipulation, on the other hand, is transformative nonaction that takes place "upstream" (Jullien 2004, 125), as Jullien explains: it references an intervention before a full conflict has come into being, at the moment of highest efficacy. This is not a seizing of the right moment or occasion, the Western event, but an efficacious, efficient inscription within the flow of things at a far remove from the situation that will eventually result from it, when the situation is still "round" (ibid., 128), before it has become "square" (ibid.). It thus stands in opposition to the Western notion of the "miracle" (on which the event is based; 134). In this logic of manipulation, one wins "without striking a single blow, since, by the time the fight at last begins, the enemy is *already* undone" (138). Whereas persuasion values speech, manipulation doesn't: the good manipulator speaks as little as possible, or when they are not seen (156).

USES IN MILITARY THEORY AND MANAGEMENT THEORY

Given the above overview, I suppose it should come as no surprise that research on Jullien will turn up articles written by both military officers and business leaders. In "Preferring Copies with No Originals: Does the Army Training Strategy Train to Fail?" (published in the journal *Military Review*), US Army Major Ben E. Zweibelson references Jullien's *Treatise on Efficacy* twice in his consideration of "other worldviews that differ from the accepted Western one" (Zweibelson 2014, 19) and especially of other theories of war. The key question in his article is whether army-training strategy should focus on those other perspectives to, as Zweibelson puts it, "achieve greater training realism" (ibid., 20). If it doesn't, US soldiers may merely be training to fight themselves—a figure that does not correspond to the enemy they will confront on the battlefield. Presumably, Jullien's treatise—as well as some of the other sources that Zweibelson mentions—could become a key text on the syllabus for such training.

Also writing in *Military Review*, Robert M. Hill (credited as "deputy chief, Leader Development, Education, and Training, Information Proponent

Office, Ford Leavenworth, KS, and a seminar leader for the Functional Area 30 Qualification Course") references Jullien's treatise as well in his article "Complexity Leadership: New Conceptions for Dealing with Soldier Suicides." In Hill's view, Jullien's observations about the Chinese tradition of thought can help soldiers in dealing with the stresses for war and its aftermath by reorienting their perspective away from the heroic agency that is central in the Western frame of mind to the silent transformations that Jullien foregrounds. In this way, soldiers would be able to recognize the complexity of their problems and realize that such problems demand complex solutions—a realization that Hill, who is relying on the work of Karl E. Weick here, labels "profound simplicity" (Hill 2011, 42).

Aside from such quick references, which have nothing to do with Jullien's actual field of study (namely, China), Jullien's *Propensity* is referenced, for example, in US Army Colonel David C. Menser's article "Did the United States Lose China Again?" published in *The Army War College Review*. Menser uses Jullien's analysis of the notion of *shi* not, as he points out, "as a mystical concept" that would "inappropriately [paint] China as an exotic other [there is a footnote here to Edward Said's *Orientalism*]" (Menser 2017, 37) but to specifically consider China's strategic approach in it and political relations to the United States. *Shi*, he argues, provides an important piece in that puzzle. Menser's focus on China brings his work closer to Jullien's actual concerns. These are just three examples of the reception of Jullien's work in military theory.

In management theory, Jullien's work is referenced more frequently, but usually with the same casualness as the examples from military theory that I have given—in other words, never as part of a sustained engagement with Jullien's work. Rather, Jullien's *Treatise* (and in some cases also other books that aren't part of the trilogy on potentiality, war, and management) is used to back up or often also illustrate a management strategy. A great example here is Dominique Poiroux's "En quête de la voie en Chine" (In search of the path in/into China), published in *Journal de l'école de Paris du management*. Poiroux is credited simply with the name of the business for whom at the end of 2002 he left to China: "Danone" (Poiroux 2007, 8). The article summarizes his experiences in eight sections whose titles operate as statements summarizing their main advice. Let me list them to give an idea of their range:

- "Cent jours pour écouter" (One hundred days for listening)
- "Prendre du recul" (Taking a step back)
- "Gagner du temps" (Gaining time)
- "Si l'ennemi ne peut être arrêté, préparer une alliance" (If the enemy can't be stopped, prepare an alliance)

- "Rester humble au quotidien" (Stay modest in relation to the everyday Chinese person)
- "Un demi-effort, cent succès; cent efforts, un demi-succès" (the Chinese proverb is included in transcribed Chinese as well: "shi ban gong bei; shi bei gong ban"; half an effort, one hundred successes; one hundred efforts, half a success)
- "Se séparer d'un collaborateur, mais rester bons amis" (Separating oneself from a collaborator while staying good friends)
- and finally "Savoir se laisser mener en bateau" (here, too, in the transcribed Chinese: "man tian guo hai"; letting oneself be guided in a boat).

Rather than explain all of these, I want to note that the first section explicitly credits a lot of these wisdoms to François Jullien, with Poiroux writing that Jullien's book *Treatise on Efficacy* will often be quoted in the sections that follow. He does not note what Jullien's book is about, only that while he will be applying it to management, "il [n'a] pas du tout été écrit dans cette perspective" (it was not at all written in that context; Poiroux 2007, 9). Apart from the fact that Poiroux does not tell us what that context was—it was, as I've discussed, military theory—it's also worth noting that Poiroux is making an overstatement here: as I've discussed, Jullien's book was framed through a question about the potential of a business, and it includes, in fact, several references to the economic realm and management strategy. That Jullien's book is a work of military theory certainly becomes visible in the short section titles that I've listed: suddenly, the Danone business leader can use the military language of "enmity" and "alliance" to summarize his management advice.[11] Remarkably, there is *no* reflection on this shift in the article: it shows to what extent the presence of military language is simply *accepted* in this context as the language of management. "Strategy" seamlessly crosses here from military into management theory, anecdotes from military history are without any friction applied in the context of management and as part of the broader project of explaining to Western business leaders how to find a "path" in or into China, as the article title puts it. The use of the term "path" is itself significant: it is a rather obvious pun on the Chinese notion of the *dao*, the path or way that is the flow of all things; but it is repurposed here as part of a Western business strategy for gaining an economic foothold in China.

If Poiroux's repurposing of the *dao* already lay included in Jullien's theory of war and his own suggestions of its economic application, it's worth pausing for a moment to consider how, exactly, this repurposing takes place in Poiroux's title. The title in fact allows for two readings: on the one hand, a "Chinese" one, which would be "in search of the path/*dao* in China." As such it would capture Poiroux's spiritual search, if you will, into the path/*dao*, and perhaps also his consideration of its relevance for his work as a manager.

However, the title also allows for a Western reading, which Jullien would argue is incompatible with the former: "in search of a path *into* China." In such a reading, "*dao*" could not be substituted for "path" since, as Jullien in his *Conférence sur l'efficacité* points out, "la voie chinoise n'est pas une voie qui 'mène à'" (the Chinese path is not a path that "leads to/into"; Jullien 2005, 9); it's the European path that has such a goal, a *telos* that will be achieved by following a model or plan (an *eidos* or ideal form). This is the path of Western philosophy, of a progress toward truth or, in this case, economic gain. Daoism, however, is a philosophy of process: "il n'y a aucune idée d'aboutissement" (there is no idea whatsoever of an end goal; Jullien 2005, 69). Whereas Poiroux's article seeks to present the reader with advice for managers in China, the title makes it quite clear that such advice ultimately takes place within a thoroughly Western thought of progress—not a Chinese thought of process. On this count we must follow Jullien's advice and take the thought of the *dao* "out of the hands of the gurus" to "return it to philosophy."

But let me return to my main point: many other articles can be found to illustrate the easy exchange between military theory and management theory, which revolves around the term "strategy." While those never demonstrate any deep engagement with Jullien's work (often they aren't even context-specific), the casual references to his thought are many and contribute to the development not only of business strategies in China specifically but—and here's where my real interest lies—*of management theory in general*. This is different from Poiroux's use of Jullien in a specifically Chinese situation. China's non-Western model of warfare as it is exposed in Jullien's *Treatise* becomes highly productive both within Jullien's work (where it leads to his *Conférence sur l'efficacité*) but also outside of it, in its reception in management studies, as part of the development of contemporary management strategies not just for China but *at large*. If military theorists are trying to argue for the inclusion of the Chinese theory of warfare (as well as other non-Western theories of warfare) into military training, to better train US soldiers to confront an enemy that does not fight like them (but not to develop a US practice of warfare that is more Chinese *in general*), the relation of management theory to the Chinese theory of warfare appears to be quite different—*there* the goal appears to be in part for management theory to become more Chinese *overall*. This difference is, I would argue, an extension of the fact that there are elements in the Chinese theory of war that resonate with the Western theory of management, a way in which the Chinese approach to "politics" (if you will—the particular sovereignty that can be found in China) resonates with Western theories of management and what one might call today's "economic government" (and I have in mind neoliberalism in particular) in the West.

Consider, for example, the chapter "Do Nothing (With Nothing Left Undone)" in Jullien's *Treatise*, where Jullien as elsewhere in his work suggests that one of the models for efficacy (both in war and elsewhere) is "the growth of plants" (Jullien 2004, 90). This is because

> one must neither pull on plants to hasten their growth (an image of direct action), nor must one fail to hoe the earth around them so as to encourage their growth (by creating favorable conditions for it). You cannot force a plant to grow, but neither should you neglect it. What you should do is liberate it from whatever might impede its development. You must *allow it to grow*. Such tactics are equally effective at the level of politics. A good prince ... is a ruler who, by eliminating constraints and exclusions, makes it possible for all that exists to develop as suits it. His acting-without-action amounts to a kind of laissez-faire but not to a policy of doing nothing at all. (Ibid., 91; emphasis original)

The idea—which has its origins in Mencius—is repeated in explicitly political terms later on, in the chapter "Allow Effects to Come About." With respect to political reality, Jullien writes,

> The excessive fullness that burdens it is, as we have seen, that of regulations and prohibitions that, as they multiply, end up weighing society down so that it is impossible for it to evolve as it should. An emptiness needs to be created, those regulations must be *evacuated*, to allow reality the space in which it can take off. For as soon as nothing is codified any more (codification being nothing but a reification of fullness), because nothing any longer bars the way to initiative, this can deploy itself *sponte sua*. In the emptiness created by the removal of prohibitions and regulations, all that is necessary is to allow things to happen, to allow them to pass through, so that action now occurs without activity. (Ibid., 112)

Even if both of these quotations seem to include an idea of freedom (with the verb "liberate" being used explicitly in the first), one should not get the wrong idea here: it is by allowing the plant to grow, and to develop *sponte sua*, that the Chinese politician exercises total control. Jullien points out that in that sense, the association with Daoism here is "a travesty": "For Daoism recommended nonaction on the part of the ruler with a view to allowing individuals to flourish, liberating them from the bonds imposed by rules and prohibitions," whereas what we get here is the "[enslavement of] the entire mass of individuals to the power of a single figure who embodies the State" (Jullien 2004, 101).

Still, it is through *laissez-faire* that the Chinese ruler governs—*sovereignly*, as Jullien emphasizes. With respect to this phrase laisser faire/laissez-faire, it is worth including a brief historical note about its origins.[12] If I focus on it here specifically because of its importance in contemporary analyses of neoliberalism, it is worth noting that the phrase supposedly originates in eighteenth-century French economist François Quesnay's writings on Chinese despotism. Indeed, laisser faire/laissez-faire is supposedly a French translation of the Chinese notion of *wu wei* (無爲), which means "without exertion" and is closely associated with the Chinese understanding of effective government.[13] Certainly when the phrase "laisser faire" appears in Jullien, in a chapter titled "Do Nothing (With Nothing Left Undone)," that is where we should situate its origins. But as such, the notion's appearance in Jullien can of course not be disentangled from its translation into the work of Quesnay, and by extension the work of the French physiocrats, whose ideas about the "natural," "spontaneously" self-regulating market producing the natural "true price" of a good, so interested Michel Foucault in both *Security, Territory, Population* (which dedicates a lecture to the physiocrats; Foucault 2007, 55–86) as well as *The Birth of Biopolitics* (which recalls Foucault's earlier discussion of the physiocrats; Foucault 2008, 30–37). (As far as I know, Foucault does not mention the phrase's origins in *wu wei*.) It is this idea of wu wei or laisser faire/laissez-faire that according to many would later on lead to Adam Smith's notion of the invisible hand, and it is present in Jeremy Bentham's notion of the panopticon as well. Apart from its liberal/neoliberal articulations—Bryan W. Van Norden notes that "in his State of the Union address in 1988, Ronald Reagan quoted a line describing *wu wei* from the *Daodejing*, which he interpreted as a warning against government regulation" (Van Norden 2017, 21)[14]—connections between laisser faire/laissez-faire and anarchocapitalism ought to be considered as well.[15]

If in the West, sovereign regimes of power have been associated precisely with the disciplinary prohibitions and regulations that, according to the standard analyses, neoliberal societies of control operate alongside of and that they *in some* (but not all—surely we have by now moved past naive understandings of neoliberalism as antisovereign? See Ong 2006) *cases* break down, the Chinese regime of sovereignty that Jullien uncovers governs neoliberally, through the lifting of prohibitions, by allowing a growth whose final outcome is fully foreseen. It's worth noting that this is not a regime that deregulates—regulation is in fact central to it.[16] This is the government through manipulation that Jullien associated with the Chinese theory of war. A person might act freely and believe they are promoting their own interest, "without realizing that in truth he is simply bolstering the power of his oppressor" (Jullien 2004, 151). This leads Jullien to identify "two principal characteristics of Chinese efficacy [that] come to operate within the political domain": "In the first place, this efficacy is indirect and stems from a process of conditioning," which means the ruler does not need to seek authority for their actions; second, and pushing this even further, "true efficacy dispenses with the need to exert oneself . . . a true tyrant can direct everything without having to make the slightest effort or even involve himself personally" (ibid., 151–52). In *Treatise*, Jullien points out that this was "accompanied by secret, subtle policing techniques that proceed, on the one hand, by means of investigations and, on the other, by the dissemination of misinformation designed to entrap people . . . The prince thus turns his position into a veritable intelligence-gathering machine. Through this relentless collection of information and this meticulous gleaning of data, from deep inside his palace he is able to 'see everything' and 'hear everything' (given that, in these circumstances, everyone 'becomes his eyes and his ears')" (ibid., 29). In the end, Jullien sums this up as the logic of totalitarianism; but it is interesting to note, I think, that beyond its association with Bentham's panopticon and disciplinary society, it includes elements of what we have come to understand as the "society of control" and neoliberal government—associated with management. The importance of laisser faire/laissez-faire for Bentham indicates as much.

When I write "society of control," I have of course in mind Gilles Deleuze's William Burroughs–inspired "Postscript on the Societies of Control," in which Deleuze pushes Michel Foucault's analysis of the disciplinary society into his own perceptive understanding of the society of control, associated with business and management. Here it is worth recalling Jullien's association of the Chinese theory of warfare and management, of knowing and living, with the serpent and especially the dragon:

> There is one image in particular, that of a snake or, better still, a dragon, that successfully conveys the mobility of mind that makes it possible to allow things to evolve freely without the slightest difficulty or effort (evolution stands in opposition to action). The dragon's flexible body has no fixed form; it weaves and bends in every direction, contracting in order to deploy itself, coiling up in order to progress. It merges so closely with the clouds that, borne constantly along by them, it advances without the slightest efforts. Its movement is hardly distinguishable from that of the clouds. In the same way, strategic intentionality should have no fixed goal, is fixed on no particular plan, and so can adapt to every twist in the situation and profit from it. The general does not act, does not dissipate or expend his energies in any predetermined action but, instead, in the manner of the infinitely supple body of the dragon, makes the most of the ever-changing situation so as to advance continually along with it, *in a state of constant evolution*. (Jullien 2004, 97)

This echoes the chapter titled "The Dragon Motif" in *Propensity*, where Jullien writes,

> The body of the dragon concentrates energy in its sinuous curves, and coils and uncoils to move along more quickly. It is a symbol of all the potential with which form can be charged, a potential that never ceases to be actualized. The dragon now lurks in watery depths, now streaks aloft to the highest heavens, and its very gait is a continuous undulation. It presents an image of energy

constantly recharged through oscillation from one pole to the other. The dragon is a constantly evolving creature with no fixed form; it can never be immobilized or penned in, never grasped. It symbolizes a dynamism never visible in concrete form and thus unfathomable. Finally, merging with the clouds and the mists, the dragon's impetus makes the surrounding world vibrate: it is the very image of an energy that diffuses itself through space, intensifying its environment and enriching itself by that aura. (Jullien 1995, 151)

Both books have, it's worth noting, dragons on the cover.

In his "Postscript," Deleuze too builds somewhat of a bestiary, associating the disciplinary society of sovereignty with the burrowing mole and the society of control with the serpent which slides across the surface (Deleuze 1992, 5). Seemingly out of nowhere, he then also offers another image of it: that of the surfer, which in Jullien's work too is brought into association with the Chinese theory of warfare and management. In the society of control, Deleuze somewhat enigmatically suggests, "surfing" (ibid., 6) has taken over from all the older sports. Odysseus, full of *mètis*, has become the dominant type. No wonder that "water" is a prominent image in the thought of ancient China (Jullien 2004, 170–83). Read through the lens of Jullien, in "Postscript" Deleuze can be said to argue that the Chinese strategy of warfare and management has become dominant.[17]

It is perhaps not surprising given all of this that in both *Treatise* and *Conférence sur l'efficacité* Jullien ends on a note that is highly critical of China: in *Treatise* he writes that the Chinese theory of warfare "kills" (Jullien 2004, 197)—it kills the subject, it true confrontation with otherness, agency, morality, et cetera. The last words of the book are in fact imagining another book, *In Praise of Counterefficacy*, that would work against Chinese strategy. In *Conférence sur l'efficacité*, we get an even stranger ending: after indicating that he is writing about Chinese strategy at a point in history when it appears to be triumphing globally, Jullien positions himself critically in relation to it and in fact begins to sing the praises of . . . Europe. It is Europe, he suggests, that confronted with the Chinese hegemon will rediscover its "importance" (Jullien 2005, 91), a certain "wisdom" in relation to the Chinese dominance (ibid., 92)—indeed that will become, as Jullien provocatively puts it, the new "Orient"—"mais de ce côté-ci," but on the European side (ibid.).[18] If this move returns us to Jullien's descriptions of his own work as turning to China in order to learn how to better read Greek, it also sheds light on the fact that the for-now final part of Jullien's trajectory has very much been focused on European thought and its possible uses in relation to Chinese thinking (for example, "the ideal" in his book on Plato). All of this indicates, in my view, that Jullien's work does not invite a sovereign decision for or against either Europe or China, even if it operates in the divergence that operates between the two. There are cultural resources on both sides that ought to be "exploited," as he puts it, and his work participates in that very process, with Jullien dancing on the tightrope suspended between both.

Finally, it seems worth asking whether the translation of *wu wei* into neoliberalism's laissez-faire can hold water. Can *wu wei* be used to refer to deregulated government? I'm not convinced this is so. Present in Confucius's *Analects*, even if it only explicitly appears in the text once (Confucius 2003, 175), *wu wei* captures the following idea, expressed in *Analects* 2.3: "If you try to guide the common people with coercive regulations [*zheng*, 政] and keep them in line with punishments, the common people will become evasive and will have no sense of shame. If, however, you guide them with Virtue [*de*, 德], and keep them in line with means of ritual, the people will have a sense of shame, and will rectify themselves" (ibid., 8). At first sight, this emphasis on virtue may not sound very neoliberal, but that could only be a provisional conclusion: scholars like Melinda Cooper and Wendy Brown have shown, in their books *Family Values* and *In the Ruins of Neoliberalism,* how crucial conservative morality is to neoliberal government. Friedrich Hayek, for example, can really sound like Confucius on this count. Today, of course, this insistence on morality has become hollowed out: Brown writes of a "contractual use" of morality by today's neoliberalism, and this is certainly one of the meanings her book's title (that we are living in the ruins of the neoliberalism that Hayek and co. started).

In the *Dao De Jing*, where one comes across the frequent use of both verbal and nominal *wu* forms, the association is made more easily—hence, no doubt, Ronald Reagan's reference to the *Dao De Jing* in his State of the Union. (Note, though, that Reagan does not make explicit that not overcooking the state means to govern by virtuous example.) In their commentary on the *Dao De Jing*, the term Roger Ames and David Hall most often use to characterize the "politics" of the old master is "anarchy": for the Daoist, there is no "overarching *arche* or 'beginning' as an explanation of the creative process" (Ames and Hall 2003, 14), a philosophical point that leads to their association of Daoism with "political anarchism" (ibid., 102) later in the book. Still, when that association is made, they add that the *Dao De Jing* "still assumes the need for a hierarchical political structure" (ibid.), something that (as Jullien notes through his emphasis on sovereignty) can in fact be found throughout classical Chinese thought. "Is Daoism a political anarchism?" Hall and Ames ask later on. "Definitely, with the proviso that there is an unquestioned assumption that rulership is a natural feature of human organization" (166). So, rather than a combination of neoliberalism and sovereignty, what we find here is a combination of anarchism and sovereignty, terms that may be more on the mark if, at least, one does not think that they exclude each other out (as many no doubt do—they would argue that sovereignty is constituted precisely by an *arche*—αρχη).

On my nonspecialist reading, the *Zhuangzi* probably goes the furthest in this anarchic direction, ending its final Inner Chapter (chapter 7) with a cautionary tale about the death of Chaos (Zhuangzi 2009, 54): as is explained in the Commentaries, Chaos dies because "Swoosh" and "Oblivion" decide to drill seven holes in him through which knowledge can enter (ibid., 212). This interferes with Chaos's connection with the flow. Better to just "Let it be!" (*yi hu*, 已乎; or *yi yi*, 已矣), as the text's central recommendation puts it. In Zhuangzi's contemporary, Mencius—a Confucian—we are on the other hand quite far removed from anarchism: one finds there prominently again the idea of governing well, noncoercively, by giving the good (virtuous) example. The book, which starts with Mencius's famous rejection of "profit" (*li*, 利) in his audience with King Hui of Liang—specifically, his rejection of profit that is put before rightness—could hardly be associated with neoliberalism (Mengzi 2008, 1).

Still, in all of these thinkers' embrace of noncoercive government there resonates something of deregulation, or—more precisely—of regulation by nonregulation, that can be associated both with certain understandings of anarchy (of democracy as an anarchic regime, for example) *and* of laissez-faire neoliberalism and as such it is worth keeping both terms (neoliberalism and democratic anarchy) in the picture as we move forward in identifying the political dimensions of Jullien's thought.

POLITICS: THE SPIRIT OR THE SHOE

> I'm told again and again that my work resides at a certain remove from politics. . . . My reply is: No. My work is political throughout.
>
> —François Jullien,
> interview with Oliver Zahm and Donatien Grau[19]

In the interview with which I began, Jullien pushes the divergence between persuasion and manipulation further, into the political realm, noting persuasion's association with democracy and manipulation's removal from that, even if he also indicates (in *Treatise*) that these are analytical distinctions and associations that truly overflow the framework within which he makes them fit. We are encountering an interesting problem here that lies at the root of my own fascination with Jullien's work: whereas the West, which operates within the logic of persuasion, has developed democratic political regimes that are—at least in theory—anarchic in the sense that they equally qualify everyone to participate without exception in their rule, the Chinese model is within the logic of manipulation and is intensely sovereign, nondemocratic, totalitarian even (in *Propensity*, Jullien points out that it is "horrified" by anarchy; Jullien 1995, 237—although it should be pointed out that what Jullien means here by anarchy is not the democratic anarchy I've just evoked but what he glosses as a "vacuum of authority"; ibid.). At the same time, Chinese thought appears to contain many nonexceptionalist elements (potentially associated with democratic anarchy; also associated with neoliberalism, as I've discussed)—Jullien points out, for example, that Daoism's association with totalitarianism is really a travesty—which nevertheless did not translate into a Chinese democratic political regime. On the Western political side, we may have accomplished political unexceptionalism (democratic anarchy; neoliberalism), but it seems that much of Western thought remains stuck within an exceptionalism that can productively be challenged from a Chinese point of view. This situation has led to exceptionalist concepts of sovereignty on the Western side, heavily indebted of course to religion (Judeo-Christianity). On the Chinese side, we get sovereignty as well, as Jullien emphasizes, but with elements of what from the Western point of view we can only read as nonsovereign elements (democraticoanarchic? Neoliberal?) mixed in. If in the West one can analytically distinguish, even if such a distinction is overdrawn, between what Michel Foucault analyzes as sovereign and governmental/biopolitical regimes of power (Foucault 1990), in China such a distinction appears impossible because the sovereignty it has developed includes governmental/biopolitical elements as its very core. It is this "other" conception of sovereignty, or, from the other side, this "other" conception of governmentality/biopolitics, that I'd like to look into now. If in the West the concept of sovereignty might be blamed on ontological/metaphysical thinking and religion (Judeo-Christianity), the question is why in China, which thinks very differently and does not have religion, no regime other than sovereignty has been possible. The answer can only lie in the fact that China developed *another understanding of sovereignty*, and it is that understanding that I want to explore.[20] For Jullien, such a project is about confronting Chinese thought and politics with the categories of European thought and politics so as to tease out the unthought of both (Martin and Spire 2011, 267).

Jullien begins to develop this other understanding of sovereignty in *Propensity*. The thinking starts from the fact that the Chinese model of propensity and efficacy, of disposition and dispositif, is "beyond good and evil"—outside of any moral content; it is purely about strategy. As such, it forms the basis of "the monarchical form of power" (Jullien 1995, 44), which in Late Antiquity was interpreted differently by various groups: as a moral authority by the Confucians, which put some content into the purely strategic approach to propensity and efficacy; or in a purely positional way, by the so-called Legalists. Jullien points out that the Legalists in truth weren't legalists at all but "theorists of *authoritarianism* and *totalitarianism*" (ibid.,

45; emphasis original), advocating a power that both "command[ed] openly" and "manipulate[d] secretly" (ibid., 49). This form of power, as I've already suggested, does not depend on the sovereign's "personal commitment" at all; instead it functions "*technically*" (ibid., 50; emphasis original). Jullien also refers to this as a "dehumanized" form of power since it's a form of power that works "autonomously and automatically" as a "product of human invention" (rather than of transcendent design) but without depending on an actual human being to exercise it (ibid.; also 53). Jullien associates this kind of power with Michel Foucault's analysis of Jeremy Bentham's panopticon and "the ideology of an absolute reign of surveillance" (ibid., 55). If Foucault, in Jullien's recollection, comments that the panopticon is "'an important mechanism, for it automatizes and disindividualizes power'" (56), Jullien adds that "No better definition of the political *shi* could be imagined" (ibid.). In the conclusion to the first part of *Propensity* from which I have been drawing, Jullien also discusses, however, "The Historical Compromise" that in his view emerged from the tension between Confucians and Legalists—namely, a sovereign power that both operated strategically, through disposition and efficacy, and had moral content—in other words that combined Confucian and Legalist tenets, the power of the panopticon and another kind of moral power that operated alongside of it. It is the particular combination of elements in this historical compromise that I now want to consider.

One of the books in Jullien's more recent work on European philosophy can be useful here. In *L'Invention de l'idéal et le destin de l'Europe* (The invention of the ideal and the destiny of Europe), a book that hasn't been translated into English where Jullien rereads Plato from a Chinese point of view, Jullien has a chapter titled "Modélisation ou regulation: la loi/le rite" (Modelization or regulation: law/ritual) that helps one further develop what I've characterized as the Chinese, neoliberal conception of sovereignty. The chapter approaches politics within the divergence that Jullien already developed elsewhere, associating Western political thought with modelization: "monarchy—oligarchy/aristocracy—democracy—tyranny" (Jullien 2017, 222). Plato's typology of political regimes favors the rupture that modelization brings about (ibid., 223). The typology has become so well established, Jullien points out, that we no longer question it. But why, the chapter asks, did China only know one of these types, monarchy, the "royal path" (*wang dao*, 王道; ibid., 225)? Moreover, because China only knew one political form, it did not think in terms of political types or ideal Forms at all, only within the distinction between order and disorder, the good and the bad prince (ibid.). So what is it in China, Jullien asks, that blocks the modelization of politics and what is the other logic that was adopted there?

One reason that Jullien gives is the preponderance of the family structure in China, and specifically of the role of the father (Jullien 2017, 226).[21] By contrast, in Greece the political structure was only able to develop by separating itself from this (ibid., 226). This separation enabled the conception of different political models, whereas China remained stuck in the family as the basis of politics. The main reason Jullien mentions, however, to explain why China did not develop a governmental apparatus properly speaking, is the Chinese reliance on regulation—the belief in the flow of things, which is naturally present in everything and is the basis of relations between people, including people in the family. It involves protection, submission, well-being, and respect (ibid., 227). This preserves a harmonious equilibrium. If there is too much forcing, too much constraint, there will be a revolution; if the people are oppressed in an irregular or unequal way, they will revolt as well; one must oppress them continuously and equally so that the oppression is considered natural. On the Chinese side, it is therefore a question of allowing political relations to operate *sponte sua* starting from the basis of family relations.

As I've already discussed, on the Western side, there is modelization; on the Chinese side, regulation. Jullien now points out that these are expressed in two different modes of social structuration and organization: laws (*nomoi*, voµoἱ) on the Western side and rites (*li*, 禮) on the Chinese side. Western laws go back to the Platonic ideal Form; they need to be related to the logic of modelization that Jullien describes throughout his work. This marks the West's originality, its innovation. Because China, however, did not have a philosophy of the ideal Form, it did not develop laws but was governed through rites. Law is theoretical, Jullien writes; rites are not. They are practical (Jullien 2017, 234). Rites in that sense connect to the practical intelligence of *mètis* and the Chinese theory of warfare. This does not mean that in China there weren't any codes of government. But, Jullien argues, these did not develop to the status of Western laws. They apply mostly to the lower classes and have a punitive function; they were apparently also often criticized for their bad influence (ibid., 235). In China, he argues, there is a set of codes that are administrative regulations rather than legal dispositions.

It's at this point that Jullien distinguishes between "legalité" and "normativité"—"legality" and "normativity" (Jullien 2017, 237)—and points out that while laws are supposed to operate on actions, rites operate on behaviors or conducts ("comportements"; ibid., 238).[22] Whereas the law commands, the rite predisposes following its normative form, not by making people obey it but by assimilating them into it. Rites provide immediate guidance. They name a normative system of governing behaviors or conducting conducts that stands apart as Jullien sees it from the obedience-demanding system of laws. Unlike laws, which derive from the ideal, rites derive from the functional: "they do not incarnate a certain intelligible, modelized and projected form, like the idea of the Good or the Just" (ibid., 240). Instead, they "serve the continuous regulation of conduct, limiting themselves to amplifying what is too constrained and reducing what would be excessive" (ibid.). Rites instruct us in "what is appropriate or adequate and what makes that we are always in phase with the demands of a situation, both privately and publicly, from a personal and collective point of view" (ibid.). Rites do not follow the logic of the *eidos* or ideal Form but operate according to polarities—the famous yin and yang, for example, that in their polarity mark the regulative process of respiration, of breathing in and breathing out (ibid.), and it's in view of this that one constantly adjusts one's position. In short, rites "canalize" Chinese civilization (ibid., 241) and guarantee its "viability" (its "life" but also its path and way, its *dao*).

Rites thus stand at the opposite of the Western model of governance, based on the metaphysics of Being. If the Western model operates through "commandment" (*commandement*), the Chinese logic is that of "conditioning" (*conditionnement*): it's about shaping dispositions, a shaping that's all the more constraining as it is discrete. Jullien points out that

> il opère en douceur, en amont, au fil des jours, orientant insensiblement la conduite avant même que nous ayons pu l'analyser: "La transformation éducative exercée par les rites est subtile: elle arrête la déprivation au stade où celle-ci n'a pas encore pris forme. Elle fait que l'homme de jour en jour tend vers le bien et s'éloigne du crime sans que lui-même s'en rende compte; c'est pourquoi les anciens souverains tenaient les rites en honneur." (Jullien 2017, 243)

> [The rite] operates softly, gradually, over the course of time, unnoticeably orienting conduct before even we were able to analyze it: "The educational transformation that rites bring about is subtle: it stops deprivation before the state where it hasn't even taken form yet. Day by day it orients people toward the good and away from crime without them even noticing it; that's why ancient sovereigns held rites in high esteem."

Whereas the law "goes back to the ideal" and "originates in a contract" (243), the rite is about "efficacy of conduct" (ibid.) and influences "through silent transformation, without being thought through, beyond our will even" (ibid.).

This culminates in the chapter in the provocative pair of the spirit and the shoe (Jullien 2017, 244). It's a very playful part of the chapter, but the play is serious, I think, and illuminating. Whereas the rite, Jullien writes—or the Chinese *li*—can be glossed as *li* (?),[23] "shoe," he suggests that the Greek *nomos* ought to be glossed through its relation to *nous* (νους), "spirit" or "intellect."[24] These two different glosses evoke, he suggests, their very different purposes: as part of a modelizing politics that operates through commandment, on the one hand, and as part of normativizing government that operates through the conditioning of conduct, on the other. In its proximity to the shoe, rather than the spirit, the rite—without commanding—makes us walk a certain way (it operates, if you will, from below, on the feet rather than on the head); the law, on the other hand, commands the intellect. It is of the order of the *eidos/telos* (ibid., 245). The former inscribe themselves into the continuity of things, whereas the latter mark a break.

Jullien develops all of this without reference to any contemporary Chinese or Western political thought, but from the point of view of contemporary Western political philosophy, it is remarkable to what extent—down to the very phrase "the conduct of conduct"—the analytical separations he sets up echo the already evoked distinctions between sovereignty and governmentality/biopolitics in the work of Michel Foucault. This is most visible in *Propensity*, which explicitly references Foucault but still remains largely implicit about the philosopher's influence in its pages. In the introduction to *Propensity*, Jullien writes that "art, or wisdom, as conceived by the Chinese, consequently lies in strategically exploiting the propensity emanating from that particular configuration of reality, to the maximum effect possible. This is the notion of 'efficacy'" (Jullien 1995, 15). Interestingly, this efficacy is marked in *Propensity* as the "dispositif" that fulfills, as the translator of the book in a note puts it, a "disposition"—also rendered as "configuration," or, I would suggest based on Jullien's other books, "situation."[25] A dispositif, the translator further clarifies, is a set-up that actualizes a situation's disposition. From *Propensity* to *Conférence sur l'efficacité*, but especially in the much later *L'Invention de l'idéal*, one finds reflected the shift from laws to norms that is crucial to Foucault's work on governmentality/biopolitics; as a paradigm one can take in this context the soft governing force of the shoe that, without necessarily disciplining, still makes people walk a certain way. The Chinese model of sovereignty is not one that operates through commandment and the power of the sword, or by taking lives, as Foucault characterizes it in the famous fifth section of his *History of Sexuality: Volume I*. Instead it operates through a regulative conditioning. Interestingly, whereas in Foucault's tracing of the emergence of the governmental/biopolitical paradigm in the West, religion, specifically Christianity's pastoral component and its interest in the governing of souls, plays a crucial role, Jullien insists that there is nothing religious about the Chinese approach and that it was cut off from theology early on (Jullien 2017, 225).

In an article titled "Biopolitical Beijing," Judith Farquhar and Qicheng Zhang consider in the sovereign context of the People's Republic of China how "power is generated, sustained, and challenged through everyday practices" (Farquhar and Zhang 2005, 303). Referencing work by Foucault and Agamben, but also explicitly taking their distance from it, they look specifically at *yangsheng* (养生) as a "practice of cultivating life in contemporary Beijing" (ibid., 306). It is worth noting that it is this notion that, in Jullien, translates as "nourrir sa vie"—"vital nourishment" (Jullien 2018, 237). As such, *yangsheng* is "older than the *techne tou biou* (τεχνη του β[ου) or art of existence Foucault finds in hellenistic culture" (ibid.) and that Westerners often find so onerous, as the authors point out (they suggest this may be because of the notion's Christian legacy). However, as a practice that includes "cultivation of the spirit," "good nutrition," and "exercise," it certainly resonates with it, even if the Chinese approach to *yangsheng* is much more cheerful. The authors' ultimate point, however, is to consider how these techniques of cultivating life operate within state power as practices of (self-) government. The argument implicitly turns neoliberal here: "Where their health is concerned," the authors write, "most people realize that they are on their own" (Farquhar and Zhang, 320). If this mode of government, which combines state sovereignty with governmental/biopolitical and neoliberal self-care, is typical of contemporary Beijing, as it is (one might add) of the West, my reading of Jullien makes one wonder whether the particular combination of power practices that Farquhar and Zhang's article considers isn't a typical feature of Chinese conceptions of sovereignty at large as always crossing the analytical distinction between sovereignty and governmentality/biopower within which Foucault's theory of Western power operates.

I ultimately don't have the expertise to assess the distinction between law and rite that Jullien offers his readers, but to the extent that it echoes Foucault's distinction between sovereignty and governmentality/biopolitics but now mobilizes it within a divergence between the West and China, I find it theoretically interesting: for it ends up describing a form of sovereignty that operates in a governmental/biopolitical way—that is most sovereignly effective, in fact, where it rules governmentally (normatively rather than through laws). It is a monarchic model but shot through with an approach to power that is not sovereign in the Western sense of the word—that is *sovereign otherwise*. If I am reconstituting Jullien's theory of such sovereignty here, it is because of its close association with management not just in his work but also in management studies overall, which has taken inspiration from the Chinese theory of warfare to design its strategies for efficacy.

It seems to me, then, that looking at these aspects of Jullien's thought helps us to uncover a number of things:

- first, another theory of war, which enlarges a gap that, at least since Clausewitz, has opened up in Western theories of war (it goes back to Aristotle's response to Plato, as Jullien points out);
- second, the connections between that other theory of war and theories of management, not just management in China but management overall; this is captured by the phrase "managers à la Sun Zi";
- third, the affinities between a Chinese approach to efficacy not just in war but in all things—a hypereconomical approach, as Jullien points out—and to management in general, allows us to see a connections between Chinese

approaches to power and contemporary structures of government, which contain—as many have pointed out—elements from both sides of the sovereignty/governmentality-biopolitics divide within which a scholar like Michel Foucault has worked (Judith Butler has pointed out the need to break down the analytical distinction to make sense of contemporary phenomena such as Guantánamo [Butler 2006], but I'm more thinking here of nuanced approaches to the governmental logic of neoliberalism that have considered the importance of the state in neoliberal governance beyond the rather facile opposition of sovereignty to neoliberalism—a good indicator here is Carl Schmitt's importance in various neoliberal theories and theories of neoliberalism; the most pertinent reference in this context would probably be David Harvey's chapter on China and "The Neoliberal State"; Harvey 2007).

What we get from Jullien, then, is partly a theory to consider the contemporary situation of government that appears to be marked by a becoming hegemonic of the Chinese situation. I don't mention this in a panicked, "yellow peril" kind of way; it simply seems to me that Jullien's work on power in China can help us understand how we are governed today. At the same time, and in the spirit of counterhegemony evoked by Jullien's own gesturing at the end of *Treatise* toward the necessary *praise of counterefficacy*, it is worth considering to what extent the West's cultural resources could be exploited, as Jullien might put it, to work against this hegemonic situation. Certainly Jullien is exploring such a project in his most recent work—he draws out, for example, the radical innovation of laws and why he prefers them to rites. At the same time, maybe the return to the West as the new "Orient," as Jullien dubiously puts it at the end of his *Conférence sur l'efficacité*, isn't the right move either. Perhaps there is a productive third that could be considered, outside of the divergence between West and East, law and rite, but also outside of the divide between sovereignty and governmentality/biopolitics. For that, perhaps the notion of democratic anarchy could provide the key.

NOTES

1. Jullien 1995, 20.
2. See, for example, Jullien 2009, 182.
3. I have found that often the takedowns of Jullien's work are misinformed. Jeffrey Richey's scathing review of *A Treatise on Efficacy* is a good example: attributing to Jullien a "psychologically, identity-obsessed set of assertions" (anyone who has actually read Jullien can only laugh out loud at this) and a "tediously essentialist and reductionist" view of China (Jullien's entire oeuvre precisely works against

essentialism; Richey 2005; 447), Richey merely reveals the remarkable limitations of his own reading. As Jeremy Henkel in another review of this same book points out, Jullien "is careful not to essentialize the two worldviews [of China and Europe]. While he is pointing out patterns and tendencies in the thinking of Europe and China, he is not positing an essential incommensurable difference between them" (Henkel 2006, 348).

4. Stone 1987.

5. It should be noted here that this parallelism between war and management, as enabled by a theory of strategy and a theory of efficacy more generally, also applies beyond the context of management. In *Propensity*, after discussing efficacy in war and politics, Jullien explores its parallel importance in art (where "the same force is at work"; Jullien 1995, 76) and history.

However, the connections are, in my view, less strong, or at least they seem very different: in art they involve, for example, how reality can effectively be rendered into a painting, not through mimesis but by allowing what is painted to express the very force that animates nature itself: "for *shi* gives depth to a representation and exceeds its concrete limitations by revealing, within the actualized static form, a dimension of perpetual, soaring flight. *Shi* is not only the internal energy from which that form has proceeded; it is also the effect of the tension this energy produces. The 'form' is seized on in all its *propensity*, which means it should be seen not merely as 'form' but also as a continuing process" (ibid., 78)—what I have elsewhere, in a political context, identified as the shift from "form" to "formation" (Boever 2016, 338–79).

Hence the importance in literature, for example, of the list, which does not operate mimetically but rather captures all the possible variations of reality (Boever 2016, 107). To speak, for this reason, of "In Art as In War," however, would be to overstate the connections, in my view, between military theory and, for example, theories of painting. I say this even if Jullien makes the parallelism explicitly in a discussion of calligraphy: "Just as for the troops 'there is no constant disposition on the battlefield,' for the ideograms rendered by calligraphy 'there is no single way, always the same, of actualizing their configuration': as with water and fire, there are multiple potentialities stemming from their disposition (*shi*), and these are 'not determined once and for all.' Literature benefits from a comparable variability" (ibid., 84).

I don't think this justifies, however, a parallelism like the one I used in my title. The parallel is strongest in the realm of management. I think Jullien realized this himself: hence the focus on business in *Treatise* and his development of the subsequent *Conférence sur l'efficacité*.

6. Detienne has also acknowledged Jullien's work on this: Detienne 2011.

7. Indeed, this is a commonly made point—that today the crossover of military theory and management theory can be found in military schools and business schools around the world. Greg Clydesdale has made the interesting observation that, while this crossover may be common today, he has found no evidence of it in the past (Clydesdale 2017, 895).

8. This dissociation of the Chinese model from *telos* is not always confirmed by what Jullien writes. In *Propensity* for example, he notes within the space of a couple of pages how the Chinese model of manipulation is about "learn[ing] how to make the

most of the tendency at work in the course of things" (Jullien 1995, 198) and about "always deriv[ing] the greatest profit" from a situation (ibid., 199). Does such a profit not constitute a *telos*?

9. Here *Propensity*'s engagement with Hegel ought to be considered. On the one hand, Jullien is writing against Hegel's racist presentation of the Orient in his work as backward (Jullien 1995, 17–18). On the other, Jullien points out certain analogies between Chinese thought—the perpetual unfolding of reality through silent transformations—and the Hegelian dialectical model; however, the analogies are shot through with difference: the Chinese model is not progress-oriented; it is not based in a means-ends logic; it involves neither "providence" nor "a concerted plan"; it is "not theological" or "eschatological"; "no final cause directs it"; "it is justified by no *telos*" (ibid., 211). All of this amounts to the claim that Chinese thought does not have "any idea of a pure, abstract future" (ibid.).

10. Jullien gives the example of aging in this context: one morning one wakes up to find oneself aged, but this process takes place as a "silent transformation," to use a phrase that is prominent in his oeuvre. The example is telling because it breaks down the Western distinction between the subject and time—and, by extension, the world—instead making the subject an integral part of time and the world. See Jullien 2016.

11. For those who want to avoid the military terms, the article "The Strategic Insights of Sun Tzu and Quality Management" provides an interpretation "of the military terminology within the context of the business environment": "battlefield" becomes "marketplace," "general/commander" becomes "manager or management," "military warfare" is "competition," "army/troops" becomes "the employees of the business," and "enemy" becomes "competitor" (Lo, Ho, and Sculli 1998, 162).

12. I want to thank Andrew Culp for pushing me in this direction and providing me with some of the references that generated this paragraph.

13. *Wu wei* is one of the verbal *wu* forms that are key to the *Dao De Jing*. Nominal *wu* forms appear in this book as well, in chapter 69 that is dedicated to military philosophy (Ames and Hall 2003, 186). For a good introduction to the *wu* forms of the *Dao De Jing*, I recommend Ames and Hall 2003, 36–53. On *wu wei* in particular, see Slingerland 2014.

14. The line Reagan quotes is, "Govern a great nation like you would cook a small fish; do not overdo it" (Reagan 1988). The line from the *Dao De Jing*—"治大國若烹小鮮" (Ames and Hall 2003, 171)—translates as "Bringing proper order to a great state is like cooking a small fish" (ibid.).

15. I am relying here on the Wikipedia entries for "François Quesnay," "Laissez-faire," and "wu wei." I hope to be able to expand my research into wu wei in future work.

16. Jullien distinguishes the Chinese regime explicitly from the "deregulation" that is often said to characterize neoliberalism and may make one reconsider this characterization (Jullien 2008, 24).

17. I know of no other approaches that explicitly establish a connection between the serpent in Deleuze's "Postscript" and the Chinese dragon. Kang Cao and Jean Hillier's "Deleuzian Dragons" considers the proximity between Deleuze's thought and Chinese thought but, in spite of what its title suggests, does not develop the connection between Deleuze and the Chinese dragon (Cao and Hillier 2013).

18. Kristeva uses this phrase prominently in her book *About Chinese Women* (see Lowe 1991, 141), and one wonders whether Jullien's use of it here might echo that problematic book.

19. Zahm and Grau 2015.

20. See Martin and Spire 2011, 198, for an interview in which Jullien himself raises these questions.

21. This goes against what Lisa Lowe has identified as "orientalist" associations of China with "the maternal," for example, in the work of Julia Kristeva (Lowe 1991, 143ff).

22. Others, too, have indicated that whereas Western philosophy is obsessed with "truth," Chinese thought is centered on "conduct": Lash 2009, 570.

23. I have been unable to confirm this gloss of *li*, "rite," as *li*, "shoe." Specifically, I have been unable to locate the Chinese character *li* that would translate as "shoe."

24. As far as I can tell, these are entirely speculative glosses, meant to draw out how exactly these two types of government—by law and by rite—operate.

25. On this, see Ames and Hall 2003, 48–53.

REFERENCES

Allouch, Jean, Alain Badiou, Pierre Chartier, et al. 2007. *Oser Construire: Pour François Jullien.* Paris: Seuil.

Ames, Roger, and David Hall, trans. 2003. *Dao De Jing: "Making This Life Significant" (A Philosophical Translation).* New York: Ballantine Books.

Billeter, Jean-François. 2006. *Contre François Jullien.* Paris: Allia.

Boever, Arne De. 2016. *Plastic Sovereignties: Agamben and the Politics of Aesthetics.* Edinburgh: Edinburgh University Press.

Bougnoux, Daniel, and François L'Yvonnet, eds. 2018. *François Jullien.* Paris: L'Herne.

Brown, Wendy. 2019. *In the Ruins of Neoliberalism: The Rise of Antidemocratic Politics in the West.* New York: Columbia University Press.

Butler, Judith. 2006. *Precarious Life: The Powers of Mourning and Violence.* New York: Verso.

Cao, Kang, and Jean Hillier. 2013. "Deleuzian Dragons: Thinking Chinese Spatial Planning with Gilles Deleuze." *Deleuze Studies* 7 (3): 390–405.

Clydesdale, Greg. 2017. "Western Perceptions of Chinese Business: Sun Tzu and the Misuse of History." *Management and Organization Review* 13 (4): 895–903.

Confucius. 2003. *Analects.* Translated by Edward Slingerland. Indianapolis: Hackett.

Cooper, Melinda. 2017. *Family Values: Between Neoliberalism and the New Social Conservatism.* New York: Zone Books.

Deleuze, Gilles. 1992. "Postscript on the Societies of Control." *October* 59: 3–7.

Detienne, Marcel, and Jean-Pierre Vernant. 1991. *Cunning Intelligence in Greek Culture and Society.* Translated by Janet Lloyd. Chicago: University of Chicago Press.

Detienne, Marcel. 2011. "De l'efficacité en raison pratique: Approches comparatives." *Belin* 3 (137–38): 231–41.

Farquhar, Judith, and Qicheng Zhang. 2005. "Biopolitical Beijing: Pleasure, Sovereignty, and Self-Cultivation in China's Capital." *Cultural Anthropology* 20 (3): 303–27.

Foucault, Michel. 1990. *History of Sexuality: Volume 1.* Translated by Robert Hurley. New York: Vintage.

———. 2007. *Security, Territory, Population: Lectures at the Collège de France, 1977–1978.* Translated by Graham Burchell. New York: Picador.

———. 2008. *The Birth of Biopolitics: Lectures at the Collège de France, 1978–1979.* Translated by Graham Burchell. New York: Picador.

Gauchet, Marcel. 2018. "Les possibles de la pensée." In *François Jullien*, edited by Daniel Bougnoux and François L'Yvonnet, 20–24. Paris: L'Herne.

Hayot, Eric. 2004. *Chinese Dreams: Pound, Brecht, Tel Quel.* Ann Arbor: University of Michigan Press.

Harvey, David. 2007. *A Brief History of Neoliberalism.* Oxford: Oxford University Press.

Henkel, Jeremy. 2006. Review of *Treatise on Efficacy*, by Jullien François. *Philosophy East and West* 56 (2): 347–51.

Hill, Robert M. 2011. "Complexity Leadership: New Conceptions for Dealing with Soldier Suicides." *Military Review* (January/February): 36–46.

Hughes, Alex. 2003. "The Seer (Un)Seen: Michel Leiris's China." *French Forum* 28 (3): 85–100.

Jullien, François. 1995. *The Propensity of Things: Toward a History of Efficacy in China.* Translated by Janet Lloyd. New York: Zone Books.

———. 2004. *A Treatise on Efficacy: Between Western and Chinese Thinking.* Translated by Janet Lloyd. Honolulu: University of Hawai'i Press.

———. 2005. *Conférence sur l'efficacité.* Paris: PUF.

———. 2007. *Chemin faisant. Connaître la Chine, relancer la philosophie. Réplique à ***.* Paris: Seuil.

———. 2008. "Umweg über China oder wie man zu den Voreingenommenheit der europäischen Vernunft zurückkehrt." In *Kontroverse über China: Sinophilosophie*, edited by Dirk Baecker, François Jullien, Philippe Jousset, et al., 7–29. Berlin: Merve.

———. 2009. "Thinking Between China and Greece: Breaking New Ground: An Interview with Marcel Gauchet." Translated by Simon Porzak. *Qui Parle* 18 (1): 181–210.

———. 2016. *This Strange Idea of the Beautiful.* Translated by Krzystof Fijalkowski and Michael Richardson. London: Seagull.

———. 2017 [2009]. *L'Invention de l'idéal et le destin de l'Europe.* Paris: Gallimard.

———. 2018. "De L'écart à l'inouï—repères III." In *François Jullien*, edited by Daniel Bougnoux and François L'Yvonnet (Cahier de l'Herne), 233–41. Paris: L'Herne.

Lash, Scott. 2009. "Against Institutionalism." *International Journal of Urban and Regional Research* 33 (2): 567–71.

Lo, V. H. Y., C. O. Ho, and D. Sculli. 1998. "The Strategic Insights of Sun Tzu and Quality Management." *The TQM Magazine* 10 (3): 161–68.

Lowe, Lisa. 1991. *Critical Terrains: French and British Orientalisms*. Ithaca: Cornell University Press.

Martin, Nicolas, and Antoine Spire. 2011. *Chine, la dissidence de François Jullien. Suivi de: Dialogues avec François Jullien*. Paris: Seuil.

Mengzi. 2008. *Mengzi: With Selections from Traditional Commentaries*. Translated by Bryan W. Van Norden. Indianapolis: Hackett.

Menser, David Christopher. 2017. "Did the United States Lose China Again?" *The Army War College Review* 3 (1): 36–40.

Ong, Aihwa. 2006. *Neoliberalism as Exception: Mutations in Citizenship and Sovereignty*. Durham: Duke University Press.

Piorunski, Richard. 1998. "Le détour d'un grec par la Chine. Entretien avec François Jullien." *Ebisu* 18: 147–85.

Poiroux, Dominique. 2007. "En quête de la voie en Chine." *Journal de l'école de Paris du management* 2 (64): 8–15.

Reagan, Ronald. 1988. "Address before a Joint Session of Congress on the State of the Union." January 25. Available online at https://www.presidency.ucsb.edu/ws/index.php?pid=36035.

Richey, Jeffrey. 2005. Review of *A Treatise on Efficacy*, by François Jullien. *The Journal of Asian Studies* 64 (2): 446–48.

Slingerland, Edward. 2014. *Trying Not to Try: Ancient China, Modern Science, and the Power of Spontaneity*. New York: Broadway Books.

Spivak, Gayatri Chakravorty. 1981. "French Feminism in an International Frame." *Yale French Studies* 62: 154–84.

Stone, Oliver, dir. 1987. *Wall Street*. Film. 20th Century Fox.

Van Norden, Bryan W. 2017. *Taking Philosophy Back: A Multicultural Manifesto*. New York: Columbia University Press.

Zahm, Olivier, and Donatien Grau. 2015. "François Jullien." Interview. *Purple Magazine* 23. http://purple.fr/magazine/ss-2015-issue-23/francois-jullien/.

Zarcone, Thierry. 2003. "China as Philosophical Tool: François Jullien in Conversation with Thierry Zarcone." *Diogenes* 50 (4): 15–21.

Zweibelson, Ben E. 2014. "Preferring Copies with No Originals: Does the Army Training Strategy Train to Fail?" *Military Review* (January/February): 15–25.

Zhuangzi. 2009. *Zhuangzi: The Essential Writings; With Selections from Traditional Commentaries*. Translated by Brook Ziporyn. Indianapolis: Hackett.

Chapter 4

François Jullien in Dialogue

> Rien qu'une écriture en marche au rhythme du Dehors. (Nothing like a writing that follows the rhythm of the Outside.)
>
> —Abdelkébir Khatibi, *Figures de l'étranger*[1]

AN ALTERNATIVE WESTERN GENEALOGY FOR JULLIEN'S THOUGHT

In this fourth and final chapter, I want to consider how the thought of François Jullien is in dialogue with the work of other scholars. Indeed, for a thinker who has turned a strong, philosophical (and political) notion of "dialogue" into a key term in his late work (as I have discussed in my introduction), Jullien has also notably been accused of not pursuing dialogue. In a scathing review of Jullien's book *The Great Image Has No Form, or On the Nonobject through Painting*, Charles Lachman minces no words when he states that Jullien's "arguments take place in an intellectual vacuum . . . without reference to almost anyone else in the field" (Lachman 2011, 233). To be fair, this criticism applies to much so-called "French theory," which often seeks to hide rather than show its references. While this can be criticized from a scholarly point of view, such a lack of references can also be read as part of a choice to write in an essayistic style, and for a general audience. Writing after Roland Barthes, who states in his *Leçon* that he has written only essays (see Barthes 1978, 7; Barthes adds that in the essay, writing enters into tension with analysis), Jullien reflects on this choice of the essay form explicitly in *In Praise of Blandness*: "How, we might ask, can one speak of blandness? Is it possible to explore it in essay form?" (Jullien 2008, 80). This leads one to conclude that his choice to omit a heavy reference apparatus should at least partly be viewed in this light.

But Jullien's explicit reasons for the lack of dialogue with critical sources, especially secondary sources, exceed such a stylistic choice as well. As Jullien himself explains, for example, in a "Notice to the Reader" that precedes *The Propensity of Things: Toward a History of Efficacy in China*,

> In the presentation of each of the areas of Chinese culture, I observe historical connections and use them to underpin the argument but do not follow them up simply for their own sake. The reason for this stricture is to allow the logical connections to emerge fully and to keep purely sinological discourse to a minimum (the contextual references are given in the notes) to make it more accessible for the nonspecialist. (Jullien 1995, 20)

Later, he adds pithily that "the omission of an index is deliberate" (ibid.), but without adding an explanation. This is perhaps because the reason for the omission is the same as the one just quoted: the index would lead the reader away from following logical connections to instead look up isolated references, which goes against the project of Jullien's book. One should note, however, how in this case "purely sinological discourse"—in other words, discourse that is relevant to the discipline of sinology alone—is left to the side in favor of pursuing "logical connections" that, within the contrast that is set up here, exceed "purely sinological discourse" and perhaps ought to be characterized rather as theoretical in a more universalizing way, or as philosophical (rather than merely sinological). One finds here very clearly, and in opposition to the "purely sinological," Jullien's preference for the concept, the fact that his work—and perhaps especially *Propensity*—revels in the (Barthesian) "pleasure of following up an idea" (ibid.). Critics have pointed out that this makes him ignore not just the work of other critics but also context. As indicated in a note in chapter 1, Jullien has responded that in this call for context, he overhears a *fear* of the concept (Martin and Spire 2011, 164). To forge a concept, he indicates in an interview, "is to forge a tool . . . is to forge a weapon" (ibid., 260). The concept is an emancipatory abstraction that Jullien defends.

This last claim echoes Gilles Deleuze and Félix, Guattari's *What Is Philosophy?*, in which Jullien's work is quoted in a discussion of immanence (Deleuze and Guattari 1996, 92). If Deleuze and Guattari have quoted Jullien, Jullien too has referenced Deleuze's work. The quotation and references hardly add up to a dialogue, however, even if an article or perhaps even a book could probably be written about Jullien's relation to Deleuze (it's interesting to see that Jullien critically distances himself from Deleuze on at least one occasion; see Jullien 2004, 83). Jullien may be stingy with references to sinology scholars, even if he of course reads closely and engages at length with primary sources in Chinese, but the references to scholars of Western philosophy are equally sparse. Jullien's relation to Western thought is largely limited to his engagement with some heavy hitters (Plato, Aristotle, Heidegger, and others; of course there are also the close affinities with Foucault or Barthes that have received plenty of attention in this book), primary sources that Jullien plays out in a divergence to Far Eastern thought. Although I am hesitant to pursue the kind of work that would follow the model of "Jullien and X," which always risks leading away from Jullien,[2] I still want to briefly address in this chapter Jullien's connections to a broader understanding of the Western philosophical tradition—more specifically, the ways in which the thinking (or at least traces of the thinking) that Jullien finds in China can already be found within Western thought. Jullien himself has in fact acknowledged such connections.

First, let me return to basic definitions that I offered earlier in this book. As I have already indicated, some ink has been spilled for good scholarly and political reasons over what Jullien means by "Chinese thought." I have already addressed his understanding of Chinese thought (or thought written in Chinese) in chapter 1. I have rarely seen it asked, however—and by "asked" here I mean more strongly "questioned"—what Jullien means by "Western thought." This seems a legitimate question as well, even if the politics of such a question aren't the same, and even if its historical import isn't equal. If we follow Jullien's understanding of Chinese thought, "Western thought" would be thought written in "Western languages," with the added caveat—which Jullien raises in his definition of Chinese thought—that saying so does not mean succumbing to linguistic determinism. But as I remarked with respect to Chinese thought previously in this book, that is a big umbrella. In the same way, then, that further nuance needed to be brought to Jullien's understanding of Chinese thought, one needs to bring further nuance to his understanding of Western thought.

Let's rehearse what Jullien means by Western thought: the notion refers for him to Greek thought, or the tradition of philosophical thinking started by Plato. Jullien's genealogies of Western thought frequently reach back to Plato and reconstruct Western thinking with a careful attunement to the differences within Western thought. While Jullien gives ample attention, for example, to Aristotle's criticism of Platonism, ultimately he seeks to show that certain aspects of Platonism continue in Aristotle and after, to the present day. Overall, however, the goal of his study is not to remain within Western thought and its deconstruction. Jullien's work, rather, seeks to enable a divergence (rather than a difference) between Western and Chinese thought, and Jullien will be attentive, for example, to elements of Chinese thought in Western thought—in, say, how Kant, Hegel, and, most frequently, Heidegger in some aspects of their work might come close Chinese thinking, even if overall they are within Western thought. These issues lead back to the methodological question of comparison and the fact that when he is "comparing" (though Jullien would likely not use that term[3]) Western and Chinese thought, Jullien is never opposing two stable entities or self-identical essences to each other. Instead, each of these thoughts needs to be considered as perpetually self-transforming, making it impossible to definitively pin them down. "It would be wrong," Jullien writes in his book *The Silent Transformations*, "to consider the diversity of cultures from the perspective of difference. This is because difference relates to identity as well as its opposite and, as a result, to the demand for identity . . . We know [by contrast] that every culture is plural, as much as it is singular, and that it is ceaselessly mutating" (Jullien 2011, 25).[4] Jullien refuses, in other words, to ontologize difference. To study two cultures next to each other is a question, rather, of drawing out what each of them leaves unthought. With Western thinking, even if it must be considered a thought in process, that unthought appears to be in part the question of process itself. It is Western thought's divergence from Chinese thinking that enables us to see this.

Going back to my remark that Jullien occasionally finds traces of Chinese thought in Western thinking, it is important to point out that it is thus *not only* Chinese thought that enables us to access the concerns that Chinese thought brings to us. Outside of the major references already given—references that explicitly appear in Jullien—there are, in fact, a number of other Western thinkers whose work reveals a proximity to Chinese thought. When in Jullien's recently translated *Living Off Landscape*, for example, "landscape" is understood "as a *process*, a process of exchange and interaction, between poles that suddenly enter *into phase*" (Jullien 2018, 50; emphasis original), readers may be reminded of the thought of Gilbert Simondon, which frequently uses the language of process and phases[5]; that suspicion seems confirmed by Jullien's discussion of the West's fear of the "apeiron" or "the inconsistency of the unlimited" (ibid., 95) later on in the same book, a notion to which Simondon also pays careful attention (see Simondon 2007). *The Great Image* picks up on this when, in its discussion of the *Dao De Jing* and the foundation (as well as source [fount]) that painting seeks to capture, it speaks of "this primordial 'there-is-not' of the undifferentiated fount [that] is not nothingness. It is rather that from which particular individualities constantly proceed, all the while becoming differentiated" (Jullien 2009, 20). Simondon, whose peculiar place in the Western philosophical tradition could via Jullien be characterized as "Chinese," writes about this as the preindividual entering into phase shift. I haven't been able to find any discussion of Simondon in Jullien's work, but even at a cursory glance the connections seem clear and could be derived from a comparative reading of Jullien and Deleuze (who is perhaps French philosophy's most famous reader of Simondon).

There are further such possible links—to the work of Jacques Derrida, for example, whose deconstruction has been characterized by another philosopher, Byung-Chul Han, as "Chinese" (see Han 2017).[6] Again, Jullien offers no detailed discussion of Derrida in his work. He largely dismisses Derrida as "too biblical," even if in *A Treatise on Efficacy* he also explicitly praises "deconstruction" (rather than destruction, as he points out; Jullien 2004, 48) as the Chinese approach to efficacy. The advantage of not pursuing these more-detailed comparative studies of, for example, Derrida's work and the work of a specific Chinese thinker, and working instead in broader strokes, is that a more general picture emerges that enables us to see how, for example, Derrida and Simondon—but also already major thinkers like Hegel or Aristotle—struggled with key issues on which Western and Chinese thinking diverge. Surely Derrida's reception in the Far East, in China but also Japan, should be considered on this count—and, similarly, the use that some contemporary Chinese thinkers have made of Simondon.[7] In other words, if a Chinese genealogy of Jullien's thought could be provided based on his work as a sinologist—a work that is on explicit display in his many books—one could just as well tease out, in parallel to such a project, a Western genealogy of Jullien's thinking—in other words, a demonstration of how much of what Jullien finds in China has been present also in Western thinking, even if it is often in those figures that haven't been central to that tradition or even if it is in those aspects of the work of Western thought's central thinkers that have been overlooked or ignored.

I suggest such a *double* genealogical work in part because it allows one to raise some important scholarly and political questions. First, might a Western genealogy of Jullien's thought cast some doubt on the exteriority Jullien attributes to China and the thought he finds in China? In other words, might a Western genealogy of Jullien's thought reveal the extent to which Jullien ultimately remains influenced by a Western tradition of thinking that persists largely silently in his work? To be clear, the Western tradition I evoke here is *not* the one to which Jullien pays ample attention in his late work—thinkers like Plato or Aristotle whose divergence to Far Eastern thought is the subject of some of Jullien's recent books. Instead, I have in mind thinkers like Deleuze, for example, who does not receive any extensive discussion in Jullien's work, or Derrida, who is perhaps all too easily—given Byung-Chul Han's book—cast aside as "too biblical" and therefore too much within the Western tradition. How exterior is Jullien's thought *really* to the alternative Western tradition that it does not acknowledge?

The second question that can be raised is political in a different way: if there are indeed connections between what Jullien understands to be Chinese thought and Western thinkers like Deleuze, Derrida, and others, how might this make us reassess the supposed "newness" or "radicalness" attributed to those thinkers and the ruptures that their work is said to have posed? As a double genealogy of Jullien's thought would make clear, the work of such thinkers can only be considered to bring a break, to qualify as radical or new, within the limits of the Western tradition—in other words, within an understanding of philosophical thought that is largely ignorant of the thinking that Jullien finds in the Far East.

Let me explain this a bit further. Reading Jullien's work on landscape, for example, one understands that some of what is currently *en vogue* in contemporary Western thought—I am thinking of object-oriented ontology, so-called "new materialism"—could be understood as unwitting "Chinese" responses to Western thought. To say that a rock is alive is news when object-oriented ontologist Timothy Morton writes it, but it isn't in China; to think of matter as vibrant, as political philosopher Jane Bennett does, could hardly qualify as a "new" materialism in the East (see also Jullien 2009, 117: "the great image [makes phenomena] vibrate").[8] Consider the centrality of the "allusive," which is all over Jullien's writings, in Chinese thought[9]; that very term takes up a central place in the work of Graham Harman, today's most important object-oriented ontologist.[10] Or think also of Manuel de Landa's "flat ontology": Chinese thought avoids ontology, as I have discussed in chapter 2, and replaces it precisely with an aesthetics of the "flat."[11] On the one hand, this explains why these kinds of thinking have been picked up in the Chinese context, where by now—recall Jullien's "steamroller of theoretical globalization"—they may have taken on some guise of the new (though only within the Western perspective that, in China too, may have become dominant!).[12] On the other, it also reveals that Western thinkers are merely struggling at sites where Chinese thinkers have been long before. In that sense, these new fashions of thought are merely symptomatic of Western thought's limitations.

In a discussion that does not include Jullien but focuses on connections between the work of Steven Shaviro and Jane Bennett and the Chinese tradition (which remains unacknowledged in these thinkers' books), Leah Kalmanson not only does important philosophical work but also intervenes politically by making a point against "academic practices that continue to define the 'new' on Eurocentric models alone" (Kalmanson 2018, 17). "In picking her way through the thicket of materialism and vitalism in Western thought," Kalmanson writes, "Bennett has unknowingly veered close to strands of Ruism [the Chinese scholarly tradition] whose roots are in China's Song dynasty and whose branches extend throughout East Asia" (ibid., 21). No one can, of course, be a specialist of everything; but Kalmanson's point is that when such work in the Western tradition characterizes itself or gets characterized as "new," the "new" only applies within a Western perspective and holds up only within a Eurocentric model of thought.

Kalmanson argues, for example, that the critical engagement with Kant's philosophy in speculative materialism/realism is entirely anticipated in a Chinese tradition of thinking that far predates the work of those major new names associated with that development in European thought. When Shaviro writes that the "speculative aesthetics" he is interested in "is still to be constructed" (Shaviro quoted in Kalmanson 2018, 23), Kalmanson points out that it can already be found "fully developed" in "Song-Ming Ruism" (ibid., 23)—in other words, that Shaviro's claim about such an aesthetic "still [needing to] be constructed" only applies in a Western context. It is perhaps the role of Alfred North Whitehead's work and process philosophy in general in some of the work associated with speculative realism/materialism that provides the most obvious grounds for this suspicion, since there is a well-developed body of scholarship on the connections between Whitehead and Chinese thought that is worth pursuing.[13]

If the problem here is the uniquely Western lineage that scholars like Bennett and Shaviro provide for their supposedly new work in philosophy, this also enables us to challenge what at times seems to be the suggestion of a uniquely Chinese lineage for the concepts that are developed in Jullien's thought. Much of Jullien's project stands or falls with his insistence on China's "exteriority" or "elsewhere," the fact that its thought developed historically as separate from Western thought. In the same way that a uniquely Eurocentric lineage for thought is problematic, a uniquely China-centric lineage for thought seems problematic as well, and while Jullien's thought has in my view avoided such a China-centrism overall—it is very explicit, after all, about how its project operates in the in-between—its insistence on China's exteriority compared to other traditions has risked creating the suggestion that China is on this count exceptional and that what can be found in China is different from what can be found in other traditions. As I have begun to suggest, however, and will explore further in my conclusion, such exceptionalism is precisely under attack in Jullien's work, and it simply will not do to accuse him of China-centrism in the context of his overall thought.

JULLIEN AND POSTCOLONIAL THEORY

Although connections between Jullien's thought and Western philosophy can certainly be found, both connections that are explicitly acknowledged in Jullien's writing and those that are implicit and left for the attentive reader to tease out, it is perhaps not so much in philosophy that Jullien's closest interlocutors operate. While Jullien's work of course raises many questions that should, from a disciplinary point of view, be recognized as philosophical—the issues in philosophical aesthetics, for example, that I discussed in chapter 2—I have tried to indicate in this book that his import, and the critical discussion about this work, should extend far beyond that—for example, into the issue of orientalism (as first theorized by postcolonial theorist Edward Said) or, for example, into economic and political thought (scholarship about neoliberalism and sovereignty, for example). This becomes most clear when one considers the kinds of questions that Jullien's work raises and that go far beyond what one might call (to turn this phrase "purely sinological" back onto Jullien) "the purely philosophical."

To elaborate this point, I would like to return to Jullien's book about Vietnam, *Le Pont des singes: De la diversité à venir* (The monkey bridge: on diversity to come), and some questions about this book that I left unaddressed when I discussed it in chapter 1. In the introductory italicized pages that function as a contextualization for that book, Jullien reports that he was invited to Vietnam by the Vietnamese Ministry of Culture. Given this context, it is perhaps not surprising, as Jullien himself notes, that there were some critical questions after his talk, which laid out a criticism of identity and specifically of cultural difference. Specifically, Jullien was asked whether he does not promote the value of French identity (Jullien 2010, 14) through his work. Jullien responds that he does not, an answer that is perfectly consistent with his position: he explains that he defends the resources of French culture, resources that are not "French" in any identitarian or essentialist way and that are open to all.

Still, one might wonder whether this position—Jullien's very criticism of the logic of identity—isn't ultimately a very French position, one that in Vietnam—a postcolonial nation-state that is not a major nation and wasn't always able to take its identity (national, cultural) for granted—makes less sense. Couldn't Jullien's argument be read as a typical case of exporting an identity in the guise of nonidentity (similar to how, according to some analyses, the secular promotes Christianity in disguise[14])? But which identity is Jullien promoting, then? If anything, it seems that Jullien's position when it comes to identity, individual and cultural, is rooted in ancient and classical *Chinese* thought. If identitarian import from France is already a sensitive issue in Vietnam due to colonial history, identitarian import from China certainly is as well. The turn to China cannot save Jullien from these questions about colonialism and its export of identity and the often-hidden ways in which such export continues today.

I have parenthetically suggested a parallel with debates about secularism (specifically secularized Christianity) in France due to a moment, early on in Jullien's text, where he notes his opposition to the veil (chador) as a marker of the inequality between the sexes that in his view makes the common impossible (Jullien 2010, 18). The veil is in conflict with what Jullien presents to be a cultural resource of the West—namely, the hard-won equality between the sexes (I have already criticized this position from the Western point of view in my introduction). For Jullien, the veil represents an "ideological regression" (ibid.) that must be resisted. However, and this is the line of critique that I want to pursue here, Jullien's position does not come with a discussion of Islam—though he notes he is not opposed to Islam—or a consideration of different significations of the veil. In fact, at several moments in his work, Jullien dismisses Islam as a site for careful study because it is, in his view, too close still to the West; for his purposes, it is not sufficiently "exterior" to the Western tradition.

That said, Jullien has of course paid plenty of attention to the Western tradition—though not the Arab world—and has in recent years even begun to write explicitly about Christianity, considering its cultural resources. It ought to be noted, however, that Jullien has paid no such attention to Islam in his work. What are Islam's resources? What might a careful study of Islam reveal about the veil as a resource? *Le pont des singes* never considers this.

The issue can be pushed further. Jullien rejects Islamic thought in this context, for example, as not being elsewhere enough, as remaining too much within the Western tradition. Jullien's own work, however, does not escape that pull of Western thought either: this is evident not only from the Western genealogy of his thinking that can be provided (and that I am trying to provide, however summarily, in this chapter) but also from, for example, the complicated role of orientalism in his work that I laid out in detail in chapter 1. Whenever Jullien indicates, for example, that Islam is not sufficiently "exterior" to the Western tradition to deserve his careful attention, this is not backed up with evidence; but even for a reader like myself, who has only read occasional works in that tradition, connections between Jullien's work and, for example, the thought of Moroccan poet and theorist Abdelkébir Khatibi, who would likely challenge the grounds of Jullien's rejection of Islam, immediately stand out.

Khatibi is, of course, hardly an innocent example in this context. In his book *Figures de l'étranger dans la littérature française* (Figures of the stranger in French literature), he begins by considering specifically exoticism in literature about both the Far East and the Arab Orient (Khatibi 1987, 9) as well as (as a point of contrast) so-called "black Africa" or sub-Saharan Africa. The latter constitutes a point of contrast, because, while Khatibi finds a positive orientalism of the Far East and the Arab Orient, he can locate no such passages about Africa, which remains, in his analysis, "vraiment un continent noir dans cet imaginaire, une sorte de planète inconnue" (truly a black continent in this imaginary, a sort of unknown planet; ibid., 10). Ultimately, he widens his scope to look at exoticism that is internal to all literature (he mentions literature's "exoticism du dedans," "exoticism from within"; ibid.) rather than just literature that looks at the Far East, the Arab Orient, or sub-Saharan Africa as external or outside. But Khatibi finds the issue especially pressing with reference to the Arab world, which is "more familiar [to him] and therefore more real and problematic" (ibid., 14).

One of the figures to whom Khatibi devotes a chapter in his book is nineteenth-century writer (and, by some accounts, sinologist) Victor Segalen, whose effort to "faire sortir la littérature française de son ethnocentrisme et de ses domaines trop nationalistes" (to make French literature leave behind its ethnocentrism and those areas where it is too nationalist; Khatibi 1987, 15) Khatibi admires. Still, Khatibi's chapter will also end up criticizing Segalen for ultimately succumbing to what Khatibi characterizes as "aristocratic atavism" (ibid., 52) and a return to some of the values and prejudices that Segalen's work also takes on.[15] Khatibi admires Segalen's attempt to subject himself to the "exigence du dehors"—the "exigency of the outside" (15), a phrase that recalls Jullien's characterization of his own method as a "deconstruction du dehors"—a "deconstruction from the outside." Indeed, Segalen and the discussion of Segalen's exoticism that is central to Khatibi's chapter are important in the reception of Jullien's work as well, where Segalen is often referenced in reviews of Jullien's books or critical articles on his work.[16] Khatibi seeks to show that, in Segalen, the *exote*—a term that is recuperated from the bad connotations of the term "exoticism"—is precisely someone who is oriented toward the outside, the *dehors* or the "ex," and this sets the *exote* apart from both the tourist and the folklorist (two other figures that Segalen distinguishes). It is, however, in view of the risk of exoticism in this "celebration of the *exote*" (which is the title of Khatibi's chapter on Segalen) that Jullien takes on the notion of "the ex-optic," proposed by Italian philosopher Remo Bodei, to distinguish his own approach from the exoticism to which Segalen's work ultimately always risks falling prey (as Khatibi's analysis makes clear).

In principle, however, the *exote*'s orientation to the outside is opposed to the folklorist's approach (which provides the pretense of "local color"; Khatibi 1987, 26) and colonial literature/tourism. Instead, it seeks to make room for the "unassimilable" (*l'inassimilable*)—for what cannot be assimilated, neither in literature nor in politics (ibid., 29). It's on this count that Khatibi establishes a connection to both the *dao*, or the path without a predetermined end goal (ibid., 29), which he then also characterizes as "*inouï*"—"unheard-of" (ibid.). Khatibi has elsewhere in his work shown himself to be very interested in Daoism, something that partly justifies my bringing his work in conversation with Jullien.

Of course, the notion of the "unheard-of" is, as I discussed in my introduction, crucial to Jullien's late thought and intimately connected to the work that Jullien has done on China. The unheard-of appears frequently in Khatibi as well, but it may be that both Khatibi and Jullien inherit it from Roland Barthes, in whose work—which is a key reference for both of them—the notion also takes up an important role.[17] In Khatibi's chapter on Barthes, which directly follows that on Segalen, he characterizes Barthes' work as being oriented toward the unheard-of (*l'inouï*; Khatibi 1987, 66) and expressing "a joy of the unheard-of" (*une joie de l'inouï*; ibid., 67). Barthes' work on the neutral—which is developed in a lecture course at the Collège de France dating some ten years before Khatibi's *Figures de l'étranger*—is tied there to "emptiness according to the Tao" and "the active emptiness" that the *dao* evokes (68 and 69).[18] In the final, more thetic part of the chapter on Barthes, Khatibi dedicates an entire section to the unheard-of, quoting from Barthes' book on Japan in which the unheard-of takes up a central place: in Bunraku theater, an unheard-of effect/an effect of the unheard-of is produced, "transforming what is silent into the unheard-of" (*Ce qui est silencieux devient inouï*; 82). It's very likely, then, that the unheard-of ends up in Jullien's oeuvre via the same path that it ends up in the writings of Khatibi: via Roland Barthes.

And "the unheard-of" is only one common term between Khatibi's work and Jullien's. Khatibi uses the notion *écart*, "divergence," as well, even if he does not elaborate it in the way Jullien does (Khabiti remains a thinker of difference and alterity influenced by Derrida as well as Maurice Blanchot and does not articulate the tension between difference and alterity and distance and exteriority in the same, elaborate way as Jullien does—this in spite of his interest in Segalen's thinking from the *dehors*, "outside"). Khatibi's *pensée-autre* (other-thinking) does, however, provide further interesting points of contact with Jullien—in particular, *critical* points of contrast. I have noted that Jullien leaves Islam aside as a site of philosophical reflection because it is, in his view, not exterior enough to the Western tradition. It is too close to the Judeo-Christian framework to constitute the outside that Jullien finds in China. However, Khatibi enables one to challenge Jullien's view precisely by "pluralizing the Maghreb"—by thinking a Maghreb that is plural, a *Maghreb pluriel*, to use Khatibi's term. (It's worth noting that Khatibi applies this to Islam as well, laying out and pursuing the task of "relire le Coran selon une pensée autre," "rereading the Koran according to other-thinking"; Khatibi 1983, 154.) This means precisely to wrest the Maghreb away *both* from how it is perceived by those outside of it (often in orientalist terms) *and* from its own ideological self-perception: this is the "double critique" for which Khatibi is calling (ibid., 12). Other-thinking leads into the "divergence" (*écart*) of the notion of the Maghreb itself, its liberation from ideological constructions from outside and within into what Khatibi with another term that is crucial in Jullien's work calls the Maghreb's *impensé*—the Maghreb's "unthought" (ibid., 14). Language and, specifically, "bilinguism" play an important role in this for Khatibi, as a pluralization of language that goes "beyond Babel" ("au-delà de toute tour de Babel"; ibid., 197) and needs to be applied to each language individually to make it decoincide with itself, to unwork it into something other than what it is (he proposes in this context the productively disorienting formulation of "traduire du français en français" [to translate from French into French], ibid., 207). This focus on language further resonates with Jullien's overall method, in which translation plays a crucial role. In Jullien's late work, it is translation that becomes the linguistic environment for "divergence" and the "in-between."

For Khatibi, importantly, such a plural thought of the Maghreb must be risked in order to "decolonize" thought (Khatibi 1983, 16). At the beginning of the chapter titled "Pensée-autre" (Other-thinking), Khatibi takes his cue from colonial scholar Frantz Fanon, who, as Khatibi recalls, "made the following appeal: 'Come, comrades, the European game is finally over, we must look for something else'" (ibid., 11). It's the search for that "something else" that drives Khatibi's critical project of pluralizing the Maghreb. "Se décoloniser, c'est cette chance de la pensée," as he writes: "To decolonize oneself is the chance of thought" (ibid., 16). This idea very much resonates with Jullien's statement that "Babel is the chance of thought," which I quoted in chapter 1. But it is important to note that Jullien's "Babel" is hardly Khatibi's "decolonization." Indeed, Khatibi points out that, for him, Babel does not go far enough, which I read as "remains too noncommittal." For Khatibi, it is the "Third World" that presents this chance of thought. Jullien, however, does not focus on the Third World and does not turn decolonization into a major concern in this work.

Khatibi's overall approach to the Maghreb thus casts some doubt on Jullien's all-too-quick rejection of Islam, or of Islam's construction from both the outside and the inside. Khatibi is precisely seeking to turn Islam into an exterior, the kind of exterior that Jullien finds in China. In other words, when Jullien speaks of Islam as being too much "within," one has to ask, *Which Islam?* Khatibi's work enables one to raise precisely this question and move toward the Maghreb's—and, by extension, Islam's—unthought. In his view, this means to pursue a "minoritarian, marginal, fragmentary and incomplete" (Khatibi 1983, 18) Maghreb; it means to move away from a majoritarian thought that is always a thought of "ethnocide" (ibid.), as he puts it. The Maghreb as a notion thus becomes what Khatibi allows one to characterize—in contrast with the ideological thought of the Maghreb by Abdellah Laroui that he criticizes—as a "horizon" of thought in a strong philosophical sense, as a notion that never quite coincides with itself, that cannot be essentialized, that is not identitarian but much closer to the active emptiness of the *dao*.[19] This is an understanding of the Maghreb as "*dao*" or "path," of the Maghreb as "method" (to use the Greek word for "path"; see Harrison 2018a), with the understanding that no predetermined goal for this method has been stated. As Khatibi summarizes in a passage that could just as well apply to Jullien's China,

> D'une part, il faut écouter le Maghreb résonner dans sa pluralité (linguistique, culturelle, politique), et d'autre part, seul le dehors repensé, décentré, subverti, détourné de ses déterminations dominantes, peut nous éloigner des identités et des différences informulées. (Khatibi 1983, 39)
>
> On the one hand, one must hear the Maghreb resonate in its plurality (linguistic, cultural, political) and, on the other hand, only an outside that is rethought, decentered, subverted, turned away from its dominant determinations, can remove us from half-baked identities and differences.

While Khatibi establishes connections to Far Eastern thought to arrive at this understanding of Islam and the Maghreb, one does not get the sense that Far Eastern thought is produced by that understanding in the way that it is in Jullien. Rather, it is Fanon who triggers Khatibi's pluralization of the Maghreb, in addition to a thinking about difference and alterity associated with deconstruction (deconstruction "from within," if we are to follow Jullien's characterization of Derridean deconstruction). Still, one can easily tease out the connections and, considering Khatibi's work on Islam and the Maghreb in this context in fact pushes questions not only in postcolonial studies but also in black studies that provide interesting—though neglected—critical angles into Jullien's work.

INDIGENEITY AND BLACK STUDIES

Before I consider some connections between Jullien's work and black studies, I want to briefly discuss some further issues related to colonialism that appear in *Le pont des singes*. These pertain to the word "indigenous," a term that, while initially used in relation to plants and animals native to a region, came to be applied to people as well during the colonial area but has very different uses in France and in the United States (from where I am writing). In *Le pont des singes*, Jullien uses the term *indigène* as part of a criticism of tourism.[20] While *Le pont des singes* is not a treatise against tourism, per se, it does decry a tourism that operates in relations of inequality, in which one population is alienated from another (Jullien 2010, 26). The book decries, specifically, a tourism that operates with a "simulacrum of strangeness" (ibid., 27). It's in this context that Jullien writes of "the theater of indigeneity": "charged with incarnating the tradition of ancestral mores, [indigenous peoples] are meant to display a pseudostrangeness" (ibid.). It's precisely *because* they are forced into alienation that as indigenous peoples they are then *forced* to produce an identity that is a *pseudoidentity*: they are forced to respond to the tourist's authenticity fetish with an identity they perform. As Jullien puts it, in French, there's *indignity* (ibid., 29) in *indigeneity*. It needs to be resisted.

In English, however, one may want to modify the pun of this last statement to "there's indignity in *this kind of* indigeneity" to allow for the different connotations that "indigeneity" carries in the United States. Whereas in the United States there has been a broad "positive" recuperation of the term "indigenous" to refer to those peoples who lived on land currently located in the United States before the white colonizers arrived, such a use of the term is extremely rare in France. In fact, no French person would refer to people living in Vietnam today using the term *indigène* or "native"; it would be considered a highly problematic, colonial/racist use of the term. One assumes that Jullien would justify his provocative use of the term in this context citing at least two reasons: first, because of France's historical colonial presence in Vietnam, which ended only as recently as 1954, and second, because of Jullien's critical construction of postcolonial tourism as a continued relation of colonialism. The provocation of the term's use in French is less legible in my English renderings of Jullien's argument.

While Jullien's criticism of the theater of indigeneity does not necessarily reject the notion of indigeneity at large, one assumes that (1) as a colonial invention and (2) as a term that is related to identity (even if it is the historically/colonially constructed identity of the indigenous person) it does not carry Jullien's favor. But it is worth pausing for a moment over the term "indigeneity" and some recent debate it has received in France. In an interview with Nicolas Martin and Antoine Spire, Jullien mentions that *Le pont des singes* got him invited to present his work "au sein d'associations qui travaillent en banlieue sur les questions d'immigration et d'intégration" (at the heart of associations that work in the banlieue on questions of immigration and integration; Martin and Spire 2011, 263). I have been unable to find any record of these presentations, but one cannot help but wonder, in view of, for example, the movement and self-declared political party Les Indigènes de la République,[21] alternatively translated as "Indigenous Peoples of the Republic" or "Natives of the Republic" (and translating the French context to the US context, perhaps the latter ought to be preferred?—the use of *indigènes* here is clearly meant to evoke colonial history), about how Jullien's rejection of indigeneity in the context of his criticism of tourism was received in view of indigeneity's reappropriation as a political identifier in the banlieue. Polemicist Houria Bouteldja and her collaborators have come to refer to themselves as *indigènes*, using the colonial term, precisely to mark their continued second-class status in the French Republic, which prides itself so much on the values of liberty, equality, fraternity. The term is not so much rejected here but recuperated as part of a project of resistance and emancipation, much in the same way that other such terms—think of "queer," for example—were recuperated as part of political struggle. I mention this because the recuperation of indigeneity by Bouteldja and company poses a challenge to Jullien's critique of identity and its rejection of indigeneity.[22] In both this case and the case of those who questioned Jullien's criticism of identity after he spoke in Vietnam, these challenges are driven by a more nuanced attunement to the colonial situation than Jullien's position on identity enables us to provide.

The set of issues that I have raised with respect to *Le pont des singes* are not, from a disciplinary point of view, philosophical questions. They are all issues, rather, that trouble the "purely philosophical" and infuse it with the impurity of history and politics, which is complicated and layered. (Separate books have, in fact, been written or are being written about each of these issues, and I can hardly be expected to do justice to them here.) If I were asked to attach a disciplinary name to these issues, one that goes beyond the vague generality of history and politics, I might suggest that they emerge from postcolonial theory (combined with feminist studies in the case of the veil, or with indigenous studies and critical race theory in the discussion of the term *indigènes*). While, as a field, postcolonial theory is arguably founded by the publication of Said's book *Orientalism* in 1978, its arrival in France (in French translation) was delayed until the 1990s, and as such it is perhaps no surprise that one sees no postcolonial theory referenced in Jullien's work. At the same time, Jullien shares some of his positions with postcolonial theory— his criticism of orientalism, for example—even if there are also aspects of his work that, from a postcolonial point of view, would demand close scrutiny. My point, however, is that, beyond Jullien's strictly speaking "philosophical" interlocutors, and beyond the philosophical questions that can be raised of his work, there is a productive conversation to be had between Jullien and postcolonial theory, and postcolonial theory enables one to ask sharp questions about Jullien's project and appreciate—critically—what it seeks to accomplish. I have tried to contribute to such a conversation, of course, through my negotiation of Jullien's orientalism in chapter 1.

Even when it comes to the philosophical stakes of Jullien's work, it seems to me that affinities can be found between his thought and thinking that is not strictly speaking characterized as "philosophical." Consider, for example, Jullien's discussion of Western ontology and of how Chinese thought escapes its logic of unified Being and presence—a point that others, before Jullien, had already made. Jullien characterizes Chinese thought as nonontological in this context and distinguishes from the logic of unified Being and presence that of "the silent transformations," the small changes of the everyday that ultimate added up to an event that, in Western thought, seems to come out of nowhere but that, in Chinese thought, began far upstream and ought to be understood and anticipated as such. Western thought quite simply does not see or hear the silent transformations (hence also Jullien's central notion of "the unheard-of"), which Jullien can hence characterize as Western thought's "unthought."

The turn toward the unheard-of, or the insistence on what was previously unheard or unseen, recalls the work of another contemporary philosopher, Jacques Rancière, who has in his books defined politics precisely as a subject acting to make something that was previously unseen or unheard seen or heard—in other words, as aesthetics, as a politics of the sensible. Such acts often take the form of a catachrestic gesture, by fusing two worlds into one that were previously thought to be separate. While this idea of fusion, and the ultimate folding of the negative into a new positive that it always entails, is much too dialectical (and Hegelian) for Jullien, Rancière's focus on what he calls a "distribution of the sensible" (Rancière 2010) in this context (a political distribution of what can or cannot be seen or heard) is helpful in terms of singling out the Western distribution of the sensible when it comes to ontology and the silent transformations that it overlooks. Clearly, however, Rancière's thought is not going to overcome such a problem, even if it contains criticisms of exceptionalism that can, I think, be brought in conversation with Jullien's thought. (Rancière distinguishes, for example, his work from that of his colleague Alain Badiou by saying that if there is an exception in his work—as there is in Badiou—it is not that of the big rupture [that, in Jullien's analysis, characterizes Western thought; Badiou is Jullien's example] but one of a "multiplicity of small displacements" [Geil 2014] [of the small transformations that Jullien associates with Chinese thought]). I bring up Rancière to consider how ontology is a distribution of the sensible and to think about Jullien's challenge to ontology (through the detour of China) as precisely a challenge to such a distribution. But this is hardly a "purely philosophical" issue.

One other contemporary thinker—critic, critical theorist, poet—who has pursued such a challenge is black studies scholar Fred Moten, who has put forth in his work a theorization of "the paraontological." Moten develops this notion (after Dimitri Nahum Chandler) in response to Western ontology, which is, he argues, a "white" ontology that under the guise of universality refuses to think blackness. As he puts it in a lengthy, beautifully lyrical, and intensely political article titled "Blackness and Nothingness (Mysticism in the Flesh)",

> Blackness is prior to ontology. . . . blackness is the anoriginal displacement of ontology . . . ontology's anti- and ante-foundation, ontology's underground, the irreparable disturbance of ontology's time and space. (Moten 2013, 739)

Blackness—both in an identitarian way, as a condition that is particularly felt by black bodies, but also in a more general sense, as a structural condition that does not depend on one's skin color (Moten distinguishes between "blackness and blacks"; Moten 2013, 749)—is precisely not covered by the ontological, and it is to move toward the philosophical thinking of blackness that Moten proposes his notion. The paraontological, in such a project, captures what resides "next to" or "para" ontology. It captures the "nothingness" of blackness, the particular "nothingness"—which is evidently not nothing—that it marks. It is on this count, perhaps not surprisingly at this point, that Moten turns to Far Eastern thought and specifically the notion of *wu* (nothing, 無) that I already discussed in chapter 3, when I commented on the legacy of the phrase *wu wei* (無爲), "do nothing," in laissez-faire economics. It's Moten who brings the "Chinese" idea of an active emptiness, also associated with the *dao* (as I have discussed), together with a black paraontology and politics of resistance that can—in his view—be associated with Frantz Fanon (ibid., 750). If Fanon was one of the counts still on which Jullien's thought, which founds its possibility in Babel, distinguished itself from Khatibi's thought, which found its possibility in decolonization and the Third World, Moten's intervention in black studies establishes a connection even on this count—between Far Eastern thought and Fanon. The thought of the *dao*, and specifically of *wu*, is a thought that puts being on hold rather than "in the hold," (ibid.) as Moten's reference to the slave ship has it. But it is also through its attention to the hold that black studies (as Moten sees it) "disrupts" (ibid., 751) the nothingness of Far Eastern thought, forcing "'the real presence' of blackness" (ibid.) back into it and working both with and against the suspension that it brings. There is, clearly, something to be learned from and resisted within the paraontological. In Khatibi's words, what's needed is a "double critique," both of the paraontological (as subject genitive: the paraontological *suspends* in the way that *wu* suspends) and of the paraontological (as object genitive: the paraontological *is suspended* by "'the real presence' of blackness").

Moten's choice (after Chandler) for the preposition "para" or "next to" in this context is worth pausing over, because it marks a moving sideways rather than up or down or inside or out. If up/down or in/out can easily be appropriated within the dialectical (Hegelian) model that I discussed in previous chapters, this is more difficult to do with the horizontal dynamic of the next-to, which posits itself on the same plane as whatever it pre-poses. Still, even in the intervention of such a sideways move, the para maintains a hyphenation to the ontological, a tie to the ontological that Jullien, in his work on China, would not be willing to grant. China is not next to ontology; it is beyond it; it never even considered it. The exteriority of its elsewhere exceeds the relationality that the "para" still maintains. Moten flirts with such an outside. "On the one hand," he writes, "blackness and ontology are unavailable to each other" (Moten 2013, 749)—and the project of paraontology seeks to remedy that situation. "On the other hand," he continues, "blackness must free itself from ontological expectation, must refuse subjection to ontology's sanction against the very idea of black subjectivity" (ibid.). The more radical conclusion would simply be to reject ontology altogether. However, Moten might consider such a conclusion irresponsible from the point of view of a history in which whiteness and blackness have been coconstituted in ontology, through ontology. In other words, while blackness might desire the outside of China, it cannot have such luxury from the point of history.[23] The question that Moten enables us to cast back onto Jullien, then, is whether China itself can ever be the site of such an outside, an outside that is of course central to its orientalist fantasy.

AT THE LIMITS OF PHILOSOPHY

These are issues that emerge at the limits of philosophy and what, in its disciplinary formation, it normally thinks. I insist on this even if of course to separate between sinology, black studies, postcolonial theory, and philosophy is problematic. One need only recall Jacques Derrida's infamous remark (made in 2001 during a lunch at the French consulate in Shanghai) that China "does not have any philosophy, only thought" (Jones-Katz 2019). The remark triggered a scandal, no doubt partly in view of Derrida's dubious use of China in *Of Grammatology*; after all, Derrida seems to suggest that there is no such thing as Chinese philosophy but that the Chinese *merely* think, perhaps think a thought that does not rise up to the standards of philosophy. But Derrida meant something quite different, as can be explained through a passage from his book *Ethics, Institutions, and the Right to Philosophy*:

> Today it's a well-known phenomenon—there is a Chinese philosophy, a Japanese philosophy, and so on and so forth. That's a contention I would resist. I think there is [too much] specifically European, specifically Greek, in philosophy to simply say that philosophy is something universal. Now saying this, I think that every kind of thinking is philosophical. I will distinguish philosophy and *Denken*, thinking. Philosophy is a way of thinking . . . so when I say, well, philosophy has some privileged relationship with Europe, I don't say this Eurocentrically but to take [history seriously]. That's one temptation, to say philosophy is universal. (Derrida quoted in Nelson 2011, 384)

In other words, Derrida pursues the risky distinction between thought and philosophy precisely *to avoid* the kinds of accusations that were thrown his way when he distinguished in Shanghai between "philosophy" and "Chinese thought." He hesitates to use the term "philosophy" to describe Chinese thought precisely to avoid bringing Chinese thought within the purview of Europe. Instead, another name must be invented. It's this challenge that the scandalous reception of his remarks all too easily overlooks.

Like Derrida, I have tried to work at the limits of philosophy and its privileged relation to Europe, suggesting that, although Jullien's thought of course connects to European thought, it resonates perhaps more with what happens at the limits of both the European and the philosophical, in postcolonial theory, for example, or black studies. This also means that, while Jullien's work is important to read for philosophers, I also think it is important to consider it in postcolonial theory and black studies, where it has not yet received the reception it deserves. Much as Jullien himself has tried to avoid his work being limited to sinology alone, and has pushed his thought into the realm of philosophy where it has increasingly begun to find a home (in part through the late phase of Jullien's work, which is focused on European thought), it is still not a very well-known reference in philosophy, and to my knowledge it has received very little, almost no, consideration in black studies or postcolonial thought outside of the one or two references that I have included in this book.[24] It's to those encounters that this book hopes to contribute.

NOTES

1. Khatibi 1987, 21.

2. In chapter 2, I pursued a comparative discussion of Jullien and Agamben because of the specific thinking on form and politics that it enabled me to open up in Jullien's thought on aesthetics.

3. I hesitate slightly because he has published a text in English that is titled "Rethinking Comparison" and suggests that it is not so much about rejecting comparison as about practicing it otherwise (Jullien 2012). The words "compare" and "comparison" appear elsewhere in his work as well as descriptors of his method.

4. Jullien has addressed this issue further in Jullien 2014 and Jullien 2016, where he distinguishes between a thought of the universal (which he claims as a "rebellious" negative that "undoes the comfort of all arrested positivity"; Jullien 2016, 27) and the ideology of universalism.

5. This echo of Simondon is strengthened in some quotations that follow from Wang Fuzhi's writing about landscape.

6. To characterize deconstruction as Chinese is nothing new: Haun Saussy writes critically of those proposing that "China is deconstruction" in his book from 2001.

7. I am thinking, for example, of the work of Yuk Hui, both Hui 2016a and Hui 2016b. Note that the role of Jullien in Hui 2016b is not reconciled, as Jullien's characterization of Chinese thought as nonontological and nonmetaphysical does not match Hui's discussion of it, even if Jullien has a role, for example, in Hui's discussion of the Chinese conception of time.

8. Peng Yu has already made this point: Yu 2016, 105.

9. See, for example, Jullien 2000, where the allusive is central to Chinese strategies of meaning.

10. Spivak notes in 1981 that according to *Tel Quel*'s Philippe Sollers in 1980, the journal's interest in China "has now been superseded" (Spivak 1981, 157). It seems it could be productive to consider, however, these new articulations of Western thought within a similar framework.

11. This is most explicit in Jullien's still-untranslated book on Chinese wisdom (Jullien 1998) in which the flat (*le plat*) appears in close connection with the "ordinary" as a theme.

12. Consider, for example, Di'an and Ga 2015. The book includes contributions by Timothy Morton and Graham Harman, among others, as well as texts by Chinese scholars and curators who establish connections between object-oriented ontology and Chinese thought.

13. See, for example, Meijun and Zhihe 2015, but there are many other articles. Jullien uses an epigraph by Whitehead and discusses Whitehead in relation to Chinese thought in Jullien 1983.

14. I am thinking here of the work of Gil Anidjar, among others.

15. It's worth noting that in the fact that it finds something useful in the orientalists it criticizes, *Figures de l'étranger* is quite different from Said's *Orientalism*.

16. I am thinking in particular of the work of Esther Lin, Jullien's Chinese translator, who wrote her doctoral dissertation about Segalen and has been exploring some connections between Segalen and Jullien in her research.

17. On the connection between Barthes and Khatibi, see Knight 1997, 137–40.

18. I've noted previously that this work is closest to Jullien's work on China—whereas Jullien is in fact very critical of Barthes' actual writings on China.

19. Interestingly, Jullien's use of the word "horizon" enables us to associate Khatibi's pluralization of the Maghreb with Jullien's critical thought of the universal: "Universel régulateur (au sens de l'idée kantienne) qui, parce qu'il n'est jamais satisfait, ne cesse de repousser l'horizon et donne indéfiniment à chercher"—"A regulative universal (in the Kantian sense) which, because it is never satisfied, never ceases to push back the horizon and indefinitely leads to further searching"; Jullien 2016, 27.

20. I would like to thank Olivia C. Harrison for advising me on this particular issue.

21. See http://indigenes-republique.fr.

22. See Harrison 2018b.

23. Robeson Taj Frazier's book *The East Is Black*, which I already discussed in chapter 1, does provide glimpses into the black experience of such an outside when it considers accounts of black Americans traveling to China and not experiencing the racism there that pervades their lives back home. In the East, blackness is not construed in the same way; certainly it is not construed by, and through, ontology, since—if we follow Jullien—Chinese thought lacks ontology (Frazier 2015).

24. One notable exception here is Coombs 2018, in which a critical dialogue is staged between the work of Édouard Glissant and that of Jullien.

REFERENCES

Barthes, Roland. 1978. *Leçon*. Paris: Seuil.
Coombs, Sam. 2018. *Édouard Glissant*. London: Bloomsbury.
Deleuze, Gilles, and Félix Guattari. 1996. *What Is Philosophy?* Translated by Graham Burchell. New York: Columbia University Press.
Di'an, Fan, and Zhang Ga, eds. 2014. *Thingworld: International Triennial of New Media Art*. Liverpool: Liverpool University Press.
Frazier, Robeson Taj. 2015. *The East Is Black: Cold War China and the Black Radical Imagination*. Durham: Duke University Press.
Geil, Abraham. 2014. "Writing, Repetition, Displacement: An Interview with Jacques Rancière." *Novel* 47 (2): 301–10.
Han, Byung-Chul. 2017. *Shanzhai: Deconstruction in Chinese*. Translated by Philippa Hurd. Boston: MIT Press.
Harrison, Olivia C. 2018a. "Maghreb as Method." *boundary 2*. https://www.boundary2.org/2018/12/olivia-c-harrison-thinking-the-maghreb-with-said-and-khatibi/.
———. 2018b. "Whither Anti-racism? Farida Belghoul, Les Indigènes de la République, and the Contest for Indigeneity in France." *Diacritics* 46 (3): 54–77.
Hui, Yuk. 2016a. *On the Mode of Existence of Digital Objects*. Minneapolis: University of Minnesota Press.
———. 2016b. *The Question Concerning Technology in China: An Essay in Cosmotechnics*. Falmouth: Urbanomic.
Jones-Katz, Gregory. 2019. "Where Is Deconstruction Today? On Jacques Derrida's *Theory and Practice* and Byung-Chul Han's *Shanzhai: Deconstruction in Chinese*." *Los Angeles Review of Books* 05/08/2019. https://lareviewofbooks.org/article/where-is-deconstruction-today-on-jacques-derridas-theory-and-practice-and-byung-chul-hans-shanzhai-deconstruction-in-chinese/.
Jullien, François. 1983. "Notes de lecture." *Extrême-Orient, Extrême-Occident* 3: 113–15.
———. 1995. *The Propensity of Things: Toward a History of Efficacy in China*. Translated by Janet Lloyd. New York: Zone Books.
———. 1998. *Un sage est sans idée, Ou: L'autre de la philosophie*. Paris: Seuil.
———. 2000. *Detour and Access: Strategies of Meaning in China and Greece*. Translated by Sophie Hawkes. New York: Zone Books.
———. 2004. *A Treatise on Efficacy: Between Western and Chinese Thinking*. Translated by Janet Lloyd. Honolulu: University of Hawai'i Press.
———. 2008. *In Praise of Blandness: Proceeding from Chinese Thought and Aesthetics*. Translated by Paula M. Varsano. New York: Zone Books.
———. 2009. *The Great Image Has No Form, or On the Nonobject through Painting*. Translated by Jane Marie Todd. Chicago: University of Chicago Press.
———. 2010. *Le Pont des singes: De la diversité à venir. Fécondité culturelle face à identité nationale*. Paris: Galilée.
———. 2011. *The Silent Transformations*. Translated by Krzystof Fijalkowski and Michael Richardson. London: Seagull.

———. 2014. *On the Universal: The Uniform, The Common, and Dialogue between Cultures*. Translated by Michael Richardson and Krzysztof Fijalkowski. Cambridge: Polity.

———. 2016. *Il n'y a pas d'identité culturelle; mais nous défendons les ressources d'une culture*. Paris: L'Herne.

———. 2018. *Living Off Landscape or the Unthought-of in Reason*. Translated by Pedro Rodriguez. London: Rowman & Littlefield.

Kalmanson, Leah. 2018. "Speculation as Transformation in Chinese Philosophy: On Speculative Realism, 'New' Materialism, and the Study of Li and Qi." *Journal of World Philosophies* 3 (Summer): 17–30.

Khatibi, Abdelkébir. 1983. *Maghreb pluriel*. Paris: Denoël.

———. 1987. *Figures de l'étranger dans la littérature française*. Paris: Denoël.

Knight, Diana. 1997. *Barthes and Utopia: Space, Travel, Writing*. Oxford: Clarendon Press.

Lachman, Charles. 2011. Review of *The Great Image Has No Form, or On the Nonobject Through Painting*, by François Jullien. *The China Journal* 66: 233–34.

Martin, Nicolas, and Antoine Spire. 2011. *Chine, la dissidence de François Jullien. Suivi de: Dialogues avec François Jullien*. Paris: Seuil.

Meijun, Fan, and Wang Zhihe. 2015. "Toward a Complementary Consciousness and Mutual Flourishing of Chinese and Western Cultures: The Contributions of Process Philosophers." *Philosophy East & West* 65 (1): 276–97.

Moten, Fred. 2013. "Blackness and Nothingness (Mysticism in the Flesh)." *South Atlantic Quarterly* 112 (4): 737–80.

Nelson, Eric S. 2011. "The *Yijing* and Philosophy from Leibniz to Derrida." *Journal of Chinese Philosophy* 38 (3): 377–96.

Rancière, Jacques. 2010. *Dissensus: On Politics and Aesthetics*. Translated by Steven Corcoran. London: Continuum.

Saussy, Haun. 2001. *Great Walls of Discourse and Other Adventures in Cultural China*. Cambridge: Harvard University Press.

Simondon, Gilbert. 2007. *L'Individuation psychique et collective*. Paris: Aubier.

Spivak, Gayatri Chakravorty. 1981. "French Feminism in an International Frame." *Yale French Studies* 62: 154–84.

Yu, Peng. 2016. "Zones of Indeterminacy: Art, Body, and Politics in Daoist Thought." *Theory, Culture, and Society* 33 (1): 93–114.

Conclusion: For Future François Julliens

> The image of what constantly flows past our feet . . . is totally unexceptional, yet its repercussions at the theoretical level are endless.
>
> —François Jullien, *A Treatise on Efficacy*[1]

THE UNEXCEPTIONAL

In the chapters that constitute this book, I have characterized the thought of François Jullien as "unexceptional." As I noted in chapter 2, "the unexceptional" is not a key term in Jullien's thought, even if it does appear in it occasionally. The term's opposite, "exceptional," appears frequently, on the other hand, when Jullien characterizes Western thought in its divergence from Chinese thought. To characterize Chinese thought, however, Jullien rarely opts for unexceptional; instead, he uses "facile" (in the final chapter of his *Treatise on Efficacy: Between Western and Chinese Thinking*, where the word "unexceptional" also appears) or, more commonly, "bland." In the last phase of his career, he has also begun to develop the word *inouï*, "unheard-of," as part of this chain.

But is "the unexceptional" the opposite of "the exceptional"? If I opt for this term here, it is precisely to avoid such an easy opposition of notions. Oppositionality is, indeed, not a very Chinese mode of relation; much in Jullien's work resists it and the dialectical operations on negativity that follow from it within the Western tradition. From China, Jullien takes, rather, the regulatory principle of respiration, which is continuously moving between breathing in and breathing out, and combines yin and yang into a dynamic unity. Jullien considers this philosophical shift to apply in the moral realm as well and embraces the dynamic unity of right and wrong rather than their opposition and the impossible, always-guilt-ridden relation to the wrong that it produces. When Jullien speaks of "the unheard-of," then, or of "the bland," "the facile," and, yes, "the unexceptional," part of the challenge is to break out of the (dialectical) logic of opposition and discover the principle of regulation within these notions, with the unexceptional always existing in a dynamic relation with the exceptional. The bland, as a name for practicing "the greatest reserve," thus reveals "the strongest presence" (Jullien 2008b, 52), as Jullien indicates in his book *In Praise of Blandness*. "The unheard-of" refers to that which is unheard-of but also to that which has never been heard of before. If "the facile" is a term that Jullien derives from his discussion of the notion of *wu wei*, of achieving one's goals by *laissez-faire*, Jullien would point out that, far from referring to an anarchic notion of freedom or what some in the context of discussions of neoliberalism may want to call "deregulation," *wu wei* needs to be understood in the context of the Chinese principle of regulation—in other words, as a form of (sovereign, in Jullien's reading) government. As such, it marks, precisely, a kind of supreme—but radically immanent—power. We are not so much operating within the logic of opposition, then, as within a more dynamic relation between terms that, in the case of the unexceptional, always requires us to think the exceptional and its unworking together.

I opt for the term "unexceptional" precisely for its resonances with the English verb "unwork," which is often used to translate the French *désoeuvrer*. Jullien himself frequently plays with the "de-": one of the subtitles he provides for his *The Great Image Has No Form, or On the Nonobject in Painting* is "an essay in de-ontology," and in several instances in this book he plays with the double meanings of the verb *depict*, translated both as "depict" or "render" and "un-render" or "un-paint." Readers may be more familiar with the noun *désoeuvrement*—translated as "unworking," "worklessness," or (most frequently) "inoperativity"—and its connections to Hegel's dialectics (it's been suggested that *désoeuvrer* is a translation of the central and polysemic dialectical term *aufheben*) as well as Protestantism (influenced by the thought of Saint Paul) (see Agamben 2005). Yet if the term "unexceptional" should be located within these resonances, it is also important to underline the distance between Jullien's unexceptional thought and Hegelian dialectics—the way in which Jullien in his book *L'Ombre au tableau. Du mal ou du négatif* seeks to save the negative from the dialectical machine.[2]

AREAS OF APPLICATION

One way to look back at the previous chapters is to suggest that in them I have pursued the notion of the unexceptional and put it to work in three related but distinct areas: first, as part of an overall divergence between Western and Chinese thought that is central to Jullien's project and methodology. This is not so much a relation of opposition but that of both a gap and a bridge that opens up and enables one to uncover, *negatively*, the unthought of each tradition and, *positively*, each tradition's cultural resources. Within this divergence, the unexceptional is the Western tradition's unthought, while the exceptional is the unthought of the Chinese tradition. Unexceptionalism is the Chinese tradition's cultural resource; exceptionalism is a Western cultural resource—even if the "oppositional" thinking that such a description risks to enable would be patently false as we should rather imagine a dynamic relation between both tendencies within each tradition. Still, this is what enables Jullien to both praise the Chinese tradition for its thinking of "silent transformations" (Jullien 2011), for example, as something that in a Western tradition focused on exceptionalism has remained largely unthought, and to praise the Western tradition for its "invention of the ideal" (Jullien 2009), a notion that is alien—Jullien argues—to Chinese thought. Jullien is able to praise both, however, as distinct cultural resources that are democratically accessible to all: exceptionalism, for the use of those outside of Western thought, and unexceptionalism, for the use of those outside of Chinese thought.

Indeed, already within Western thought one can distinguish unexceptionalist thinkers who, in the challenges they pose to the foundations of Western thought, can be characterized as "Chinese." Korean-German philosopher Byung-Chul Han has, in this context, presented Jacques Derrida's "deconstruction" as "Chinese" (Han 2017), a description that Jullien may very well agree with, even if he might point out that Derrida arrived at deconstruction always from within the Western tradition, without ever truly stepping outside of it. Derrida's interest (which was both biographical and philosophical—and political, one might add) in Islam, for example, ultimately remains for Jullien "too biblical" (Jullien 2008a, 155) to truly offer an outside. Still, and perhaps surprisingly, Derrida's ideas are very close to what Jullien discovers in the Far East, suggesting that if Jullien was able to arrive at his own thought through the detour he made via China's "exteriority," certainly the thought that he built from this is not unique to that detour and can also be arrived at in other ways, through other cultural resources. Indeed, one might ultimately argue that there is nothing particularly "Chinese" to Jullien's thinking, if one considers that thought as separate from the contributions it has made to sinology. The overall methodology it proposes—the language of divergence, for example, or Jullien's criticism of the universal—certainly is not unique to the Chinese context, as I have shown in chapter 4.

The second realm in which I've sought to pursue and apply the notion of the unexceptional in Jullien's work is that of philosophy, and specifically philosophical aesthetics. This approach focused on the challenges that the notion of the unexceptional poses to Western metaphysics and ontology. It breaks, for example, with metaphysics, in that it does not tie the aesthetic judgment of something as beautiful to a hidden (behind or above) notion of the beautiful or beauty, some ideal form that could be divined (for this logic is also theological, as Jullien argues) within any beautiful thing. Chinese thought is unexceptional, rather, in that it never developed such a thought of the ideal form. In addition, it also breaks with ontologies of being, choosing process and flow—the path of the *dao*—over unified stability.

Certainly in posing those challenges, unexceptional Chinese thought is not alone; within the Western tradition already, several philosophers and philosophical schools have challenged metaphysics and ontology. It is interesting to note in this context that among those there is a tradition of turning to China to develop such a challenge, a turn that only rarely comes with a careful study of the Far East. Jullien both criticizes such "Chinese utopias" and distinguishes his approach from them and nevertheless arrives at some of the same conclusions—criticism of metaphysics and ontology, for example—that philosophers like the already-mentioned Derrida or Jean François Lyotard and Gilles Deleuze also propose (see Spivak 1981). Still, he does articulate the differences between his thought and that of Derrida and Deleuze, for example; also, from the disciplinary point of view, he develops his conclusions as a sinologist—that is, through the lifelong study of the Chinese language and Chinese thought. So even if Jullien may share some conclusions with other philosophers who did not carefully study China, it is worth noting that he arrives at those conclusions in an entirely different way, thus giving them a different grounding and substance. Some have, of course, disputed Jullien's conclusions and cast doubt on his study of the Chinese language and Chinese thought; but such disagreements can be found within any discipline and do not, in my view, invalidate Jullien's project. There is much evidence that his work has found a receptive audience both in the West and in China, Taiwan, and Japan—not to mention other countries like Vietnam.

In the realm of aesthetics, it is the Chinese landscape—specifically the landscapes of the Southern so-called "literati" school of scholar-painters—that comes to be closely associated with the unexceptional; the exceptional, by contrast, is captured by the Western tradition of the nude, which (as Jullien as well as others have observed) is absent in China. Here, too, the deconstructive approach should be clear: rather than opposing China and the West on these aesthetic counts, it is obvious that there is a tradition of painting landscapes in the West as well and that naked bodies can be found in Chinese art history. Rather, Jullien is offering here in very broad strokes a characterization of Western and Chinese art history that can be tied to his characterization of the thoughts that underlie them. In other words, if the centrality of landscape to Chinese art history and the nude to Western art history can operate as a visualization of the divergences between Chinese and Western thought, the transcendental condition for this aesthetic distribution is philosophical and lies in the divergent thoughts that have been developed in China and the West. The Chinese landscape, then, is both the product and the figure of Chinese unexceptionalism; the Western nude, of Western exceptionalism. Aesthetics provides a particularly fruitful pathway into this philosophical divergence.

Finally, I have also pursued and applied unexceptionalism in the realm of politics and economics, and it's on this count that I want to expand my approach in this conclusion. I've discussed at length how the Chinese thought of *wu wei*, or action through nonaction, has found a reception in contemporary management studies. Jullien's thought includes this shift with his thinking on efficacy morphing from a dense scholarly book on the Chinese notion of *shi* into a short treatise on the Chinese art of war and ultimately a lecture for managers. It's not entirely clear to me what the purpose of Jullien's lecture for managers is: on the one hand, it seems he welcomes the invitation to consider the relevance of his thought on efficacy in the context of management studies; on the other, he is also very critical of "loose" uses of Chinese thought, for example, in the service of neoliberal projects of deregulation or the pervasive self-help culture that Jullien frequently rejects as based on incorrect understandings of Chinese thought. But at the same time as he works to wrest Chinese thought away from the management gurus, he also delivers it to them—including specific passages on the Chinese understanding of contracts, for example. Moreover, he indicates that he has accompanied French managers in China to help them negotiate business deals. It's perhaps not so much a question of being critical of management, then, but of the erroneous uses that are made of Chinese thought in management.

Similarly, but Jullien himself has not engaged with this aspect of his work's reception, Jullien's writings about the Chinese art of war have found an audience in military studies, where Jullien's work is quoted in both reflections on, for example, the United States' relations to China specifically and more general considerations of how to best prepare soldiers for a confrontation with an enemy who battles in a way that is truly foreign or strange to those soldiers' own mode of waging war.

My discussion of Jullien's reception in management studies has led, in chapter 3, to a consideration of the importance of his work both in the understanding of the operations of contemporary sovereignty and the economico-political mode of government that is referred to as "neoliberalism." Whereas those two terms—sovereignty and neoliberalism—are sometimes opposed, scholars have come to resist such an opposition and have drawn out, rather, the way in which the sovereign and neoliberal (governmental/biopolitical) models are imbricated into each other. (One can find such adjustments to Michel Foucault's overdrawn analytical distinction between sovereignty and governmentality/biopolitics in the work of Wendy Brown, for example, and how it then gets picked up and developed in Judith Butler's analysis after the 9/11 terror attacks of the Guantánamo Bay detention camps; Butler 2006.) In typical deconstructive fashion, Jullien's discussion of efficacy helps one think, rather, both another form of sovereignty (that would operate precisely through the laissez-faire that is usually associated with governmentality/biopolitics) and another form of neoliberalism (that operates as sovereign); as such, the conclusions that I draw from Jullien's work on efficacy echo the scholarship of many theorists of neoliberalism who have paid attention to its close connections to sovereignty (rather than its all-too-easy opposition to it).

Still, if I've raised some doubts here about unexceptionalism and its association with both particular kinds of sovereignty and neoliberalism, I have foregrounded the notion in part because of its useful divergence with the exceptionalism that structures the Western notion of sovereignty. Not so long ago, sovereignty was considered dead as a result of the post–World War II development of human-rights politics or, for example, the politics of European integration. But that postsovereign position proved to be an illusion in the aftermath of the 9/11 terror attacks, to which the United States responded with an intensification of sovereignty. Theories of sovereignty revived in response to these real-world transformations, and Carl Schmitt's exceptionalist theory of sovereignty was considered particularly relevant. Schmitt, a German constitutional scholar who was disgraced due to his affiliation with Nazism, had suggested in 1921 that "sovereign is he who decides on the state of exception" (Schmitt 1985, 5), a phrase that took on new meaning in the aftermath of the 9/11 attacks—both in view of the emergency they marked and the sovereign response they triggered.[3]

With Schmitt's exceptionalist theory of sovereignty, which, of course, many also dispute, there was a concomitant rise of philosophies of the event, which can be read as another name for the exception. As I've indicated elsewhere (Boever 2016, 290–98), the link between such philosophies and Schmitt is rarely made explicit, even if some have pointed out that it is structurally present (Lyotard, for example, has suggested this about Alain Badiou's theory of the subject; Lacoue-Labarthe et al. 1989); structure, of course, is neither history nor politics (at least, that is how it wants to present itself!), and it is not because philosophies of the event have some structural affinity with Schmitt that they share Schmitt's political affinity with Nazism; not all events or exceptions are "fascistic." In the case of Badiou, for example, who has written appreciatively about Jullien, Badiou's philosophy of the event is tied to a communist politics; others like Bonnie Honig have tried to wrest away sovereign exceptionalism from Schmitt to rearticulate it democratically (Honig 2014), as a project of popular sovereignty (a rearticulation that scholars like Andreas Kalyvas may argue lies included in Schmitt's work itself;

Kalyvas relies heavily on Schmitt's *Constitutional Theory* to make this case; Kalyvas 1999–2000). Still, in the guise of the event the exception has thrived in contemporary Western thought, which thus contributes (knowingly or unknowingly) to Western thought's investment in sovereign exceptionalism.

A scholar like Bonnie Honig knows that and has sought to counter sovereign exceptionalism with a theory of sovereign unexceptionalism, a theory of the sovereign ordinary, if you will, that she associates with second-wave feminism and its skepticism of masculinist heroism (Rossello 2015). If Honig, in spite of everything, holds on to the notion of sovereignty in this context, it is because she sees its benefits and argues that it is needed, in its popular form, to be politically effective. There are other contemporary political philosophers who share this view (Judith Butler, for example, even if Honig also has disagreements with Butler)—or also a political journalist and activist like Naomi Klein, whose changing position on the state has perceptively been analyzed by literary critic and theorist Bruce Robbins (Robbins 2017, 93–115). Certainly, all of this proves that sovereignty is hardly dead; rather, the power that is called sovereign is very much still with us, often in guises that prevent us from recognizing it, and mostly in new, contemporary formations that require theoretical reelaboration rather than hasty declarations of sovereignty's demise (to recall Foucault's woefully outdated solicitation that we cut off the head of the king in theory, just as we had done in practice in the French Revolution). Jullien's work can, in my view, make a significant contribution to this.

That contribution consists, first, in seeing how Chinese unexceptionalism can unwork the sovereign exceptionalism that pervades Western thought and politics (the nude is its figure in aesthetics; and as is obvious from Schmitt, who defines sovereignty in a book about political theology, this sovereign exceptionalism is profoundly "biblical"—so it has an intensely theological dimension as well). Such an unworking seems important both philosophically and politically, to break out of Western metaphysical and ontological thinking (which seems necessary to me in view of what they do not allow us to think—silent transformations, for example) and work against, say, the decisionism of Schmittian thought (which eclipses deliberative models of sovereignty) or also the abuse that sovereign exceptionalism often facilitates. In other words, unexceptionalism can help with rendering sovereignty democratic—with unworking sovereignty's exceptionalist core into what scholars like Emily Apter (2018) or Stathis Gourgouris (2013) might call unexceptionalist democracy. At the same time, and as scholars like Honig or Butler might argue, sovereignty is also a Western cultural resource, one that—especially in its popular form—is there for democratic exploitation by all (in the context of popular revolutions, for example). Sovereign exceptionalism can also be a resource in particular in a context where the unexceptional is dominant. If the Chinese model risks ignoring individual agency, for example, or (along more political lines) the rupture of revolution, then the Western model can introduce this into it.

Let's not forget, also, that while I just associated democracy with unexceptionalism, democracy is certainly not a given in the Chinese context: if Chinese thought may be unexceptional through and through, it is interesting to note—and this is something like the foundational enigma of this book— that this hasn't translated into political democracy, whereas it's the Western exceptionalist context that has yielded this political regime. I would argue that, in this situation, "neoliberalism" has played an important role on both sides: on the Western side, it has hollowed out democratic unexceptionalism into plutocracy, a regime of "petty sovereigns" wielding discretionary power without electoral votes to back them; on the Chinese side, unexceptional thought has operated in close connection to sovereignty to produce a contemporary, nondemocratic neoliberal state that comes to resemble more and more—but from the other side—today's Western states, that present a similar mixture of exceptionalist and unexceptionalist elements. In response, I suspect we are going to see at least two developments: on the one hand, "Western" left-liberal reclaimings of sovereignty against neoliberalism, of course in critical ways (Brown, Honig, Butler, Klein, and more), and, on the other, "Chinese" recuperations of unexceptionalism from neoliberalism against sovereignty, in the name of democratic developments. (These are, of course, only two options that I consider here within the framework of this book; but there are many more.) These will not necessarily happen exclusively on either the Western "side" or the Chinese "side"; rather, one might see some of the latter in the West—but at great political risk, since the struggle for popular sovereignty is more important in this context. Or one might see some of the former in China, at an equally great risk: it may lead to the reinforcement of authoritarian sovereignty.

It seems to me that what must be accomplished, then, is to bring both these philosophies and politics together as part of a unified process of regulation or respiratory movement, where the one leads into the other and back without ever stabilizing on either side, or without either side ever being stable as a "side." Such an accomplishment would within the framework of this book have to be read as "Chinese," for it moves away from the Western model of opposition into another mode of relation that, through Jullien, I've come to associate with China. A similar conclusion applies to Jullien's work as a whole. While Jullien claims that as a sinologist he was never fully sinized, and develops—in the late phase of his work—the cultural resources of European thought in their divergence with China, one would still have to conclude that his overall position and method is closer to Chinese thought than it is to Western thought. It is true that he mobilizes Western cultural resources in a productive divergence with Chinese thought, but overall his thought nevertheless strikes one as what we within Jullien's own framework can characterize as Chinese—and this creates certain problems, for example (as I discussed in chapter 4), when Jullien presents his work in Vietnam, which has a tense colonial history with China. I don't think there is any way out of this; this situation is due, as I see it, to the fact that Chinese thought is quite simply closer to nature and therefore was bound to ultimately dominate over a Western thought that in its invention of the ideal, for example, always operated with a degree of friction in relation to reality. At the same time, it is no doubt the proximity of Chinese thought to nature, the absence of productive friction, that has prevented the unnatural democratic break from sovereignty to come about in the Chinese context; there is, precisely, no artificial universalizing ideal (of liberty, for example) that could have forced such a development into Chinese politics. If the overall gesture of bringing Chinese thought and Western thought together as part of a single respiratory movement strikes one as Chinese, then, such a reading would have to be nuanced by drawing out the role of Western thinking within such a dynamic unification that draws the overall characterization of this gesture as Chinese into question.

A PROVOCATION

In the end, of course, my use of the term "unexceptional" to describe Jullien's thought is meant to provoke. On the one hand, the term names a core element of Jullien's work—namely, a preference for the unexceptional, the facile, the bland, and the unheard-of that arrives in his work through China but also exists independently from it as something he values. In that sense, I use "the unexceptional" as a strong philosophical notion that is central to Jullien's work in the divergence between China and the West. On the other, I am using the term also to draw out how unexceptional Jullien's turn to China in order to discover the unexceptional is: as I've already pointed out, many others have gone there—although they often, and unlike Jullien, have not *truly* gone there—and in a sense there is nothing unexceptional about Jullien's Chinese detour and the conclusions to which it has led. I have to that extent sought to inscribe Jullien's thought here (and distinguish it from) a longer history of French fascinations with China, both to show how aspects of Jullien's work fit into that (and are, in that sense, unexceptional) and also to show how Jullien's work differs from those other examples.

Certainly, Jullien himself would insist on the difference, perhaps even argue that he has nothing to do with those "Chinese utopias" that he frequently rejects and the orientalism that often characterizes them: instead, he considers China as heterotopia. But even this claim, as I discussed in chapter

1, does not fully free him from the charge of orientalism and the ties between his work and other approaches to China in the French tradition. The idea of making a detour through China to better understand the West is certainly also not a new idea in the history of French thought. If Jullien, as an orientalist, might not be an orientalist, traces of orientalism arguably still remain in his thinking, which is in that sense unexceptional as well. I've tried to draw out those traces and read them in context. At the same time, Jullien's work is also more than those traces, and by developing the notion of the unexceptional as a strong philosophical category in his work's many pages, his oeuvre has also come to stand out as an unheard-of adventure between Chinese thought and Western thought that has pushed thinking on both sides of this divergence further. In the same way that Jullien critically reappropriates the bland from Roland Barthes' rather negative (and uninformed) assessment of China, I am reappropriating the notion of the unexceptional from the negative connotation that it generally has, and mobilizing it as a critical term—philosophically and politically.[4]

To have one's thought be called unexceptional, then, is to have one's thought be praised, but critically. It's to see one's thought praised for providing a thorough development of the notion of the unexceptional as part of a criticism of exceptionalism that has all too often led to a universalization of Western thought and the forgetting of what falls outside of it (which is a lot), of a Western politics of sovereignty associated with decisionism (rather than deliberation) and the possibility of authoritarian abuse (which occurs frequently). But it's also to see one's thought be criticized for its soft orientalism or its unresolved relation to neoliberalism. If the notion of the unexceptional in this context is meant to provoke, however, I hope it will be clear I used it here to provoke my readers into the reading of François Jullien rather than away from it. I am sure that, for many, Jullien is still a thinker that they've never heard of, a sinologist whom they may never read because they do not work on China or have no general interest in it (who even knows what "sinology" means?); but my book has meant to shed light on how Jullien in today's theoretical landscape also stands out, by doing something that is—increasingly—"unheard-of": working between two different cultural resources, spending ample time with both, carefully studying their languages and thought.

It's Marcel Gauchet who, in his contribution to *Cahier de l'Herne* on François Jullien (the book with which I began), suggests that Jullien may be one of the last of his kind. This is so, according to Gauchet, because increasingly universities as the major centers of learning are reorganized (and he clearly has in mind their neoliberalization) so as to make it impossible for a thinker like François Jullien to come about: "Les réformes universitaires qu'on nous impose sont très exactement conçues pour empêcher l'apparition de futurs François Julliens" (The university reforms that have been imposed are conceived precisely to prevent the appearance of future François Julliens; Gauchet 2018, 20). Gauchet is talking about the situation in France, but the "sad reason" he mentions for this impossibility applies to the United States, from where I am writing, as well: who still lands the job that would enable the research that Jullien pursues? Who even can still conceive of research in this way, with such ambition? (I note that in certain parts of the West, very few academics still have the ambition to write a book or think the kind of thought that requires book-length development. This is because their status depends on the publication of a number of articles every academic year—articles that, once published, often can't be republished as part of a book; the university presses just won't have it. The number of articles to write is so high that it makes any other writing impossible. But these material, economic conditions have real consequences on the scope of thought and, by extension, cultural diversity.) Which doctoral programs support this kind of research? Which universities support their faculty to pursue it? How many external grants support it? How much deep language-learning support is provided in undergraduate and graduate programs or to faculty who want to start research in a new language? Most importantly, how much time do departments make available for faculty to work on these kinds of projects and to have the interdisciplinary conversations that foster them?

By all accounts, the situation is grim: more and more time gets sucked up by mind-numbing administrative tasks; teaching loads grow heavier and heavier, pushing one's research onto the backburner; more and more frequently, summer research and writing time gets colonized by administrative tasks; time off for language-learning or research abroad is difficult, if not impossible, to come by; to find a job, it is generally better to not be too "comparative" in one's approach and certainly not too "theoretical"—there aren't any jobs for people doing that kind of work. (And all of this applies to those who actually have a full-time academic job; we aren't even considering the research ambitions of those who don't.) And so, truly, Jullien's critical comments about the theoretical steamroller of globalization flattening out all relief between cultures and promoting a kind of falsely peaceful and egalitarian notion of "difference" expressed mostly in "global English," or "globish," has largely arrived: one can't teach the dead white guys who wrote in any of the European languages (even if one knows the European languages and can actually read those texts in the languages in which they were originally written), but neither does the university provide support for faculty to expand their teaching canon through deep language-learning, study abroad, and the familiarization with other traditions of thought. And so "difference" ends up being realized on the course syllabus by adding some work of "world literature" in English (or available in English translation), and truly—and out of poverty—one stays at home rather than thinking outside of one's culture.

At least today, one can still read the work of thinkers like Jullien to try to lift oneself outside of such a situation, even if taking Jullien's word on China is obviously also not enough. But what will this situation look like when the Julliens of the world have disappeared and all that remains is a ghettoized understanding of one's own culture and superficial appreciation of the supposed "alterity" of others? This will be the end of any cultural exteriority as heterotopia (never mind its orientalist associations) and every culture's realization as stupidity in the dystopia of the reformed, neoliberal university. We will all be very busy performing our administrative tasks and teaching courses that project the illusion of diversity. But in truth, we will have been deprived of our own cultural resources and those resources of cultures elsewhere, and what we imagine as the face of the other will merely be a much impoverished version of what could be the living resource of our own.

NOTES

1. Jullien 2004, 184.
2. In view of my discussion of the "paraontological" in chapter 4, "paraexceptional" is another term that could have been considered here to describe Jullien's thought and mark specifically its difference from Hegelian dialectics and the trace of Hegel in *désoeuvrer* or "unwork." But the disadvantage of that term is that it does not have the double meaning of the "unexceptional" as being both ordinary and the remarkable philosophical and political counter to Western exceptionalism.
3. See Boever 2016.
4. I've already explored its uses in the context of aesthetics elsewhere, in a short book that was written in anticipation of this longer study on Jullien and includes a minimal engagement with his thought. See Boever 2019.

REFERENCES

Agamben, Giorgio. 2005. *The Time that Remains: A Commentary on The Letter to the Romans*. Translated by Patricia Dailey. Stanford: Stanford University Press.

Apter, Emily. 2018. *Unexceptional Politics: On Obstruction, Impasse, and the Impolitic*. New York: Verso.

Boever, Arne De. 2016. *Plastic Sovereignties: Agamben and the Politics of Aesthetics*. Edinburgh: Edinburgh University Press.

———. 2019. *Against Aesthetic Exceptionalism*. Minneapolis: University of Minnesota Press.

Butler, Judith. 2006. *Precarious Life: The Powers of Mourning and Violence*. New York: Verso.

Gauchet, Marcel. 2018. "Les possibles de la pensée." In *François Jullien*, edited by Daniel Bougnoux and François L'Yvonnet, 20–24. Paris: L'Herne, 2018.

Gourgouris, Stathis. 2013. "The Question Is: Society Must Be Defended Against Whom? Or What?" *New Philosopher*, May 25. http://www.newphilosopher.com/articles/the-question-is-society-defended-against-whom-or-what-in-the-name-of-what/.

Han, Byung-Chul. 2017. *Shanzhai: Deconstruction in Chinese*. Translated by Philippa Hurd. Boston: MIT Press.

Honig, Bonnie. 2014. "Three Models of Emergency Politics." *boundary 2* 41 (2): 45–70.

Jullien, François. 2004. *A Treatise on Efficacy: Between Western and Chinese Thinking*. Translated by Janet Lloyd. Honolulu: University of Hawai'i Press.

———. 2008a. "Eine Dekonstruktion von aussen: Von Griechenland nach China und zurück." In *Kontroverse über China: Sinophilosophie*, edited by Dirk Baecker, François Jullien, Philippe Jousset, et al. Berlin: Merve. 133–59.

———. 2008b. *In Praise of Blandness: Proceeding from Chinese Thought and Aesthetics*. Translated by Paula M. Varsano. New York: Zone Books.

———. 2009. *L'Invention de l'idéal et le destin de l'Europe*. Paris: Seuil.

———. 2011. *The Silent Transformations*. Translated by Krzystof Fijalkowski and Michael Richardson. London: Seagull.

Kalyvas, Andreas. 1999–2000. "Carl Schmitt and the Three Moments of Democracy." *Cardozo Law Review* 21 (1525): 1525–66.

Lacoue-Labarthe, Philippe, Jacques Rancière, Jean François Lyotard, and Alain Badiou. 1989. "Liminaire sur l'ouvrage d'Alain Badiou 'L'être et l'évènement.'" *Le Cahier* (Collège Internationale de Philosophie) 8: 201–68.

Robbins, Bruce. 2017. *The Beneficiary*. Durham: Duke University Press.

Rossello, Diego. 2015. "Ordinary Emergences in Democratic Theory: An Interview with Bonnie Honig." *Philosophy Today* 59 (4): 699–710.

Schmitt, Carl. 1985. *Political Theology: Four Chapters on the Concept of Sovereignty*. Translated by George Schwab. Cambridge: MIT Press.

Spivak, Gayatri Chakravorty. 1981. "French Feminism in an International Frame." *Yale French Studies* 62: 154–84.

Index

About Chinese Women (Kristeva), xix, 3, 72, 99n18
absence, 41, 42
action, 45, 78
Adam and Eve, 46, 63n16
An Aesthetic Education in the Era of Globalization (Spivak), xxvii
aesthetics, 35–37, 52, 109, 127–29
Agamben, Giorgio, 48–50, 95
agency, 132
alphabet, 37
alterity, xvii, 14, 71, 113, 136; Chair of Alterity, xi, 12; China as, 30n16, 63n16; rejection of, 13
Analects (Confucius), 89
anarchism, 89
anarchy, 90, 97
anatomy, 38, 61n5
ancestrality, 25
antiorientalism, 3
application areas, 126–33
appropriation, xxvii
archetype, nude and, 47
Aristotle, xxv, 75, 105
The Army War College Review, 82
art, xviii, 36, 38, 43–44, 46, 48, 60, 98n5, 128, xxixn18
Art of War (Sun Zi), 77
As is (Tel Quel), xxiii, 2

atopia, 4
Augustine (Saint), 47
authoritarianism, 91
autocritique, of Jullien, xvii
awards, xi

Babel, 14, 114, 119
Badiou, Alain, xv, 44, 51, 118, 130
Baecker, Dirk, xxiv
Baldwin, James, xxvii
Bandung conference, 6
Barthes, Roland, xxiii, 2–4, 28n5, 28n6, 37, 62n12, 103, 113, 134, xxixn22
beautiful, 35, 43–44, 46, 49, 64n22
Beecroft, Vanessa, 49
being, xv, 16
Bennett, Jane, 108, 109
Bentham, Jeremy, 55, 86, 92
Bernstein, Leonard, 7
beyond, 43–45, 49
bilingualism, 114
Billeter, Jean-François, xvi, xx, 19–20, 57, xxixn13, xxixn18, xxviiin7; attack by, 63n16; debate with, 71–72; Jullien response to, 29n12
"Biopolitical Beijing," 95–96
The Birth of Biopolitics (Foucault), 86
blackness, 122n23

"Blackness and Nothingness (Mysticism in the Flesh)," 118–19
Black Panthers, 7–8
black studies, 115–20
black subjectivity, 120
bland (*dan*, 淡), xxiii–xxv, 125
blandness, xxiii, 46, 53
Bodei, Remo, xvii
body, 22, 38, 43, 59
Book of Beginnings (Jullien), xiv, 11, 30n13, 44–45, 57, 62n12
Borges, Jorge Luis, 9, 29nn8–9
Bouteldja, Houria, 116–17
Braque, Georges, 62n10
breath, 59
bridges, 22–23
Brown, Wendy, 130
Buddhism, xv, 42
business, in China, 69–73, 80
Butler, Judith, 130

Cahier de l'Herne, xii, 72, 134
Capital (Marx), 60
capitalism, 60
Catholicism, xxvi
Catholic schools, xxv–xxvi
Chair of Alterity, xi, 12
chance, war and, 77
chaos, 42
Chaos (Greek mythology), 89–90
Chemin faisant (Step-by-step) (Jullien), xv, 71
Cheng, Anne, 21
Chesneaux, Jean, 2, 6, 7, 8
children, heterotopias and, 10–11
China: as alterity, 30n16, 63n16; business in, 69–73, 80; Chinese thought and, xxxn25; contract in, 80; detour through, xii, xv–xvi, xviii, xxv, xxvi, 13, 30n16, 54, 70, 118, 127, 133–34; as elsewhere, 20, 30n16, 63n16; exoticization of, xxi; exteriority of, 107, 109, 119, 127; Foucault on, xii, 9–10; as heterotopia, 8–18, 28n4, 133; holism of, 19; internal coherence of, 24; Jullien and, 9; Lacan and, 3; language of, xx, 10, 128; neoliberalization of, 56; phantasmatic constructions of, 17; philosophy in, 69–73; pictorial theories in, 39; politics of, xix, 8, 56–57, 84; in *Propensity of Things*, culture of, 104; regulation in, 93; sovereignty in, 84; theory of war in, 76–77, 79, 84, 86, 88, 98n8, 129; time in, 131n7
"China as Philosophical Tool," 71
Chinese art: history, 36, 128, xxixn18; landscape painting, 35, 37, 39–40, 61n4, 128, xxviiin5; sketching, 42–43, 62n9
Chinese Cultural Proletarian Revolution, 8
Chinese Dreams (Hayot), 3
Chinese thought, xxixn17; being and, 16; blandness and, xxiii, 46, 53; in *Book of Beginnings*, 62n12; Braque and, 62n10; China and, xxxn25; classical, 30n18; coherence of, 17; conditioning in, 94; defining, 12; early, 19; essence in, 59; essentialization of, xvi; European thought and, xv, 12, 132; event in, 44; exceptionalism in, 54; future in, 99n9; generalization of, xvi; German Romantic tradition and, xxixn15; in *The Great Image Has No Form, or On the Nonobject in Painting*, 11, 40; Hegel and, 31n24; Jullien on, xv, 14; landscape in, 37–39, 41, 45; management and, 129; metaphysics and, xviii, 43; ontology and, 41–42, 117, 121n12, 122n23; philosophy and, 120–21; politics in, 56; preference for, 51–52; transcendence in, 54–55; unexceptional and, 37, 52; unthought of, xxiv, xxv, 21, 127; as untranslatable, xiv; Western thought and, xiii, xx, xxiv, 11, 13, 17, 19–20, 37, 40, 50, 52, 65n26, 70–71, 96,

105–6, 117–18, 126–27, 129, 132–34, xxxn25
Chinese utopias, 2, 6, 11, 17, 72, 74, 128, 133–34
Chow, Rey, 6
Christianity, xxv, 29n12, 58, 64n22, 91, 110, 111
Clausewitz, Carl von, 75, 76, 96
clothing, 49
cognition, embodied, 19
colonialism, 116
commandments, in Western thought, 94
commodity, utopia and, 24
communism, 6, 29n12
comparison, 11, 12, 29n12, 40, 106, 121n3
composition, landscape and, 37–38
conditioning, in Chinese thought, 94
Conférence sur l'efficacité (Lecture on efficacy) (Jullien), xviii–xix, 57, 73–75, 78–81, 84, 88, 95, 97
Confucianism, xv, 12, 56, 65n27
Confucius, 53, 65n27, 89, 92
connivance, 23–27, 40
Constitutional Theory (Schmitt), 131
constructivism, 20
contract, in China, 80
Contre François Jullien (Billeter), xvi, 57, 71, xxixn18
correlation, xviii
countersovereignty, 63n16
counter-spaces, Foucault on, 10
Critical Inquiry, 31n24
Critical Terrains (Barthes), 3
criticism: of *The Great Image Has No Form, or On the Nonobject in Painting*, xvi, 103, xxixn18; of tourism, 116; of *A Treatise on Efficacy*, 97n3
Critique of Postcolonial Reason (Spivak), xxvii
cultivation of spirit, 96
cultural diversity, 13
cultural identity, 23
cultural resources, 21, 111, 127

culture, 14, 24, 106, 135–36
cunning intelligence (*mètis*), 30n20, 88
Cunning Intelligence in Greek Culture and Society (Detienne & Vernant), 31n21, 75

Damascus, 63n14
dan, 淡 (bland), xxiii–xxiv, 125
dao, 30n18, 36, 55, 119; nothingness and, 16; ontology and, 44; path and, 83–84, 114–15, 128; translation of, 19–20; war and, 77
Dao De Jing, 12, 35–36, 42, 89, 99n13, 99n14, 106, xxixn23
Daoism, xv, 12, 42, 65n27, 65n30, 85, 91
de Beauvoir, Simone, 7
decisionism, 134
de-coincidence, existence and, xiv
decolonization, 114
deconstruction, in *A Treatise on Efficacy*, 107
degree, xi
Deleuze, Gilles, xix, xxiv, 28n66, 65n30, 88, 99n17, 104, 128
De l'Intime (Jullien), 63n14
democracy, 70, 90, 132
Deng Xiaoping, 56
deontology, xxviii, 40, 126, xxxn24
deregulation, 126
Derrida, Jacques, xvii, xxvii, 13, 28n3, 71, 107, 113, 120, 127, 128
despotism, 86
Detienne, Marcel, 30n20, 31nn21–22, 75
dialogue, xiii, 15, 20, 103
Dickinson, Emily, xxiii
difference, 14, 30n17
disengaged from the vital, 26, 27
distance, 113
distribution of sensible, 118
divergence, 17, 26–27, 52, 54, 65n26, 113; aesthetics, 35–37, 129; culture and, 14; in-between and, 23, 114; language of, 127

Divergence and the in-between (L'écart et l'entre), xvi, 12–13
diversity, 136
divine, 44, 46
Dong, Shu-bao, 65n30
dragon, 87–88, 99n17
dreaming (*songer*), 22
dream logic, 3
Droit, Roger-Pol, xix, xxviiin3
dualism, 19

early work, xxv
The East Is Black (Frazier), 7, 122n23
Ebisu, 69
écart (gap), xiii, xviii, 28, 113, xxixn21
L'écart et l'entre (Divergence and the in-between), xvi, 12–13
economicopolitical aspects, 70
economics, 6, 60–61, 129, 135
efficacy, xviii, xix, 107; action and, 45; of conduct, 94; effort and, 86–87; personality and, 78; plants and, 85; war and, 74; in Western thought, 75
effort, efficacy and, 86–87
effraction, 23
eidos (form as idea), 47–48, 50
embodied cognition, 19
Empire of Signs (Barthes), 3
energy, 59
English, globalization and, xiii, 25, 135
Enlai, Zhou, 6
Enlightenment, xxv, xxvi
l'entre. See the in-between
epics, 62n12
equality, xxvi
Erasmus, xxiii
escape, 26–27
essence, 42, 45, 48, 59
essentialism, 19
essentialization, xvi, 19, 36–37
ethics, xvi
Ethics, Institutions, and the Right to Philosophy (Derrida), 120
ethnocentricity, 24
ethnocide, 114

Étiemble, René, 21–22
Europe, 38
European painting, 46
European philosophy, xix
European reasoning, 11
European thought, xv, 12, 70, 109, 121, 132
event, 44–45, 50, 55–56, 79
evolution, 13–14
exceptional, xxv, 125
exceptionalism, xxiii, xxv–xxvi, 14, 37, 51–54, 63n16, 91, 129, 136n2, xxixn23
exercise, 96
existence, de-coincidence and, xiv
exoptic, xvii, 20
exote, 112
exoticism, xvii, 11, 18, 20, 23, 36, 111–12
exteriority, xvii, 107, 109, 113, 114, 119, 127

facility, xxiii, xxiv, 52, 78
Fanon, Frantz, 114, 119
Far Eastern thought, 105, 115, 119
Farquhar, Judith, 95–96
feeding life, 58–60
femininity, 63n16
feminism, xix, 3, 63n16, 72, 131
feminist studies, 117
Figures de l'étranger (Khatibi), 103, 111, 113, 122n15
finality, 41
flat ontology, 108
floating, 59
flow, 59
forced assimilation, xiii
Forest, Philippe, 5
form, 46; essence and, 48; ideal, 48, 50, 64n22, 75, 84, 92, 93, 128; in *The Impossible Nude*, 50–51; nude and, 47
forma, 47
form as contour (*morphe*), 47
form as idea (*eidos*), 47–48

formation (*xing*) (形), 48
Foucault, Michel, 27, 28n6, 29nn8–9, 55, 86, 97, xxixn13; Bentham and, 92; on China, xii, 9–10; on counter-spaces, 10; governmentality/biopolitics and, xix, 129–30; on heterotopias, 9–11, 14, 17; imaginary and real melding and, 5; power and, 91; on same and other, 9
Frazier, Robeson Taj, 7, 122n23
freedom, 85, 126
French, Patrick, 5
French Centre for Research on Contemporary China, xi
"French Feminism in an International Frame," xix, 3, 72
French Republic, 116–17
French Revolution, 131
French theory, 103
future, in Chinese thought, 99n9

gap (*écart*), xiii, xviii, 28, xxixn21
Gauchet, Marcel, 72, 134–35, xxxn25
Gekko, Gordon, 73
gender, 3, 17, 46, 110–11
geometry, 75
German Romantic tradition, xxixn15
Glissant, Édouard, xxi
globalization, English and, xiii, 25, 135
goals, 84
God, xv, 42
good and evil, 56
governance, 94
governmentality/biopolitics, xix, xxvi, 58, 91, 95–97, 129–30
Grau, Donatien, 90
The Great Image Has No Form, or On the Nonobject in Painting (Jullien), 106; Chinese thought in, 11, 40; comparison in, 12; criticism of, xvi, 103, xxixn18; deontology in, xxviii, 126, xxxn24; in-between in, xviii; landscape in, 35, 39; mathematics in, 61n5; noncontradiction in, 41; objects in, 41; Western thought in, 11, 40, 43

Greek: literature, 31n21; myths, 31n21, 89–90; philosophy, xxi; politics, xix; thought, 70, 75
Guattari, Félix, 65n30, 104
Guillain, Robert, 6

Han, Byung-Chul, 46, 107, 127
happiness, Christianity and, 58
Harman, Graham, 108
Harrist, Robert, xvi
Hayot, Eric, 3, 5
health, 61n5
Heaven (*tian*, 天), xxiv
Hegel, G. W. F., xiv; Chinese thought and, 31n24; dialectics of, 31n24, 126, 136n2; Jullien and, xix; racism of, 31n24, 99n9, xxviiin8
Heidegger, Martin, 23, 48, 64n22
heroism, 78, 131
heteros, 14
heterotopias: children and, 10–11; China as, 8–18, 28n4, 133; Chinese utopias and, 11; culture and, 14; Foucault on, 9–11, 14, 17; syntax and, 9–10
Hill, Robert M., 81–82
History of Sexuality: Volume I (Foucault), 95
Hokenson, Jan Walsh, 28n5
holism, 19
holistic orientalism, 19
Homer, 69–70
Homo Sacer (Agamben), 48
Honig, Bonnie, 63n16, 130
horizon, of thought, 114
Hughes, Alex, 6–7, 22, 72
human form, 41
human rights, 21, 130
humble orientalism, 31n23

idea, 46, 69, 104
ideal form, 48, 50, 64n22, 75, 84, 92, 93, 128
identity: colonialism and, 116; critique of, 117; cultural, 23; logic of, 110; pseudoidentity, 116
image, 46, 125

imaginary, real and, 5
imagination, xxii–xxiii
immanence, xxiv, 40, 54, 58, 65n30, 104
The Impossible Nude (Jullien), xviii, 36, 38, 39–40, 46, 50–51
the in-between (*l'entre*), 28; Chinese utopias and, 17; divergence and, 23, 114; in *The Great Image Has No Form, or On the Nonobject in Painting*, xviii; language of, xiv; Western thought and, 16
India, 42
indigeneity, 115–20
indigenous, 25
inequality, 110–11, 115
l'inouï (the unheard-of), xxi–xxv, 28n6, 112–13, 125
In Praise of Blandness (Jullien), xxiii, 35, 37, 52–54, 62n12, 103–4, 126
In Praise of Counterefficacy (Jullien), 88, 97
"In Praise of Facility," 52
In Praise of Folly (Erasmus), xxiii
In Praise of Shadows (Tanizaki), xxiii
integration, 14, 23, 30n17
intellectual vacuum, xxi, 103
intelligence, 23, 30n20, 75–76, 88, 93
internal transcendence, xxiv
interventionism, 55
L'Invention de l'idéal et le destin de l'Europe (The invention of the ideal and the destiny of Europe) (Jullien), xii, 92
invisible hand, 86
irrationalism, 58
Islam, xvii, xxvi, 111, 113–14

Japan, 4, 28n5, 28n6
Journal de l'école de Paris du management, 82–83
Judaism, xxvi
Judeo-Christian tradition, xvii
Jullien, François. *See specific entries*

Kantian categories, xxv
key terms, 18
Khatibi, Abdelkebir, xxi, 103, 111–15, 119, 122n15, 122n19
Klein, Naomi, 131
Kristeva, Julia, xix–xx, 2, 3, 6, 57, 72, 99n18

Lacan, Jacques, 3
laisser faire/laissez-faire, xix, 55, 85–87, 89–90, 119, 126
Landa, Manuel de, 108
landscape: in Chinese thought, 37–39, 41, 45; composition and, 37–38; in *The Great Image Has No Form, or On the Nonobject in Painting*, 35, 39; nude and, 38; in *Vital Nourishment* (Jullien), 54
language: of China, xx, 10, 128; of divergence, 127; of the in-between, xiv; of management, 83; pluralization of, 114
Laroui, Abdellah, 114
late phase, xii, 21, 62n9, 114, xxviiin3
laws, 93, 96
laws of dialectics, xiv
Leçon (Barthes), 103
Lecture on Efficacy (Jullien). *See Conférence sur l'efficacité*
Legalists, 91, 92
library, xv
life, xiv, 58–60
Lin, Esther, xvii, 122n15
lineage, 25
linguistic determinism, xv, 14, 17, 105
Lingyun, Xie, 39
literature, philosophy and, 42
Living Off Landscape or the Unthought-of in Reason (Jullien), 24, 25–27, 37–39, 40, 106
logic of identity, 110
logos, xxv
Longxi, Zhang, 9, 29n9

Lowe, Lisa, 4, 8, 25
Lyotard, Jean-François, xix, 57, 128, 130

Maghreb pluriel, 113–15, 122n19
management, xix, 59–60; Chinese theory of war and, 84; Chinese thought and, 129; effective, 78; language of, 83; military theory and, 81–90, 99n11; in *A Treatise on Efficacy*, 84–85; war and, 73–74, 79, 98n5, 98n7; Western, 84–85
manipulation, 81
Mao, 7
Maoism, 29n7
Martin, Nicolas, xiii, xvii, 116
martyrdom, 63n16
Marx, Karl, 60
Marxism, 6
Marx-Scouras, Danielle, 5
masculinity, 63n16
materialism/realism, xxi, 65n30, 108–9
mathematics, 61n5
matter, 59
meaning, space and, 4
Mencius, 90
Menser, David C., 82
metaphysics, xxvi, 12, 16; Chinese thought and, xviii, 43; event and, 44; in *The Impossible Nude*, 46; nude and, 46, 47; *This Strange Idea of the Beautiful*, 43; unexceptional and, 128; Western thought and, xix, 43, 63n16
mètis (cunning intelligence), 30n20, 88
mètis (practical intelligence), 75–76, 93
Military Review, 81–82
military theory, 75, 81–90, 98n5, 99n11
Mind and Body in Early China (Slingerland), xxixn14
mind-body holism, 19
miracle, 81
misinformation, 87
modelization, of politics, 92, 93

modern art, xviii
Møllgaard, Eske, 64n22
The Monkey bridge (Jullien). *See Le pont des singes*
morphe (form as contour), 47–48, 50
morphology of capital, 57
"Morrison Lecture," 8
Morton, Timothy, 108
Moten, Fred, xxi, 118, 119–20
Murakami, Haruki, xxiii
museums, 44
mysticism, 25

narration, 62n12
nature, 25, 54–55, 98n5
Nazism, 130
Needham, Joseph, 38
negative, 126; insufficient, xiv; negative, xiv, xxv; silent transformations and, xix; universal, 15
neoliberalism, 56, 86, 89, 90, 97, 129–30, 132, 134
Neoliberalism as Exception (Ong), 72
neo-orientalism, 31n23
The Neutral (Barthes), xxixn22
new materialism, 108
9/11 terror attacks, 56, 130
noncontradiction, 41
Norden, Bryan W. Van, 86
nostalgia, 11
nothing (*wu*, 無), 119
nothingness, 16, 118–19
novel form, 43, 62n12
nude, xviii, 36, 37, 48, 51, 61n4, 129; Agamben and, 49–50; archetype and, 47; beautiful and, 46, 49; clothing and, 49; in European painting, 46; event and, 50; form and, 47; landscape and, 38; metaphysics and, 46, 47; in Western thought, 45, 49
The Nude (Jullien), 37
"Nudity," 49
nutrition, 96

Il n'y a pas d'identité culturelle (There is no cultural identity) (Jullien), xvi, 2, 19, 28
Nylan, Michael, 21

objectification, 41
Oblivion, 89–90
occidentalism, 37
Oceanos, 75
Odysseus, 75–76, 88
Of Grammatology (Derrida), xxvii, 28n3, 120
Olympics, 56
L'ombre au tableau (Jullien), xiv, 31n24, 126
Ong, Aihwa, 72
On the Universal (Jullien), xvi, 2, 15–16, 21
ontology, xviii, xxvi, 12, 16, 59, 119; Chinese thought and, 41–42, 117, 121n12, 122n23; *dao* and, 44; event and, 44; flat, 108; in *The Impossible Nude*, 46; theology and, 43–44; unexceptional and, 128; unthought of, 44
opposite, 25–27, 56–57, 125
Order of Things (Foucault), 9–10, 11, 27, 29n8
ordinary, 122n11
orientalism, xvii, xxi, 11, 28n5, xxixn15; holistic, 19; humble, 31n23; neo, 31n23; neoliberalism and, 134; positive, 111; radical, 1–8; risk of, 18–28, 31n24, 36; of *Tel Quel* (As is), 8; traditional, 4; as writing strategy, 4
Orientalism (Said), 18, 29n9, 117
orientalists, 1–2
Oser construire, 71
other, unthought of, 11
others, 9, 65n37, 136

panopticon, 92
paraontology, 119, 120, 136n2
Paris, Chinese quarter in, 56–57

passion, 65n37
path, *dao* and, 83–84, 114–15, 128
pensiero debole (weak thought), 29n12
perception, 12, 39
personality, efficacy and, 78
persuasion, 81
philosophy: in China, 69–73; Chinese thought and, 120–21; European, xix; Greek, xxi; limits of, 120–21; literature and, 42
Picasso, Pablo, 42
pictorial theories, in China, 39
Piorunski, Richard, 69
plants, 85
Plato, xxv, 48, 64n22, 75, 105
Platonic ideas, xxiv, 46
Platonism, 105
pleasure, 65n37, 69, 104
Pleynet, Marcelin, 2
Plotinus, 47
poetics of escape, 4
points of reference, xii, xiv, xvi, xviii
Poiroux, Dominique, 82–83
politics, xvi, 90; of China, xix, 8, 56–57, 84; in Chinese thought, 56; governmentality/biopolitics, xix, xxvi, 58, 91, 95–97, 129–30; Greek, xix; modelization of, 92, 93; Rancière on, 118; regulation and, 93; in *Silent Transformations*, 55–56; sovereignty and, 85, 134; unexceptionalism and, 51–61
Le pont des singes (The monkey bridge) (Jullien), xvi, 1–2, 21–24, 27, 110–11, 116–17
Porkert, Manfred, 38
positive orientalism, 111
postcolonial theory, 109–15, 117
postcolonial tourism, 116
postmodernism, 18, 20–21, 29n12, 62n12
potentiality (*shi*, 勢), 73, 98n5
power, 5, 91–92
practical intelligence (*mètis*), 75–76, 93
presence, xviii, 41

probability theory, 76
Procès ou création (Jullien), 28n6, 35
process, subject-hood and, 43
Propensity of Things (Jullien), xviii, 55, 73–74, 76, 77, 95, 98nn8–9; Chinese culture in, 104; dragon in, 87–88; sovereignty in, 91; war in, 98n5
Protestantism, 126
pseudoidentity, 116
pseudophilosophy, 58
psychological war, 79

Quesnay, François, 85–86

racism, 122n23
radical chic, 1–8
radical orientalism, 1–8
Rancière, Jacques, 118
Reagan, Ronald, 86, 89, 99n14
real, imaginary and, 5
reality, war and, 77
rebellion, 79
regulation, 60; in China, 93; Chinese theory of war and, 86; politics and, 93; universal and, 15, 122n19; war and, 77
releasement, 64n22
religion, 91
respiration, 57, 94, 125–26, 132
Ressources du Christianisme (Jullien), 63n14
reverse image, of self, 30n16
rhetoric, 62n12
Richey, Jeffrey, 97n3
Rihua, Li, 42
rites, 93–94, 96
Robbins, Bruce, 131
Roland Barthes by Roland Barthes (Barthes), 4
Ruism, 108
Russia, 56

Un sage est sans idée (Jullien), 28n6
Said, Edward, 5, 18, 29n9, 62n9, 117
same, other and, 9

Sartre, Jean-Paul, 7
Schlegel, xxixn15
Schmitt, Carl, 130–31
science, 25–26
second life, xiv, xxii
second-wave feminism, 63n16, 131
Security, Territory, Population (Foucault), 86
Segalen, Victor, 112
self, 30n16, 60
self-care, 96
self-government, 96
self-orientalization, 18
self-perception, 113
separated, 26–27
Shanzhai (Han), 46
Shaviro, Steven, 108–9
shi, 勢 (potentiality), 73, 76, 77, 82, 98n5
silent transformations, xix, xxiii–xxiv, 43, 45, 56, 61, 62n12, 63n14, 82, 99nn9–10, 117–18, 127
Silent Transformations (Jullien), 43, 51, 55–56, 63n14, 106
Simondon, Gilbert, 106–7
sinologists, xii, xx
sinophilia, 3, 6
sinophobia, 3
sketching, 42–43, 62n9
Slingerland, Edward, 18, 19–20, xxixn14
Smith, Adam, 86
social domination, 5
social system, 3
Sollers, Philippe, 2–3
songer (dreaming), 22
soul, body and, 59
sovereignty, xix, xxvi, 63n16, 75, 89, 95–97; capitalism and, 60; in China, 84; governmentality/biopolitics and, 129–30; politics and, 85, 134; in *Propensity of Things*, 91; unexceptionalism and, 131; in Western thought, 130–31
space, meaning and, 4

speculative aesthetics, 109
Spire, Antoine, xiii, xvii, 116
Spivak, Gayatri Chakravorty, xix, xx, xxvi, xxvii, 3, 6, 57, 72
sponte sua, 85, 93
state power, 5
Step-by-step (Jullien). See *Chemin faisant*
sterile negative, xiv
strategy, 84
strong mode, comparison and, 11, 29n12
style, xxi
subject, time and, 99n10
subject-hood, 39, 43
subjectification, 41
subjectivity, 65n37, 120
Sun Bin, 76
Sun Tzu, 73, 99n11
Sun Zi, 76, 77, 96
surveillance, 92
Swoosh, 89–90
symbolic system, of Japan, 28n6
symbols, 61n4
syntax, heterotopias and, 9–10
synthesis, 37

Tanizaki, Jun'ichirō, xxiii
telos, 64n22, 75, 77–78, 84, 94, 98n8, 99n9
Tel Quel (As is), xxiii, 2–3, 5, 6, 8, 72, 122n10
Les Temps Modernes, 7
tension, 39
terrorism, 130
theology, 41, 43–44
There is no cultural identity. See *Il n'y a pas d'identité culturelle*
thing itself, 45
This Strange Idea of the Beautiful (Jullien), xiii, 12, 35–36, 41, 43, 46
thoughts-in-progress, xx
tian, 大 (Heaven), xxiv
time, 43, 99n10, 131n7
Titaness Metis, 75

Ton Yeou-Ki ou le nouveau singe pèlerin (Étiemble), 21–22
totalitarianism, 55, 91
totality, 15
tourism, 23–24, 115–16
transcendence, 54–55, 64n22
translator, xiii–xiv, 30n18, 43, xxviiin7
A Treatise on Efficacy (Jullien), xviii, xxiii, 52, 55, 62n12, 65n37, 73–74, 98n5; action in, 78; Chinese theory of warfare in, 88; criticism of, 97n3; deconstruction in, 107; image in, 125; management in, 84–85; war in, 75, 82
Trésor de la langue française, xxii
truth, xv
Trying Not to Try (Slingerland), 20

Ulysses, 76
uncertainty, war and, 77
unexceptional, xxiv, xxv, 37, 52, 125–26, 128
unexceptionalism, xxvi, 51–61, 127, 129, 131–32
the unheard-of (*l'inouï*), xxi–xxv, 28n6, 112–13, 118, 126, 133–34
universal, xxv, 15, 21, 122n19
universalism, 15, 121n4
unthought, xii, xv, xxii, 28, 91, 106, 113; of Chinese thought, xxiv, xxv, 21, 127; of Islam, 114; of ontology, 44; of other, 11; of Western thought, xxiv, 13, 21, 118, 127
utopias: Chinese, 2, 6, 11, 17, 72, 74, 128, 133–34; commodity and, 24. *See also* heterotopias

van der Poel, Ieme, 7
Vattimo, Gianni, 29n12
Vernant, Jean-Pierre, 30n20, 31nn21–22, 75
"Victor Segalen Lecture," 8
victory, war and, 78
Vietnam, 24, 110, 133
virtue, 89

vitalism, 108
Vital Nourishment (Jullien), 41, 54, 56–61, 61n5

Wahl, François, 2–3
Wall Street (Gekko), 73
Wang, Xing, 31n23
war, xix; art and, 98n5; chance and, 77; in China, theory of, 76–77, 79, 84, 86, 88, 98n8, 129; *dao* and, 77; efficacy and, 74; gambling in, 76; management and, 73–74, 79, 98n5, 98n7; motivation of soldiers, 77; outcome of, 77; in *Propensity of Things* (Jullien), 98n5; psychological, 79; reality and, 77; regulation and, 77; theory of, 73–74; in *A Treatise on Efficacy*, 75, 82; uncertainty and, 77; victory and, 78; Western theory of, 76
weak mode, comparison and, 11, 29n12
weak thought (*pensiero debole*), 29n12
Weick, Karl E., 82
Western art history, 48
Western ideology, 4
Western management, 84–85
Western theory of action, 62n12
Western theory of war, 76
Western thought, xvi, 12, 36, 105, 108; beautiful in, 43; Chinese thought and, xiii, xx, xxiv, 11, 13, 17, 19–20, 37, 40, 50, 52, 65n26, 70–71, 96, 105–6, 117–18, 126–27, 129, 132–34, xxxn25; commandments in, 94; efficacy in, 75; exceptionalism in, 54, 91, 136n2; in *The Great Image Has No Form, or On the Nonobject in Painting*, 11, 40, 43; the in-between and, 16; metaphysics and, xix, 43, 63n16; nude in, 45, 49; pseudophilosophy in, 58; sovereignty in, 130–31; universalization of, 134; unthought of, xxiv, 13, 21, 118, 127
Whitehead, Alfred North, 109
without exertion (*wu wei*, 無爲), 86, 119
Wolfe, Tom, 7
Woman and Chinese Modernity (Chow), 6
women, xxvi
world, time and, 99n10
world literature, 135
Worthy, William, 8
wu, 無 (nothing), 119
wu wei, 無爲 (without exertion), xix, 79, 86, 99n13, 119, 126

Xi Kang, 59
xing (形) (formation), 48

Yantu, Bu, 42

Zahm, Oliver, 90
Zarcone, Thierry, 1, 13, 71
Zeus, 75
Zhang, Qicheng, 95–96
Zhou, Shen, 41
Zhuangzi, 56, 59, 64n22, 89
Zong Bing, xiii
Zweibelson, Ben E., 81

About the Author

Arne De Boever (PhD Columbia, 2009) teaches American studies in the School of Critical Studies and the MA Aesthetics and Politics program at the California Institute of the Arts and has held visiting professorships at the University of California–Los Angeles, and the Central Academy of Fine Arts, Beijing. He is author of *States of Exception in the Contemporary Novel* (2012), *Narrative Care* (2013), *Plastic Sovereignties* (2016), *Finance Fictions* (2018), and *Against Aesthetic Exceptionalism* (2019). He is editor or coeditor of *Gilbert Simondon* (2012), *The Psychopathologies of Cognitive Capitalism: Part 1* (2013), and *Bernard Stiegler* (2017). De Boever also edits the critical theory/philosophy genre section of the *Los Angeles Review of Books* and is a member of the *boundary 2* editorial collective.

Printed in Great Britain
by Amazon